Malachi
Then
and Now

Malachi
Then
and Now

An Expository Commentary
Based on Detailed Exegetical Analysis

Allen P. Ross

LEXHAM PRESS

Lexham Press, 1313 Commercial St., Bellingham, WA 98225
LexhamPress.com

First edition by Weaver Book Company.

Unless otherwise noted, all translations are the author's.

Print ISBN 9781683591429
Digital ISBN 9781683591436

Cover: Frank Gutbrod
Interior design and typesetting: {In a Word}
Editing: Line for Line Publishing Services

24 vii / US

Contents

Preface

The book of Malachi is one biblical book that receives very little attention, apart from the occasional use of a line or two exhorting tithing. This is a pity because if the original audience needed to hear these messages from God as they waited for the coming of the Messiah, the modern professing churches need to hear them all the more because the warnings have been ignored and the failures and violations have continued in spite of the fulfillment of Malachi's prophecy of the coming of John the Baptist and Jesus the Messiah. It is a book that should be studied regularly by Christians, or, better yet, preached often in the churches with all the passionate intensity of the prophet.

Malachi must not be passed over as just another historical collection of messages from ancient Israel's prophets. It is the word of God, true and trustworthy in all it says, and timelessly relevant in its admonitions and warnings. The messages are addressed to all who profess to be the people of God, some of whom truly believe and others who actually do not believe in the LORD; but the messages are applicable to everyone because they come with the warning of the final judgment that will separate the righteous believers from the unbelievers.

A brief overview of the messages in Malachi will show clearly how important they are to the way Christians think and live now:

1. The prophet has to remind that people who were living in troubling times that God's everlasting love chose them and would see them through the difficulties of this life.
2. The prophet admonishes the people to replace cheap, contemptible, and meaningless ritual with worship that honors God.
3. The prophet denounces ministers for ruining the ministry by causing people to stumble in the faith because of their failure to teach the word of the LORD correctly and impartially.

4. The prophet condemns those who profane the holy covenant of marriage by divorcing their legitimate spouses and marrying pagan unbelievers.

5. The prophet answers the foolish charge that God was not just in dealing with sinners by declaring that no one can withstand the imminent coming of the Lord to purge sin and judge the wicked.

6. The prophet rebukes the people for robbing God and challenges them to trust his faithfulness by faithfully bringing their tithes and offerings.

7. The prophet instructs the people to heed the warnings of the coming messengers to repent before the great and terrible day of the Lord comes when he will separate the righteous from the wicked.

The seven messages uncover the failures of the people: they forgot the love of God and were troubled by events in the world, they ruined worship with their quick and easy participation, the word of God was not being declared with power and clarity, holy marriage had been profaned by choosing corrupting pagan partners, they had become self-righteous in charging God with failing to judge the wicked and needed to be reminded of the promise of his coming to judge sin, they robbed God by failing to give him their tithes and offerings and as a result did not receive his untarnished blessing, and they were complaining that they did not benefit much by following the Lord and had to be reminded of the great day of the Lord that would destroy the wicked and set the righteous free.

All these messages are greatly needed today. They are timeless, even though some of the circumstances have changed over the years. For example, we do not bring animal sacrifices today for our worship service, but the principle of giving our best to God applies to every offering we make, and the fulfillment of the typology of the sacrificial Lamb is central to all truly Christian worship.

God's people are in a similar position today as the people were then: we too are desiring the coming of the Messiah to deliver his people from the bondage of the world and destroy wickedness. His messengers will prepare people for the coming by calling them to repent; but it will not be John, for that prophecy was fulfilled at the first coming of our Lord. We are now waiting for the second coming. Thus we live on the other side of the Lord's coming to his temple; the fulfillment of that prophecy should inspire greater hope as we await the fulfillment of the second.

This commentary is designed to provide two helpful resources for the expositor and serious student of the Bible. First, it is a commentary on the book of Malachi. But second, it demonstrates the process of developing the exposition from the exegetical analysis of the text. As a commentary, the work will benefit anyone who wants to understand Malachi; but as a study guide, the material will be of greater use to the expositor who has had training in biblical exegesis.

For years I have used the book of Malachi in teaching Hebrew exegesis in seminary. In class use the students would be given assignments on each step and in each passage and then out of those assignments form the exegetical basis and the expository format.

But organizing the material for publication provided a different challenge; only the conclusions of the analysis of the text and the preparation of the exposition could be included. At an early stage the idea of putting the exegetical material in footnotes to the exposition of the book was abandoned for the simple reason that it seemed to lessen the importance of the exegetical material. Moreover, people often do not read the footnotes. The present format not only presents the exegetical analysis as important as the final commentary, but demonstrates the movement from exegesis to presentation as well.

For each passage there will first be a translation of the text with a few footnotes that deal with textual difficulties or provide explanations for the translation of the Hebrew text. This will be followed by exegetical observations on the text, discussions of the grammar and syntax that are necessary to understanding the translation and its meaning. Some of these notes will include more information relevant to the resolution of textual difficulties. Common aspects of the grammar and syntax will not be given much attention. Then after this a detailed exegetical outline will be provided so that the argument of the passage can be understood in its development. An exegetical summary of the unit will then be provided. At this point the reader will have a clear understanding of the way the text was written in the original language, as well as the meaning of the words, the syntax, and the contextual ideas.

Then the material will be recast in the form of a complete and clear commentary on the passage. But the commentary will be laid out in the form of an exposition. To relate the exposition to the analysis of the text, the outline will now be changed into an expository outline. The details of the Hebrew exegesis will not be repeated mechanically here; the meaning of the text will be presented, and only where there are major differences in views will the analysis of the text be applied more deliberately. The basic meanings of key words will be presented in the commentary; but the most important words will be given a more thorough analysis at the end of each unit. The conclusion of each exposition will include the theological meaning, the correlation to the New Testament, and practical applications. These may not need a great deal of elaboration since the passages are prophetic messages and include the applications very powerfully. And this is the reason for developing the exegesis into its exposition. The modern expositor will readily recognize the "sermonic" form of Malachi. What is needed is the detailed explanation of the text and the relevant use of it in the modern day.

The exegetical observations of the text necessarily use Hebrew in the discussion so that those who can use the language will be able to see the forms and the constructions. In the commentary section for each passage the Hebrew has been kept to a minimum, usually retained in parentheses so as not to interrupt the flow of the English sentence. Those who have not studied the language will find the discussion easy to read and understand.

In a few places the interpretation of the text is very difficult. The translation is clear, but its meaning open to several views. For the most part the different interpretations do fit the context, so the general idea is not lost. But in a few places the changes do affect the interpretation of the passage, and there I have spent more time with the views and the arguments. I was first confronted with this problem when I was teaching the Bible with a team in Kiev. When I came to the end of the section on divorce, I read the verse as it is usually translated, the LORD's saying, "I hate putting away" (i.e., divorce). This caused quite a stir among the pastors and teachers, for the Russian Bible says, "If any man hates his wife let him put her away," close to other readings that say "If a man hates his wife he puts her away with violence." Obviously we had to stop and take some time on the passage, and on translations in general (without destroying their confidence in using their Bible). But our concern always has to be what God was saying through Malachi at the time, and here or there that will take more research to come to the most likely conclusion. Even then the results must be presented with an irenic spirit, because very fine exegetical expositors may have come to a different conclusion.

I am thankful to Jim Weaver for taking on this project and providing helpful suggestions for its present format and presentation. I believe it is a much-needed book and will prove beneficial to those who want to understand and apply these ancient prophetic oracles. I must also acknowledge the contribution of my students to the writing of this book, even though they did not contribute knowingly or perhaps in some cases willingly. But the interchange in class over the text and its use today is very helpful for anyone trying to write a commentary and guide people through the process. Many of them I am sure will recall some of the class discussions as they have opportunity to read this commentary.

Introduction

The Format of This Commentary

This commentary has been written for the purpose of helping people develop biblical expositions from a solid exegetical analysis of the text. I have chosen the book of Malachi because it is short and can be easily expounded in a short series, and because it has a good variety of forms and constructions that provide test cases for a practicum in exegetical exposition; but most of all, because the messages recorded here are needed just as much today as in Malachi's day.

There are a number of commentaries available that are helpful for obtaining the message and theology of the book; and there are a couple of books that analyze the technical aspects of the Hebrew text apart from the exposition. This commentary analyzes the technical, exegetical material of the text with the theological analysis, but it does so in a way that helps the expositor learn how to develop the exposition in an effective way. It will therefore demonstrate how the technical exegetical ideas should be expressed in a practical exposition, how the structure and theology of the passage should be developed, how an expository outline can be easily developed from the exegetical outline, and how the main message should be expressed in a timeless, theological principle, correlated with the New Testament, and applied specifically today. But in the final analysis, this book will provide people with a commentary on the book of Malachi that will deal precisely with the interpretation of the text but that will also lead naturally into the formation of the exposition, whether for preaching, teaching, or writing.

This commentary is written with two readers in mind. First, with the Hebrew student in mind, the analysis of the forms and constructions of the Hebrew text have all been included for the entire book. For the most part, the technical material, that is, the analysis of the verbs, the labels for the syntactical constructions, the descriptions of the poetic elements, and the etymology and usage of key words, has been included. On occasion a word, a grammatical form, or a classification of a noun or verb, or figure of speech, will be retained in the commentary itself, but in a way that will not interfere with the straightforward reading of the commentary material. Not all the categories and labels for classification are explained in the book because exegesis students will be using different resources as they work through the text. But the commentary will show how the analysis of the text leads to the interpretation, without dragging too much technical terminology into the message.

Second, with the Bible expositor in mind, one who may or may not know Hebrew, the commentary has been written in a popular style that should be easy to follow. The translation, outlines, and the important introductory material for each passage is clear and straight to the point. There are not many textual variants, but when they occur they will be in the footnotes of the translation rather than the body of the commentary, unless they lead to different interpretations in modern translations and commentaries. Any folks looking for the interpretation or the flow of the passage will find it easy to discover in reading the commentary (and then if they want the exegetical support for the interpretations, the exegetical details will be there for use).

For each passage there is an exegetical section followed by an expository section. In the exegetical section the detailed analysis of the text is presented. There is a translation laid out in poetic form with footnotes on difficulties in the text, variant readings, or rare and problematic words and constructions. There is a brief discussion of the context and construction of the passage, which is followed by an exegetical outline and an exegetical summary of the passage.

This is followed by the expository presentation. The expository outline is developed from the exegetical outline, and then inserted into the exposition in the proper places. The exposition explains the text but does not include all the technical grammatical, syntactical, and philological observations — only what all of that showed us about the meaning of the text. The conclusion of the exposition presents the expository idea, the thesis statement of the message/passage. The exposition should lead to this conclusion, showing how the idea was developed. The conclusion then states the basic theological message of the passage and derives specific applications from the text for clear instructions. Then the message and the applications are correlated with the New Testament in order to show that the message is timeless. In making the correlation the expositor will have to be mindful of the changes between the testaments, for many things were done away with while others were merely modified. Along the way in the conclusion of each passage suggestions for the unifying expository theme or idea as well as significant applications are provided. There are other ways to express some of these expository outlines and points, but the following development offers ways it can be done clearly and effectively in order to provide samples of the process.

At the end of each passage I have included brief word studies on the most important words in the passage. Even though Hebrew forms and their basic meanings may be included in the discussion of the text, the studies of these words from the passage will fill out the ideas more.

The commentary does not say everything that could be said or needs to be said on the book of Malachi. But it analyzes the text thoroughly and develops the exposition from the exegetical study. This should be sufficient to get the expositor well under way and to inspire further study so that more can be discovered and used in the explanation of the text.

The Book of Malachi

The book of Malachi begins with "A burden, the word of Yahweh to Israel by the hand of Malachi." And that is all the information we have. Other prophetic books often tell when the prophet wrote, that is, during the reigns of certain kings. As we shall see, though, there were no kings in Israel when Malachi delivered his messages — they were a thing of the past, and of the future. There was only a governor. So how can we date this book? What clues do we have?

Date and Authorship

To answer some of these questions we can only look at the contents of the book and make an estimation of the date of its composition. A quick read through the book will tell us that the messages are intensely practical about sacrificial worship, priestly ministry, marriage and divorce, tithing, and the preparation of the coming of the LORD to judge the world and fulfill the promises of the covenants. We can conclude from the contents that there was no problem with idolatry in the nation — it too was a thing of the past. In fact, there is no mention of God's judgment on Israel for idolatry, namely, the Babylonian captivity. That was a thing of the past as well, long since forgotten by these folk. But they did have a temple and a functioning priesthood, even though it was not functioning correctly. On the basis of these observations we would date the book in the early post-exilic period.

The exile in Babylon ended in 536 BC. Many of the people returned to the land under the leadership of Zerubbabel, an heir apparent to the throne if there ever was one to inherit; Joshua the High Priest; and the prophets Zechariah and Haggai. By March 515 BC they had rebuilt the temple in Jerusalem, a major triumph for the people of God, but also a disappointment for those old enough to remember the splendor of the old temple that was destroyed. As the people settled in the land and tried to make a life for themselves, they became discouraged and disillusioned because the glorious prophecies about their re-gathering to the land and the building of the city and the temple seemed not to be fulfilled. And so in time as their confidence in the promises weakened, their commitment to the covenant began to lag as well.

About 455 BC Ezra returned to the land and promptly began a revival to bring the people back to the faith. The results of that spiritual work did not last very long, for in 444 BC Nehemiah was sent as governor and he found the same sins being committed that Ezra had tried to correct. Nehemiah's task was to continue the reforms and rebuild the walls of the city of Jerusalem, while enemies attacked them and their project. Nehemiah was called back to the palace in the East about 433 or 432 BC and remained there a few years. It seems most plausible to put the ministry of Malachi close to the time of Nehemiah's reforms and then his absence, because the messages address the same problems that Nehemiah had been working to correct. In Nehemiah we find that many had taken alien wives (13:23), and so too do we find this in Malachi (2:11); in Nehemiah the people were withholding their tithes (13:10), and so too did they violate the tithing laws in Malachi's day (3:8); Nehemiah had to deal with the divorce of legitimate wives (13:23, 27) and so did Malachi (2:15–16); and Nehemiah spoke of the neglect of temple service (13:4–5, 11), and so did Malachi (1:12–13). We may conclude that while Nehemiah was there his reforms began to take hold, but when he was recalled there was a relapse, for he returned to find things had deteriorated again.

All this would suggest that Malachi wrote approximately between 440 and 420 BC. He was the last of the prophets to write, and his writing predicted the next great prophet who was to come to prepare the way of the Lord — John the Baptist. But we must remember that when we say he was a post-exilic prophet, we must note that he actually came a good hundred years after Zechariah and Haggai, and almost a generation after Ezra. Malachi is the last of the twelve minor prophets, but those twelve prophets stretch over a period of 400 years.

Malachi delivered his messages to expose and rebuke the sins of the people and admonish them to change. He found in the people an outward appearance of faith expressed in a perfunctory service but with no inward conviction or devotion. There was widespread skepticism as well, for the people complained that the earlier prophetic promises had not been fulfilled and divine justice was not present. So they were impatient for God to judge their enemies, especially the Gentiles, as well as those Jews whom they believed rebelled against the Lord, and as a result to deliver them from their current difficulties. But the prophet cut to the core of their problems — sin.

There are other suggestions that have been made over the years but they are not very compelling. One suggestion places Malachi as a contemporary of Haggai and Zechariah, or about 520 BC.[1] Another[2] puts him in the first half of the fourth century, but there is no reason to date it that late.

The Style and Structure of the Book

The style of the book of Malachi is clear and direct — it is the style of prophetic sermons with a few predictions included. Commentators have debated whether his style is more poetic or prosaic. It is not classical poetry, but its lines often follow a rhythmic and poetic style. It is a series of oracles written in free verse.

The nature of the contents of the book of Malachi is prophetic. Malachi may not have had the lofty style and poetic imagination of an Isaiah, but he is nonetheless profound and effective. He is more of a preacher who reasoned with the people than a poet, and that is what was needed for these people. His style is simple, smooth, concise, and forceful — and at times eloquent. His description of the ideal priest in 2:5–7 is powerful as well as poetic; and his description of the coming of the Lord in 4:2–3 includes some of the most beautiful imagery found in the prophets. We just do not have much of his work to make any significant comparison with other prophets.

Because Malachi's audience was skeptical, he chose to use interrogation and reply as the way to get through to them. The material has been des-

---

1 This was the view of A. C. Welch, *Post-Exilic Judaism* (Edinburgh: Blackwood, 1935), pp. 113–25.

2 C. C. Torrey, "The Prophecy of Malachi," *Journal of Biblical Literature* 17 (1989): 14–15.

ignated as prophetic disputation because of this. In each point he knew what they were thinking and so dealt with them with both the questions and the answers. The language of the book frequently draws on Deuteronomy — ideas such as love, fear, faithfulness, tithes in the storehouse, and Levitical priests all tie his messages to the authority of the Law. The book can easily be divided into prophetic messages:

I. The everlasting love of God that chose Israel and destroys her enemies (1:1–5).
II. The corrupt worship that defiles God's sanctuary and is rejected (1:6–17).
III. The perverted teaching of the Law that God rebukes and removes (2:1–9).
IV. The destruction of marriage through divorce and illegitimate marriages that God hates and will judge (2:10–16).
V. The announcement of God's messengers who will prepare the way for the coming redemption and judgment (2:17–3:5).
VI. The failure of the people to honor God with their tithes and their decision not to serve him (3:6–12).
VII. The deliverance of the faithful people of God who are prepared for the coming of the LORD (3:13–18 and 4:1–6).

With topics like the love of God, corrupt worship, faithful teaching of God's word, marriage and divorce, tithing, the justice of God, the coming of the LORD, John the Baptist and Elijah, and the final judgment of the wicked, the value of the book for Christian exposition is obvious.

The Method of Exegetical Exposition

The following survey will lay out the process of doing exegetical exposition in a logical, step-by-step order. However, in the practical use of the procedure the steps in the process overlap a good deal once a certain level of expertise is reached. For example, when solving a textual problem it will often be necessary to consider the syntax, the meaning of the word, and the poetics. Moreover, not every step will apply fully to every passage of the Bible. But for the purpose of training people to do this kind of biblical study, we usually have to work with each discipline separately at first. After a while the method becomes a way of thinking when studying the text, and the research in one area will contribute to the study of another.

The word "exegesis" is the standard term that we use for careful, biblical studies. It basically means that our study leads the interpretation out of the text — the interpretation emerges from the text. The opposite, which we try to avoid, is called "eisegesis." This is where an expositor reads a preconceived idea into the text, an idea that is simply not there. Unfortunately this is easy to do, and so it is done very frequently. The task of the preacher or teacher is to deliver a clear interpretation of the passage, showing how the exposition came from the passage.

The following aspects of the study are essential to the correct interpretation of the text, even though some of them may not be necessary in some passages.

1. Determining the Literary Unit to Be Studied

The material for the exposition must come from the text, the whole text being studied. It is possible to deliver an exposition of a single verse, of course, but in so doing the meaning of the context will be a controlling factor in the interpretation. The most effective expository preaching or teaching, however, will focus on the full literary unit.

The expositor must therefore study the passage to identify the literary structure and motifs that form the unit. Apart from the book of Psalms you cannot rely on the chapter divisions because they often mark off sections that include several stories or oracles. So here you are looking for structural markers that will mark a new beginning and an end to the unit. These will be key words or phrases that are repeated, syntactical forms that are repeated, shifts in subject matter, or the presence of repeated ideas or refrains. Some of these will be transitional markers to the next passage, and so you will have to decide where to make the break for your message. While the chapters of the Bible often include more than one literary unit, you may choose to do the longer section and relate the units in it. This is workable, but it is much harder to do well because it involves several exegetical studies. If the book of Malachi is divided into larger units, such as taking chapter 2 as one unit, and then 3:6–4:6 as one unit, it will be almost impossible to deal with the material in a standard exposition. There are links between the sections in these places, but they are not strong enough to require all the sections be taken as one unit. Chapter 2 has two very distinct messages, and 3:6–4:6 also can be easily subdivided.

It may be helpful to take into consideration the literary genre of a passage to form the substance of the exposition. The identification of a genre will require comparing the passage with other passages that are similar in form and function. It will take some time and practice to get used to the biblical genres so that you can identify the expected structure and parts. And there are some pitfalls here. One temptation is to use classical genres for Hebrew literature, things like heroic literature, or comedy and the like. If they fit, fine; but if you find yourself changing the meaning or even skipping part of the passage so that it fits the category, then the study will be contaminated. It is better to use the attested categories of the Bible itself. Even here you will find that the genres are never stereotyped and predictable. They may have similar features, but in different order and with different lengths. As a result the commentaries will often disagree on the genre. Nevertheless, the detailed analysis of vocabulary and motifs in a passage will help separate the literary unit.

The subject matter will be one of the more helpful ways of isolating the passage. In Malachi we are dealing with prophetic oracles. But having said that, a prophetic oracle could take any literary form. So structural markers, repeated expressions, and subject matter will be the strongest evidence. You will soon learn how Malachi likes to begin an oracle with principles and then challenging questions. And in them you will see if the subject is worship, teaching, divorce, tithing, or the coming of the day of the Lord.

Once you have separated the unit and identified its nature and subject matter, you should try to determine its relationship to the argument of the book, how the passages flow in the sequence of the arrangement. Until you have worked through the whole book, you will have to rely on the works of other people to help you get started with the whole context in a helpful way. In a series of prophetic oracles the sequence of ideas may not be that clear or helpful; they may simply help you understand why the prophet takes up the next subject.

In any exegetical study you may find in the process that you have to rethink your division of the unit, perhaps linking the next few verses with it, or perhaps leaving a few verses for the next section. Or your exposition might seem to be too much for an ordinary exposition. For example, the section in Malachi on tithing is part of a larger section on the prophet's rebuke of the people. But you may find that the smaller section within the unit is a sermon of its own. That can be easily done, as long as the section is related to the context.

2. The Preliminary Observation of the Passage

This is an essential step in the process, for it will enable you to plan your studies within the time you have to work, and in line with the purpose of your exposition (i.e., knowing your audience).

First, read the passage in several English translations to see where there are major differences that will have to be studied and explained. In particular, read the text in the translations that you know your audience will have. Do not just read the passage once in each version; read it many times to become more familiar with it and the ways it has been translated (interpreted). At this stage you should begin to form a general idea of the central theme, that is, discover the angle that your exposition should take.

Second, note any major textual differences that will need more attention. Translation choices are not textual difficulties (for example, "dwell" and "live" are simply different ways the versions express the same thing). Do not work with paraphrases at this stage; they do not follow the text as closely and so you could not tell if there was a different textual tradition or a loose paraphrase.

Third, list key words that you think will need to be studied — theological words that have bearing on the message of the passage, words that are repeated, or problematic words. You will have a list of more words than you can actually study, so you will have to prioritize them. Then when you study the words, you will only take the study as far as you need to in order to make its meaning clear.

Fourth, make a list of the poetic devices and figures of speech in the passage, and mark those that will need to be explained in the exposition. Some poetic expressions are self-evident (but do not assume people will know them); but other expressions will need explanation. When you analyze the poetical expressions and devices in your study, you will have to be clear on all of them in case people ask; but you will work more on those that will be part of the exposition.

Fifth, note any unclear or difficult grammatical or syntactical expressions that will need to be studied and explained. Pay particular attention to the different ways verbs have been translated, and watch for translations that smooth out the difficult grammar to communicate. You can make use of both the literal and the smooth translations in your exegesis and exposition.

Sixth, as you begin to formulate the theological subject matter that is present (in time this comes much more readily), you will have to think ahead to New Testament correlations. Note if there are New Testament quotations for the text; or, if not, think about New Testament passages that address the same issues or the same theology.

These are the things to be noting as you read through the passage in English translations a number of times. Your observations will determine what you study in your preparation. The more you use the exegetical procedure the more familiar you will become with the categories and the findings. For example, the more words you study the less you will have to do in other passages, especially where the words reappear.

3. Resolving Critical Matters

The first step in the procedure, necessarily, is to determine as well as possible the precise and original form and occasion of the Hebrew text by using the accepted methods of higher and lower criticism. Higher criticism is determining the date, author, and occasion of the passage; this you may have done in earlier studies and will not need to do it with each passage. Lower criticism is textual criticism; this is our main concern in this step. It is necessary to know what the text actually says before you develop the exegetical exposition (and not simply to choose the reading you like best, or that fits your sermon the best). This step may not seem that important to some preachers, but to the careful expositor it will be obviously clear in that the people will have a variety of translations and paraphrases.

There will be some textual problems that may not be significant enough to discuss in the exposition, minor variants such as a plural noun for a singular, or a different preposition, or an archaic spelling. But the expositor will want to work through them apart from the sermon in order to have in mind what the correct text is.

In dealing with textual variants, that is, places where the Hebrew text (the Masoretic Text) has one word or form and the ancient versions (such as Greek, Aramaic, Latin) have a different one. Do not assume that the Masoretic Text is the inspired text, or that it is always going to have the right reading. It is a rugged and therefore reliable text, but it does not always have the better reading.

The procedure of doing textual criticism requires you to reconstruct the probable Hebrew form that the ancient versions may have been looking at in their translation work, and then assess the difference. Often the Hebrew letters will be the same, but the variant reading assumed different vowels than were preserved in the Masoretic Text. Once you understand the exact difference between the readings, then you have to determine which one was the original and which the secondary reading. The fundamental rule to follow is that the reading that best explains the other reading is probably the correct reading. Here you have to get into the mind of the scribes and test each reading — if reading #1 was the original, what would have led the scribe of the other reading to have another reading? Then you would do the same with reading #2. Using your understanding of scribal tendencies and contextual clues, you will be able to discern the most likely original reading. And the original reading will usually be the more difficult form, because scribes tended to smooth out the text for clarity. Many modern versions have done the same thing, that is, choose the reading that seems to be clearer and easier to understand rather than the more difficult reading. But that leaves the question unanswered: if the smooth reading was the original, why would a scribe change it into a difficult or even impossible form?

You may find yourself coming back to rethink your decision the more you study the passage and see how the words and the syntax are being used.

In delivering the exposition you must use wisdom in dealing with a textual difficulty. There will be times when you will have to explain what the text actually says, and then offer an explanation of how some of the versions made their translations. At such times it is always helpful to emphasize that this problem may in fact be the only word in the whole chapter that is a problem, or to note that the overall meaning of the passage is not normally changed. But you will probably have to train people to study the Bible using different translations and study notes if they want to be precise.

4. The Study of Words

There are two types of word studies that will need to be done when studying any passage: the study of common theological words, and the study of rare or problematic words. The study of the theological words will be a rich study; and it will be helpful in the exposition (do not assume that people know what words like "righteousness," "holy," "glory," or "wisdom" actually mean). A clear explanation of these key words will help people understand the passage as well as theology. And once you have done a study, say, for a word like "holy," then in subsequent expositions where the word occurs you can draw upon your earlier work. Soon you will have a working knowledge of all the key theological terms.

The procedure to follow is straightforward. Using a concordance (that simply gives the biblical references where the word is found) you will look up the passages to see how the word is used, write a description of the use, and start to place the uses in categories or denominations (e.g., "create" might divide into categories where the word describes God's creation of the universe and everything in it, or God's formation of the nation of Israel, or God's renewal of the spiritual life of the penitent). If the word has too many references to check, then you can check selected passages in the categories of the dictionaries or word study books to be sure those are legitimate categories, and then decide which nuance fits your passage.

The study of rare and difficult words is more challenging. Here we are often dealing with a word that occurs only once or a few times, and so concordance study will not be as important as etymological studies — analyzing the form of the word, comparing the word to similar words in the other Semitic languages, tracing the development of the word in different texts, and with caution seeing how the ancient versions translated the word (caution because in many places the word was just as difficult for them as it is for us). Here you will see that the commentaries and modern translations may do a good degree of re-interpreting a word, or connecting it to another word group. You have to know enough of the process to evaluate what they are writing in the commentaries or presenting in their translations.

For the most part you will probably not do this etymological work, not having the tools or training in comparative philology. But you will have to evaluate the suggestions that commentaries make to determine if that was the original and true meaning of the word. You are more likely to see such etymological proposals in poetic sections of the Bible, but on occasion in narrative sections as well. If a change in meaning is being proposed, you first have to ask if it is necessary, and then if it is following sound reasoning. For significant changes (those that will change the text you are expounding) you may have to look at a couple of commentaries to get all the proposals and the pros and cons for each. Good, up-to-date tools will make your analysis much easier.

If you are going to plan a series of expository sermons on a book in the Bible, study the main theological words in that book well in advance. This will make the week-by-week preparation easier. For example, if you had studied "bless," "curse," "holy," and "profane" before beginning a series on Malachi, you would have a good start on the exegesis of the individual passages.

In the regular preparation for exegetical exposition, you will have to prioritize the words you study and determine how much time you can take in explaining them in your exposition. Some passages may have twenty to thirty very important words; you cannot do them in one preparation. So choose the words that are most important to the interpretation of the passage, words that are found in explanatory sections, admonitions, or theological propositions. Then do as much study of these words as you need to in order to be able to explain and perhaps illustrate the meanings clearly.

In this commentary on Malachi, words of passing importance are discussed in the body of the commentary. But key theological words have been selected from each passage and given a more thorough discussion at the end of the section. These are not meant to be complete word studies, but helpful starters for your study.

5. *The Analysis of the Grammar and Syntax*

Courses in exegesis usually spend a good amount of time analyzing the grammar and syntax. This includes the interpretation of the uses of nouns, whether in the nominative, accusative, or genitive locations; the application of the different nuances of the perfect tense and the imperfect tense; the range of meanings for the volitive, the imperative, the jussive, and the cohortative; the distinct uses of participles and infinitives in different contexts; and of course the ways that *waw* can be used. Much of this classification will depend on the correct identification and parsing of the forms in question. And so in most classes in Hebrew grammar and syntax, all these things are emphasized. In using all that material in exegesis the expositor will quickly see what the most frequently used categories are. Accordingly, the forms and functions will be learned the best by doing exegesis.

Also of great importance is the ability to identify and explain the various subordinate clauses. In interpretation these clauses often carry the most significance; they will give the circumstances, causes, results, conditions, and explanations of what is being said. Even a rough sentence diagram will reveal how these clauses contribute.

Poetic passages and recorded dialogue will require the greatest attention to syntax. In poetry, especially Psalms and Proverbs, the English versions will have very different translations of the tenses of the verb, requiring the expositor to know the options and then determine from the context how the forms should be interpreted. This is crucial, because with a different category the interpretation could change from a prayer to a praise, or from a universal truth to a wish. In poetry and dialogue the sentences here can be cryptic, and so the expositor will have to be able to explain how the clauses and phrases work in the sentences.

Of course all of this will have to be done in the preparation; in the presentation there is no good reason to refer to adverbial accusatives, jussives, gnomic truths, and the like. Just translate the line as it should be and then explain what it means. The categories are for your thinking through the choices. Do not tell people that their Bible is wrong, or you could destroy their confidence in reading the Bible. The way they translate a verb is basically an interpretive choice. You can offer your interpretation and the reasons for it. Most of the time the difference will be minor, or the choice obvious.

6. *The Analysis of Poetics*

Now we have to consider the structure and texture of the passage. Some passages will lend themselves to this readily, or necessitate it; in other passages it may seem incidental, but nonetheless will have to be explained.

Study the structure of the passage. Here you are looking for signs that will indicate the structure. Look for narrative with dialogue inserted throughout, or repetition of words or structural markers, especially if at the beginning and ending of parts (called inclusios), or for reversals in the order of the material (called chiasms), and determine how they influence your analysis, or more practically, your outlining of the passage.

You may also be able to compare the passage with others that have a similar structure, similar vocabulary, or a comparable setting or occasion. You may have a distinct genre to work with, and if so, that may help you understand the function.

More importantly, and certainly more frequently, you will need to deal with the texture of a passage — the figures of speech. Usually these will be covered in classes in biblical interpretation, hermeneutics, or principles of exegesis. But unfortunately, they often are not — not in seminary, college, or high school. You will have to study them if you have no understanding in this because so much of the Bible is written with poetic expressions. Even basic things, such as "This is my body" will require this analysis. Is it literal or figurative? And if figurative, what figure of speech do we have, and what does it mean?

There are figures of comparison that are used very often: the metaphor, the simile, the implied comparison in which only the figure is stated (called a hypocatastasis), personification, anthropomorphism, and zoomorphism. In each case the word has to be explained by the category; and in the exposition the explanation made clear without using the technical label. When Malachi says, "The sun of righteousness shall rise with healing in his wings," you should be able to explain that sun is an implied comparison (called a hypocatastasis), comparing the appearance of the Messiah in glory with the glistening sun in the morning. And you should be able to say that the word "wings" is drawn from the animal world (called a zoomorphism), comparing the rays of the morning sun in the sky to wings of a giant bird. Just as the sun and its rays bring life to all creation, so the appearance and influence of the Messiah will bring healing.

A second group of figures are those that are substitutions. Something that is related to the topic in some way is stated, but you have to discover what is meant. In these cases there is included a literal aspect to the figure, whereas in the above group there is not. Above, a figure of comparison as in "dogs have surrounded me" compares the enemies to dogs, but he is not surrounded by dogs. But here, a statement such as "the grave cannot praise you" means that if the speaker dies and is put in a grave, he cannot praise God, but there would be a grave in which he would be placed. It takes some practice for people to get used to the language of poetry, but once they do, their expositions will flow clearly and powerfully.

In this group then we have the metonymy (several different kinds) in which things loosely connected are stated for what is meant, as in "they have Moses and the prophets." They don't have Moses and the prophets; they have what those people wrote. There is also synecdoche (several kinds) in which the figure is more closely linked to the intended meaning, often generically, as in "their feet are swift to run to evil," in which case more than their feet is involved. Then there is the merism in which opposites are stated to signify the totality; the hendiadys in which one of two words modifies the other; and symbols and types.

Then there are figures of addition or intensification (such as repetition, parallelism, word plays, hyperbole, or rhetorical questions), as well as suppression or understatements (such as ellipsis, understatements, or cutting off words or sentences due to intense feelings).

These are the most common figures, but there are many others. There are good reference books for these figures; but however you acquire a working knowledge of them it will greatly enhance your exposition of Scriptures.

7. Developing an Exegetical Outline and Summary

Today people have an aversion to making outlines; they actually do not know what one should look like. But both the exegesis and the exposition outlines will make what you are doing very clear and help people to follow you section by section. The audience is always happy to have some idea where you are in your message.

I teach people to make two outlines, the first is the exegetical outline (and it is rather easy to do) and the second is the expository outline (and it is easy to do if you did the exegetical outline). I demand that in both outlines people use full sentences in order to convey a complete idea. Here I will focus on the exegetical outline.

This outline is essentially a point-by-point summary in your own words of what each part of the passage is saying. You may see the pattern and nature of the exegetical outline in each of the passages in Malachi in this commentary; or you may look at others in each passage in Genesis, Leviticus, and Psalms in my commentaries. To construct an exegetical outline you simply put in your own words what each sentence or major clause is saying, then group similar ideas together for each section and write a summary statement for each of the larger sections. In this way the summaries of the lines will become (when edited) the sub-points A, B, and so on, and the summary statement of the group will become the Roman numeral point.

Then you take these statements of larger sections, the Roman numeral points, and write them together. Then you edit them into one full sentence which will be your summary message of the entire passage. If you do this well, the outline will include every idea in the passage, and it will show the relationships between the sections. The statements will all be full sentence descriptions of what the lines and sections are saying. If you do this in the relaxed atmosphere of your study, it will go fairly easily. And then you will discover that it will enable you to think through the passage by memory. If you cannot do this at first in your study, you will not be able to do it extemporaneously from the pulpit. It is always helpful in delivering an exposition to be able to say in your own words what the next section is saying. Then you can point out the things in those verses that contribute to the interpretation.

8. Determining the Theology of the Passage

If it has not been gradually emerging all along the way, the theology of the passage must be uncovered and stated in a propositional form — this is what God is saying to us in this passage. What the theology takes into consideration is what the passage says about God, his names, his nature, his acts, and what it says about people, their names, natures, actions, and finally what it says about the relationship of God with his people, or his creation. This relationship often focuses on covenants God made with people — his promises and their requirements.

Put your exegetical findings in theological statements and condense them into one summary idea for the whole passage. In most cases the theological statement will be similar to the expository idea. The statement should be about ten or fifteen words in length, easy to hear and remember. Then in your exposition you do not simply preach your idea, but the whole passage, using the summary idea to keep you on track and to help the people see the theological message emerging from the text step by step.

A very important part of developing the theology of an Old Testament passage is the correlation of that passage with the theology of the whole Bible, especially the New Testament. Be sure to explain how the New Testament uses the Old Testament, whether your passage is a direct prophecy, or a type, or simply an analogical application.

Where there is a major change in the New Testament, or there is not citation from it in the New, you still must find the corresponding theological idea that informs the text. You will have to find a place where the same theology is being taught, albeit now through the grid of the new covenant. Be careful not to read New Testament ideas into the Old Testament; derive the theology first and then find the corresponding New Testament connection. Do not simply explain the Old Testament passage and then preach and apply the New Testament passage; show the connection and development.

9. Developing the Expository Outline and Idea

Now we want to change the exegetical outline into a homiletic one. It is much easier to write a homiletic outline if you already have the exegetical one, because you simply have to edit it by shortening it, expressing it in timeless and more universal expressions, and stating it as a theological principle.

Condense and edit each point in your exegetical outline to make an expository outline. This outline will have shorter sentences, it will state clearly in propositional, theological statements what each line meant to the original audience as well as to your audience, and it will provide you with an easy transition to specific applications. This outline I would use in the pulpit because the points are theological principles that each section is providing. In my discussion of Malachi to follow, I have inserted my expository outline into the commentary part, which is where it should be if your exposition will work through the passage. You can compare the wording of the exegetical outline and the expository outline to see the difference.

Some folks think this is too much work. That may be true if you have never made an outline before; but once you develop the procedure, it will come much more easily. The practical value for you is that all the exegetical material you discover will be arranged in a clear and organized way. Too often sermons today are presented as a stream of consciousness or a general discussion with a verse from the passage thrown in every so often. We can do better.

Finally, work with the theological idea you have written and form it into an expository thesis statement, which is a propositional statement that will form the heart (not the totality) of your exposition. The finished product must do the following:

1.   adequately account for the contents of the entire passage;
2.   be worded in the form of a timeless truth, not in the form of a history lesson about Israel, nor in the form that would exclude the Old Testament meaning entirely;
3.   be stated in a way that is applicable to the original audience, the New Testament audience (where it correlates), and the current audience;
4.   be ten to fifteen words that can be understood and retained on one hearing (if you cannot even read it clearly so that people can remember it, it is probably too rough); and
5.   not be so general that it fits hundreds of passages and says little about your passage.

If you have an expository outline that you will use in presenting the exposition, it is easy to develop this expository idea, the main statement in which you state what you believe God is saying to us in this text. It is, after all, the message of the entire passage in a memorable statement. You do not expound your statement; you expound the text, but the statement will keep your exposition focused and clear.

10. Completing the Exposition

With all this material in mind you should know the passage very well and know exactly what angle your exposition will take. With the main theme and the theology in mind, you now are ready to write the conclusion. This will include a brief review of the passage, very brief, a clear statement of the central theme or idea that emerges, one or two very clear New Testament correlations, and then specific applications — that is, what you want the people to know, what you want them to believe, and what you want them to do. The applications should clearly emerge from the text; but now you will state them as principles and then add your suggestions of how they might be implemented (not specifically in this text, but perhaps by correlation). The applications can be short and precise if you have done your work for the exegetical exposition.

Now you are ready to write an introduction because you know where your exposition is going. The introduction should not start with the historical background of the passage since that often comes across as boring and irrelevant. First, raise some issues that you know this passage is going to address, and then in transition to the exposition relate a few important details of the historical context. Here you can learn a good deal from Malachi the preacher. He raises general principles that the audience would affirm; then he raises questions concerning their failure to live by them; and then when he has their attention, he states clearly the problem and what God's word says about it. It would be a good practice in each of these passages to see how Malachi arranged his sermons. You could not improve on the way each is developed and presented. You are actually preparing exegetical expositions of sermons.

Bibliography

1. Commentaries

Baldwin, Joyce C. *Haggai, Zechariah, Malachi: An Introduction and Commentary.* Tyndale Old Testament Commentary. London: Tyndale Press, 1972.

Glazier-McDonald, Beth. *Malachi: The Divine Messenger.* Society of Biblical Literature Dissertation Series 98. Atlanta: Scholars Press, 1987.

Hill, Andrew E. *Haggai, Zechariah, Malachi.* Tyndale Old Testament Commentaries. Downers Grove, IL: IVP Academic, 2012.

———. *Malachi*. Anchor Bible 25. New York: Doubleday, 1998.

Kaiser, Walter C., Jr. *Malachi: God's Unchanging Love*. Grand Rapids: Baker, 1984.

Merrill, Eugene H. "*Malachi*," in The Expositor's Bible Commentary. Grand Rapids: Zondervan, 2008.

Morgan, G. Campbell. *Malachi's Message for Today*. Grand Rapids: Baker, 1972.

Packard, Joseph. *The Book of Malachi*. Lange's Commentary. New York: Scribner, Armstrong & Co., 1876.

Smith, Ralph L. *Micah-Malachi*, Word Biblical Commentary. Waco, TX: Word, 1984.

Verhoef, Peter A. *The Books of Haggai and Malachi*. New International Commentary on the Old Testament. Grand Rapids: Eerdmans, 1987.

Wolf, Herbert. *Haggai and Malachi: Rededication and Renewal*. Chicago: Moody Press, 1976.

2. Related Books and Articles

Althann, R. "Malachi 2:13–14." *Biblica* 58 (1977):418–21.

Baldwin, J. G. "Malachi 1:11 and the Worship of the Nations in the Old Testament." *Tyndale Bulletin* 23 (1972):117–24.

Bamberger, B. J. "Fear and Love of God in the Old Testament." *Hebrew Union College Annual* 6 (1929):39–53.

Chisholm, Robert B., Jr. "A Theology of the Minor Prophets." In *A Biblical Theology of the Old Testament*. Edited by R. B. Zuck. Chicago: Moody Press, 1991. Pp. 418–33.

Clendenen, E. Ray. "The Structure of Malachi: A Textlinguistic Study." *Criswell Theological Review* 2 (1987):3–17.

Deuel, David C. "'Book of Remembrance' or Royal Memorandum? An Exegetical Note." *The Master's Seminary Journal* 7 (1996):107–11.

Dumbrell, William J. "Malachi and the Ezra-Nehemiah Reforms." *Reformed Theological Review* 35 (1976):42–52.

Eybers, I. H. "Malachi : The Messenger of the Lord." *Theologica Evangelica* 3 (1970):12–20.

Fischer, James A. "Notes on the Literary Form and Message of Malachi." *Catholic Biblical Quarterly* (1972):315–20.

Fuller, Russell. "Text-Critical Problems in Malachi 2:10–16." *Journal of Biblical Theology* 110 (1991):45–57.

Glazier-McDonald, Beth. "Intermarriage, Divorce, and the *bat 'el nekar:* Insights into Malachi 2:10–16." *Journal of Biblical Literature* 106 (1987):603–11.

———. "Malachi 2:12: *'er we'oneh* — Another Look." *Journal of Biblical Literature* (1986):295–98.

Jones, David Clyde. "A Note on the LXX of Malachi 2:16." *Journal of Biblical Literature* (1990):683–84.

Kaiser, Walter C., Jr. "The Promise of the Arrival of Elijah in Malachi and the Gospels." *Grace Theological Journal* 3 (1982):221–33.

Kooy, V. H. "The Fear and Love of God in Deuteronomy." In *Grace Upon Grace*. Festschrift for L. J. Kuyper. Edited by J. I. Cook. Grand Rapids: Eerdmans, 1975.

Malchow, Bruce V. "The Messenger of the Covenant in Mal. 3:1." *Journal of Biblical Literature* (1984):252–55.

McKenzie, Steven L., and Howard N. Wallace. "Covenant Themes in Malachi." *The Catholic Biblical Quarterly* 45 (1983):549–63.

Myers, J. M. *The World of the Restoration*. Englewood Cliffs, NJ: Prentice-Hall, 1968.

Petersen, D. L. *Late Israelite Prophecy*. Atlanta: Scholars Press, 1977. Pp. 38–45.

Redditt, Paul L. "The Book of Malachi in Its Social Setting." *The Catholic Biblical Quarterly* 56 (1994):240–55.

Robinson, A. "God, the Refiner of Silver." *Catholic Biblical Quarterly* 11 (1949):188–90.

Sutcliffe, E. F. "Malachi's Prophecy of the Eucharistic Sacrifice." *Irish Ecclesiastical Review* 5 (1922):502–13.

Swetnam, J. "Malachi 1:11: An Interpretation." *Catholic Biblical Quarterly* 31(1969):200–209.

Torrey, C. C. "The Prophecy of Malachi." *Journal of Biblical Literature* 17 (1989):1–15.

Verhoeff, P. A. "Some Notes on Mal. 1:11." *Die Ou Testamentiese Werkgemeenskap in Suid-Afrika* (1966):163–72.

Waldman, N. M. "Some Notes on Malachi 3:6; 3:13; and Psalm 42:11." *Journal of Biblical Literature* 93 (1974):543–49.

Weiner, A. *The Prophet Elijah in the Development of Judaism*. London: Kegan Paul, 1978.

Welch, A. C. *Post-Exilic Judaism*. Edinburgh: Blackwood, 1935.

Wendland, Ernst. "Linear and Concentric Patterns in Malachi." *The Bible Translator* 36 (1985):108–21.

3. Exegetical Resources

There are so many fine books and resources available today that it is often difficult to know what to buy, especially since almost no bookstore carries an array of the finest resources for this level of study. I have listed here the books and tools that I have found most useful in teaching the exegetical procedure. There are others that are also excellent, and their omission from the list should not be taken to mean they are not worth having. The expositor needs to find what is personally the most useful and then make the purchases. These are the standard works; become familiar with them. Then you will be able to evaluate the electronic programs you might have to see what they include.

EXEGETICAL METHOD

Chisholm, Robert, Jr. *From Exegesis to Exposition: A Practical Guide to Using Biblical Hebrew.* Grand Rapids: Baker, 1998.

Smith, Gary V. *Interpreting the Prophetic Books: An Exegetical Handbook.* Handbooks for Old Testament Exegesis, edited by David M. Howard Jr. Grand Rapids: Kregel, 2014.

Stuart, Douglas. *Old Testament Exegesis: A Primer for Students and Pastors,* 2nd ed. Philadelphia: Westminster Press, 1984.

See also John H. Hayes and Carl R. Holladay, *Biblical Exegesis: A Beginner's Handbook,* 3rd ed. (Atlanta: John Knox, 2007); and *The Interpreter's Dictionary of the Bible,* Supplementary Volume, (Nashville, Abingdon, 1962), pp. 296–303, s.v. "Exegesis" by K. L. Keck and G. M. Tucker.

HERMENEUTICS

Bright, John. *The Authority of the Old Testament.* Nashville: Abingdon, 1971.

Bullinger, E. W. *Figures of Speech Used in the Bible.* 1898. Reprint, Grand Rapids: Baker, 1968.

Caird, G. B. *The Language and Imagery of the Bible.* Philadelphia: Westminster Press, 1980.

Doeve, J. W. *Jewish Hermeneutics in the Synoptic Gospels and Acts.* Assen, Amsterdam: Van Gorcum Press, 1954.

Goldingay, John. *Approaches to Old Testament Interpretation.* Downers Grove, IL: InterVarsity Press, 1981.

INTRODUCTIONS

Arnold, Bill T., and Bryan E. Beyer. *Encountering the Old Testament: A Christian Survey.* 3rd ed. Grand Rapids: Baker, 2010.

Dorsey, David A. *The Literary Structure of the Old Testament.* Grand Rapids: Baker, 1999.

Harrison, R. K. *Introduction to the Old Testament.* Grand Rapids: Eerdmans, 1969.

Kitchen, Kenneth A. *Ancient Orient and Old Testament.* Chicago: InterVarsity Press, 1975.

———. *The Bible in Its World.* Downers Grove, IL: InterVarsity Press, 1978.

Other works worthy of consulting include William Sanford LaSor, David Allen Hubbard, and Frederick William Bush. *Old Testament Survey: The Message, Form, and Background of the Old Testament.* 2nd ed. (Grand Rapids: Eerdmans, 1996); Brevard S. Childs, *Introduction to the Old Testament as Scripture* (Philadelphia: Augsburg Fortress Press, 2011); Raymond B. Dillard and Tremper Longman III, *An Introduction to the Old Testament.* 2nd ed. (Grand Rapids: Zondervan, 2006). For a classic liberal approach, see Otto Eissfeldt, *The Old Testament: An Introduction* (New York: Harper & Row, 1965). For a non-conservative, Catholic approach, see J. Alberto Soggin, *Introduction to the Old Testament: From Its Origins to the Closing of the Alexandrian Canon.* 3rd ed. (Philadelphia: Westminster, 1989).

TEXTUAL CRITICISM

Brotzman, Ellis R. *Old Testament Textual Criticism.* Grand Rapids: Baker, 1994.

Klein, Ralph W. *Textual Criticism of the Old Testament.* Philadelphia: Fortress, 1974.

McCarter, P. Kyle, Jr. *Textual Criticism.* Philadelphia: Fortress, 1986.

Tov, Emmanuel. *Textual Criticism of the Hebrew Bible.* 3rd ed. Minneapolis: Fortress, 2011.

Würthwein, Ernst. *The Text of the Old Testament.* Translated by Erroll F. Rhodes. 2nd ed. Grand Rapids: Eerdmans, 1995.

GRAMMAR AND SYNTAX

Kautzsch, E., ed. *Gesenius' Hebrew Grammar.* Translated by A. E. Cowley, 2nd English ed. Oxford: Clarendon Press, 1910.
Waltke, Bruce K., and M. O'Connor. *An Introduction to Biblical Hebrew Syntax.* Winona Lake, IN: Eisenbrauns, 1990.

WORD STUDIES

Barr, James. *Comparative Philology and the Text of the Old Testament.* Rev. ed. Winona Lake, IN: Eisenbrauns, 1987.
———. *The Semantics of Biblical Literature.* Oxford: Clarendon Press, 1961.
Botterweck, G. Johannes, and Helmer Ringgren, eds. *Theological Dictionary of the Old Testament.* 12 vols. Translated by John T. Willis. Grand Rapids: Eerdmans, 1974–.
Harris, R. Laird, Gleason Archer, and Bruce K. Waltke, eds. *Theological Wordbook of the Old Testament.* 2 vols. Rev. ed. Chicago: Moody Press, 2003.
Jenni, Ernst, and Claus Westermann, eds. *Theological Lexicon of the Old Testament.* Peabody, MA: Hendrickson, 1998.
Van Gemeren, Willem, ed. *The New International Dictionary of Old Testament Theology and Exegesis.* 5 vols. Grand Rapids, Zondervan, 1998.

BIBLICAL THEOLOGIES

Eichrodt, Walther. *Theology of the Old Testament.* 2 vols. Philadelphia: Westminster Press, 1961.
Hasel, Gerhard. *Old Testament Theology: Basic Issues in the Current Debate.* 3rd ed. Grand Rapids: Eerdmans, 1975.
House, Paul R. *Old Testament Theology.* Downers Grove, IL: InterVarsity Press, 1998.
Oehler, Gustav F. *Theology of the Old Testament.* Translated and edited by George E. Day. 1874. Reprint of English edition. Grand Rapids: Zondervan, 1955.
Von Rad, Gerhard. *Old Testament Theology.* 2 vols. New York: Harper & Row, 1962.

If you want a good study of the history and the development of biblical theology, see John Hayes and Frederick Prussner, *Old Testament Theology:*

Its History and Development (Atlanta: John Knox Press, 1985). Von Rad is excellent for textual discussions of individual themes, but of questionable value for the understanding of the origins of theology.

HISTORY OF THE ANCIENT NEAR EAST

Hallo, William W., and William K. Simpson. *The Ancient Near East: A History.* New York: Harcourt, Brace, Jovanovich, 1971.
Moscati, Sabatino. *Ancient Semitic Civilizations.* New York: G. P. Putnam's Sons, 1957.
Wiseman, D. J., ed. *Peoples of Old Testament Times.* Oxford: The Clarendon Press, 1973.

HISTORY OF ISRAEL

Bright, John. *A History of Israel.* 4th ed. Philadelphia: Westminster Press, 2000.
Merrill, Eugene H. *Kingdom of Priests: A History of Old Testament Israel.* 2nd ed. Grand Rapids: Baker, 2008.

Other helpful resources include John H. Hayes and J. Maxwell Miller, eds., *Israelite and Judean History* (Philadelphia: Westminster Press, 1977), which gives a collection of studies on the subject; and Martin Noth, *The History of Israel* (New York: Harper & Row, 1960), which gives a clear presentation of a view that became a major force in Old Testament studies.

CUSTOMS AND MANNERS

Aberbach, Moshe. *Labor, Crafts, and Commerce in Ancient Israel.* Jerusalem: At the Magnes Press, 1994.
de Vaux, Roland. *Ancient Israel.* Volume 1: *Social Institutions.* Volume 2: *Religious Institutions.* 3rd ed. New York: McGraw-Hill, 1997.
Noth, Martin. *The Old Testament World.* Philadelphia: Fortress Press, 1966.

Also to be recommended are the following: W. Corswant, *A Dictionary of Life in Bible Times* (Bungay, England: Hodder and Stoughton, 1960); and M. S. Miller and J. L. Miller, *Encyclopedia of Bible Life* (New York: Harper & Row, 1955).

ARCHAEOLOGY

Aharoni, Y. *The Archaeology of the Land of Israel.* Philadelphia: Westminster, 1982.

Albright, W. F. *Archaeology and the Religion of Israel.* 5th ed. Baltimore: Johns Hopkins Press, 1968.

Avi-Yonah, Michael, and Ephraim Stern, eds. *Encyclopedia of Archaeological Excavations in the Holy Land.* 4 vols. Jerusalem: Massada Press, 1975–1978.

Currid, John C. *Doing Archaeology in the Land of the Bible.* Grand Rapids: Baker, 1998.

Kenyon, K. *Archaeology in the Holy Land.* 4th ed. New York: W. W. Norton & Company, 1979.

Lance, D. *The Old Testament and the Archaeologist.* Guides to Biblical Scholarship: Old Testament Series. Philadelphia: Fortress Press, 1981.

Further works include P. Lapp, *The Tale of the Tell*, Pittsburgh Theological Monograph Series 5 (Pittsburgh: Pickwick Press, 1975), which gives a treatment of how archaeologists work. For current discussions, subscribe to journals like *Biblical Archaeology Review* and *Bible Review*. And for topical treatments, for example, water systems, town planning, etc., see S. Paul and W. Dever, eds., *Biblical Archaeology* (Jerusalem: Keter, 1973).

ISRAELITE RELIGION AGAINST THE WORLD

Mullen, E. T. *The Assembly of the Gods: The Divine Council in Canaanite and Early Hebrew Literature.* Harvard Semitic Monographs 24. Chico, CA: Scholars Press, 1980.

Oppenheim, A. L. *Ancient Mesopotamia: A Portrait of a Dead Civilization.* Revised and completed by Erica Reiner. Chicago/London, 1977 (1964).

Pritchard, J., ed. *Ancient Near Eastern Texts Relating to the Old Testament.* 3rd ed. with supplement. Princeton: Princeton University Press, 1969.

Also of value, and perhaps more affordable (but in no way complete) are the following works: Helmer Ringgren, *Religions of the Ancient Near East* (Philadelphia: Westminster Press, 1973); John Day, *God's Conflict with the Dragon and the Sea: Echoes of a Canaanite Myth in the Old Testament* (Cambridge: Cambridge University Press, 1985); J. Gibson, ed., *Canaanite Myths and Legends* (Edinburgh: T & T Clark, 1977); and, if available, especially

New Larousse Encyclopedia of Mythology (New York: Hamlyn Publishing Group, 1968).

JEWISH BACKGROUND TO THE NEW TESTAMENT

Blackman, Philip, ed. *Mishnayoth.* 6 vols. New York: Judaica Press, 1973.
Bloch, Abraham. *The Biblical and Historical Background of Jewish Customs and Ceremonies.* New York: KTAV, 1980.
Cross, Frank Moore Jr. *The Ancient Library of Qumran and Biblical Studies.* New York: Doubleday, 1961.
Lightfoot, John. *A Commentary on the New Testament from the Talmud and Hebraica.* 4 vols. 1959. Reprint, Grand Rapids: Baker, 1979.
Patai, Raphael. *The Messiah Texts.* Detroit: Wayne State University Press, 1979.
Safrai, S., et al. *The Jewish People in the First Century.* Vol. 2. Assen, Amsterdam: Van Gorcum Press, 1974.

BIBLE DICTIONARIES

Buttrick, George A., ed. *The Interpreter's Dictionary of the Bible.* 4 vols. plus Supplement. Nashville: Abingdon Press, 1962.
Douglas, J. D., ed. *The Illustrated Bible Dictionary.* 3 vols. Leicester, England: Inter-Varsity Press, 1980.
Tenney, Merrill C., and Moisés Silva, eds. *The Zondervan Encyclopedia of the Bible.* 5 vols. Rev. ed. Grand Rapids: Zondervan, 2009.

HEBREW AND GREEK (OT) CONCORDANCES

Even-Shoshan, A. *A New Concordance of the Bible.* Jerusalem: Kiryat-Sepher, 1977.
Hatch, Edwin, and Henry Redpath. *A Concordance to the Septuagint and the Other Greek Versions of the Old Testament.* 2 vols. 1897–1906. Reprint, Grand Rapids: Baker, 1983.
Lisowsky, G. and L. Rost. *Konkordanz zum Hebraischen Alten Testament.* Stuttgart: Wurttembergische Bibelanstalt, 1958.
Mandelkern, S. *Veteris Testamenti Concordantiae: Hebraicae atque Chaldaicae.* 4th corrected edition. New York: Schocken, 1958.
Wigram, George V. *The Englishman's Hebrew and Chaldee Concordance of*

the Old Testament. London: Samuel Bagster & Sons, 1890. (Many reprints.)

ATLASES

Aharoni, Yohanan. *The Land of the Bible. A Historical Geography*. Revised and enlarged. Translated by A. F. Rainey. Philadelphia: Westminster Press, 1979.
Aharoni, Y., and M. Avi-Yonah, eds. *The Macmillan Bible Atlas*. 3rd ed. New York: Macmillan, 1993.
The Collegeville Atlas of the Bible. Collegeville, MN: The Liturgical Press, 1998.

THE OLD TESTAMENT IN THE NEW TESTAMENT

Baker, D. L. *Two Testaments, One Bible*. 3rd ed. Downers Grove, IL: InterVarsity Press, 2010.
Bruce, F. F. *New Testament Development of Old Testament Themes*. Grand Rapids: Eerdmans, 1968.
France, R. T. *Jesus and the Old Testament: His Application of Old Testament Passages to Himself and His Mission*. London: Tyndale Press, 1971.
Johnson, S. Lewis, Jr. *The Old Testament in the New: An Argument for Biblical Inspiration*. Grand Rapids: Zondervan, 1980.
Longenecker, Richard N. *Biblical Exegesis in the Apostolic Period*. Grand Rapids: Eerdmans, 1975.
Moo, Douglas J. *The Old Testament in the Gospel Passion Narratives*. Sheffield, England: Almond Press, 1983.

TIME-SAVING TOOLS

The more exegetical expositions one develops the easier it becomes. But at the outset the process can be time-consuming and therefore off-putting. The standard lexica provide a tremendous amount of information once you learn how to use them easily. The standard lexicon by Brown, Driver and Briggs is still very helpful and a good starting point — and the least expensive. More comprehensive lexica are Koehler and Baumgartner (4 vols.) and Cline (8 vols.).

There are translation and parsing resources available that speed up the process and enable you to find the word in the dictionaries more quickly: *A Reader's Hebrew-English Lexicon of the Old Testament*, 4 vols., edited by

Armstrong, Busby, and Carr (Zondervan); *Analytical Key to the Old Testament,* 4 vols., ed. by Owens (Baker); and *The NIV Interlinear Hebrew-English Old Testament,* ed. by Kohlenberger (Zondervan). And for Malachi, the detailed analyses of the text by James N. Pohlig, *An Exegetical Summary of Malachi* (Summer Institute of Linguistics); and Terry W. Eddinger, *Malachi: A Handbook on the Hebrew Text* (Baylor) will prove very helpful. Computer programs are also excellent in facilitating the various searches necessary for exegesis. Bible Works for Windows (Hermeneutika Computer Research Bible Research Software) and Bible Windows (Silver Mountain Software) are excellent tools for IBM-PC users. For Mac users, Accordance (Gramcord Institute) would be worth having. The computer programs serve the exegetical process very well, although for more detailed research other resources not included will have to be checked.

The modern expositor has more resources available for the study of the text than at any time in history. Individuals must discover what combination of books and programs are most helpful for their needs and abilities; having the right resources readily available will expedite the process.

COMMENTARY ON
THE BOOK OF MALACHI

1   *God's Faithful Covenant Love*

(MALACHI 1:1–5)

Introduction

Translation and Textual Notes

[1]   A burden — the word of the LORD unto Israel by[1] Malachi.[2]

[2]   "I have loved you," says the LORD.
> But you say, "Wherein have you loved us?"
> "Is not Jacob Esau's brother?" is the oracle of the LORD,[3]
>> "Yet I have loved Jacob, [3] but Esau I have hated.
>> I have made his mountains a desolation
>> and[4] his heritage for jackals of the desert."

[4]   If Edom says, "We are shattered but we will rebuild the ruins,"
> the LORD of armies says, "They may build, but I shall tear down;
> and they will be called 'the wicked country,'
> and 'the people with whom Yahweh is angry forever.'"

[5]   Your own eyes will see this, and you will say,
> "Great is the LORD beyond the border of Israel!"

---

1   Literally "by the hand of," which is idiomatic for "by means of."

2   The Greek has ἀγγέλου αὐτοῦ, which represents "his messenger." This is clearly an interpretation of the word and not a representation of a personal name. The Greek then adds a line from Haggai 2:15, 18, saying, "Lay it, I pray, to your heart."

3   The editors of the printed edition propose deleting "is the oracle of the LORD" for metrical reasons (to make a better balanced line). However, since there is no manuscript support for this it is not a textual problem, only a conjectural emendation that may be rejected.

4   The editors propose adding a verb here, נָתַתִּי or the like, based on the Syriac: "I have given."

(Malachi 1:1–5)

Context and Composition

Malachi came on the scene to assist in bringing about the needed reforms permanently. But he found a spirit that would later be expressed in Pharisaism and Sadduceeism, a spirit of outward perfunctory service with little inward repentance or devotion. Not only that, there was widespread skepticism and resignation. The people complained that the earlier prophetic promises had not been fulfilled, and they were impatient for God to judge their enemies, especially the Gentiles, as well as those Jews whom they believed had rebelled against the LORD. And so Malachi had serious issues to address, but he was exactly the right man for the job.

This first brief oracle sets the tone for the entire collection of his messages. In it the prophet tried to lay a foundation for his appeals — to convince the people of God's love for them. But it had been some time since a prophet had been heard in the land, and the people to whom he preached reacted with a belligerent antagonism. The people simply challenged his assertions.

Because Malachi's audience was so difficult, he chose to use interrogation and reply as the way to get through to them. In each point he could express what they were thinking, and so he anticipated them with both the questions and the answers. Concerning God's love for them, they had focused on trivial things that they thought brought the teaching into question and had missed the main point. And so the prophet contrasted the way that God dealt with them with the way he dealt with Edom — and would continue to deal with them in judgment.

Exegetical Comments

1:2

"I have loved." The declaration of God's love is expressed with אָהַבְתִּי, the *qal* perfect, first person common singular. The verb אָהַב means "to love," very often with the special sense of choosing. If God loved Israel, it meant he chose them for himself; there was affection for sure, but divine election lay behind it all. The nuance here is probably present perfect: "I have loved you" — a love that has continued to the present in spite of all that has happened to the people.

"Wherein." The anticipated response from the people is a challenge: בַּמָּה

34

is simply "in what?" It means "in what way?" or "wherein?" This will be a repeated response of the people according to Malachi. Their question is a demand for the prophet to prove God loved them, but it is addressed to God: "wherein have you loved us?"

"oracle."   The reply is an oracle from the LORD through the prophet: it begins in verse 2 and extends to verse 3. The text has the noun נְאֻם, "an oracle." It would be rendered: "[is the] oracle of Yahweh," but most translate it simply with "says." But the idea of "oracle" is much stronger than "says."

"Is not Jacob Esau's brother?"   The oracle reads literally, "Is not Esau a brother to Jacob?" meaning, "Is not Jacob Esau's brother?" This rhetorical question was designed to reaffirm that Esau was Jacob's brother, and this statement was then to be the foundation for the next.

"Yet I have loved."   The next clause begins with the preterite with *waw* consecutive, וָאֹהַב. Recall that *I-'aleph* verbs like this have a prefix vowel *holem,* and in the first person common singular form the root letter *'aleph* drops out to avoid having two identical letters back to back. The clause in the sequence could be rendered, "and yet I have loved Jacob."

1:3

"I have hated."   Then, in the next clause (v. 3a) the verb is a perfect tense שָׂנֵאתִי, because the clause begins with a noun (and therefore cannot use the *waw* consecutive): "but Esau I have hated." Both verbs should receive the present perfect nuance: "I have loved . . . I have hated." The verb "to hate" is the opposite of "to love"; it has the sense of reject, usually with strong feelings. Here God chose the line of Jacob, but did not choose the line of Esau. And as time passed, God's love for Israel grew as they sought to serve him, whereas Esau rebelled.

But we must keep in mind that God's choosing of the line of Jacob did not mean that everyone in Israel would be a redeemed believer; neither did the rejection of Esau's line mean that no Edomite ever came to faith.

"Jacob" and "Esau."   The names "Jacob" and "Esau" are metonymies of cause: the ancestors' names are given, but the people who came from them are the intended meaning.

"desolation." The rest of verse 3 reminds the people of the devastation that God brought on the descendants of Esau. God made their mountains a desolation, and their heritage for jackals in the desert. Their place was destroyed and left desolate.

1:4

"Edom." In verse 4 the text refers to the descendants of Esau as "Edom." The word אֱדֹם, "Edom," means "red." The name was probably originally given to the region because of the very red color of the type of rocky soil in that region, soil that had shifted north when there was a split in the earth's crust. But there is a popular etymology in Genesis 25 that puns on the name of Esau as "Edom" because Esau was reddish at birth, and then he wanted the red stew from his brother. The text is showing that this person was well-suited to the red lands of Edom.

"If Edom says." Verse 4 records Edom's resolve to rebuild their land, a resolve that God would not allow to happen. This is all set in a conditional clause: "If Edom says, 'We are shattered but we will rebuild the ruins.'" The verb in their determination, "we will rebuild," could be classified as a simple imperfect, expressing their plan to rebuild. But the context calls for something stronger, the cohortative. Normally the *qamets he'* would be present with a cohortative, but on *III he'* verbs it never is, and so the verb may not have it in this construction. Thus, "we will rebuild" means, "we are resolved to rebuild." The translation "rebuild" is drawn from the verbal hendiadys, וְנָשׁוּב וְנִבְנֶה, literally, "and we will return and build," or, "we will build again."

"Then the Lord of armies says." The clause answering the conditional clause records the Lord's resolve: "If they say . . . , then the Lord of armies says . . . 'I shall tear down.'" The word "hosts," צְבָאוֹת, means "armies." The designation includes all armies at God's disposal—celestial or terrestrial. Whenever prophets use this expression they are announcing some stern message that God will enforce because he has all the power to do it.

In this verse the Lord says, "They may build." יִבְנוּ is a *qal* imperfect, third person masculine plural, from בָּנָה. Here it has the modal nuance of possibility—"they may rebuild." The use of the independent pronouns heightens the contrast: "*They* may build, *but I* (as for me on the other hand) I shall tear down." The verb אֶהֱרֹס is the *qal* imperfect, first person common singular; here it is the simple future tense.

"and they will be called."   The LORD's resolve continues in the rest of verse 4. He announces appropriate names for them. The naming formula is simply, "and they will be called." The verb is וְקָרְאוּ, a *qal* perfect, third person common plural, with a *waw* consecutive. When there is no expressed subject the verb can be treated as a passive voice: "and they will call to them" becomes "and they will be called," rather than supplying a subject to identify what other people will call them this name. The first name is "the wicked country," with "country" being a metonymy of subject, meaning the people in the country. And the effect of this wickedness forms the other description given to Edom: "the people with whom Yahweh is angry forever." Because of their great sins and their attempt to bring Israel down for good, they must endure under God's anger forever. Individuals could escape the wrath to come, but most of the Edomites remained enemies of Israel, and therefore of God as well.

1:5

_____

"Your own eyes will see."   In verse 5 the prophecy is declared that Israel will see the devastation of Edom and will praise the LORD's greatness in the world. The people that Malachi was addressing would not see it necessarily; other people of Israel would see it. Likewise in Matthew 24 and 25 (the Olivet Discourse) Jesus gives the signs of his coming to the disciples in the form of "when you see . . ." But some of what he described lay far off in the future. It essentially means, "when *you* (believers in the age to come) see it."

"Great is the LORD."   Then people will no longer doubt God's love for them. They will see what he will do to those that he hates, the wicked of the world! And they will be thankful for his love. Their trivial protests will cease to matter in that light. They will acclaim the LORD's greatness beyond the border of Israel.

Exegetical Outline

Once the basic interpretation of the passage is determined, the expositor is ready to write an exegetical outline. Here the contents of each line or verse are summarized in the expositor's own words, and then the sections are put together and a general summary written for those associated verses. The sentences are historically descriptive — it is simply restating what Malachi was saying. Doing this helps the expositor be able to state clearly what the text says and divide it into its parts.

The exegetical outlines I have written in these passages have been carefully edited, but the basic outline need not be this polished:

> PROLOGUE: The word from the LORD to Israel by Malachi was a burden (1).
>
> I.   When the people challenge his love for them, the LORD reminds them how he chose them but rejected and judged the descendants of Esau (2–3).
>
>   A.   The people challenge God's declaration of love for them (2a).
>
>   B.   The LORD reminds them that he chose them over Esau and destroyed the descendants of Esau in their hill country (2b–3).
>
> II.   When the Edomites try to rebuild their ruins, the LORD promises his people that he will destroy anything they build for a perpetual reminder that they were the wicked people whom God judged (4).
>
>   A.   The Edomites resolve to rebuild their ruins.
>
>   B.   The LORD will destroy anything they build so that they will be remembered as a wicked nation that God judged.
>
>   1.   The Edomites will try to rebuild their ruins.
>
>   2.   The LORD will tear down what they build.
>
>   3.   The Edomites will be remembered as a wicked people God judged.
>
> III.   When the people of God witness this judgment they will acknowledge the greatness of the LORD in the world (5).

Exegetical Summary

Once the exegetical outline is written, the next step is to unite the major points of the outline to form a single summary sentence of this passage (the exegetical summary). This may seem an unnecessary step, but the process will make it easy for the expositor to summarize the contents of the passage clearly and easily. And putting it into one sentence forces the expositor to determine what the main section is — that will become the independent clause of the summary, and the other sections subordinate clauses. The following exegetical summary statement has also been edited and revised for this publication:

> When the people question the LORD's love for them, he reminds them that he chose them to be his people and not Edom whom he destroyed and will destroy in the future so that they will be known as a wicked people judged by God, a prospect that will bring praise from the people of God.

Commentary in Expository Form

Prologue: The divine message is a burden (1).

The title of the book characterizes this prophecy as a "burden" (מַשָּׂא). The oracles included here will be heavy and stern. But the messages are also consolatory: they are not *against* Israel, but *to* Israel. And there are hopeful notes of forgiveness and blessing and joy — if the people will heed the warnings.

But we still have no information about the man himself other than his name is Malachi (מַלְאָכִי), "my messenger." It may be that this was an abbreviated name from Malachiah, "Messenger of Yah," meaning "Messenger of the LORD."[5] Or the name might even have been a pen name, summarizing the heart of his message. But the prophets did not do that, as far as we know. Most likely the name was his actual name, and it was in the present form, "my messenger"; nevertheless, this name like so many names of the prophets provides a major unifying theme for the book: the prophet is a messenger, the priests are messengers, the forerunner is a messenger, and Messiah is a messenger. And so we should not be surprised to see his name as an "incarnate word."

I.   *God has an abiding love for his chosen people (1:2a).*

The book opens with the declaration of the word of the LORD: "I have loved you." This affirmation of God's choice of and affection for the nation of Israel provides a powerful beginning to the oracles in the book, for on the

---

5   The development might follow other names such as Abi, which was also spelled Abijah (see 2 Kings 18:2 and 2 Chron. 29:1). But we have no evidence this happened with Malachi.

one hand it will soften the tone of the messages — they will be delivered in love, but on the other hand it will underscore the nation's ingratitude. Even though God loved them, they had failed to show any appreciation for it or any response to it. In fact, even when the prophet declared this message, the response was a skeptical challenge for Malachi to convince them that God loved them.

If people are in any way open to the word of God, the constantly repeated message of God's faithful love for his people should inspire greater devotion and service. But the appeal of Malachi will be even wider than that, for the object of God's love in this passage is the whole nation — some unbelievers and some believers. Even the unbelievers would have to acknowledge that they were part of a special people whom God loved and desired to use, if they would only believe and follow his word. So Malachi began with the most powerful motivation that he could use to appeal to the people: the love of God.

II.   *God's love is demonstrated by his choice of his people (1:2b–3a).*

The people were not immediately convinced of this declaration. Primarily because of their state of spiritual rebellion, it sounded good but was not convincing, not convincing because things in their lives had not worked out to their satisfaction. "Wherein have you loved us?" is the prophet's anticipated summary of their arrogant response. And his reply to their response reminded them of their historical status as the chosen people of God: "Was not Esau Jacob's brother?" says the LORD. "Yet I have loved Jacob, but Esau have I hated." The prophet reminded the people that God's choice of Jacob's line and his rejection of Esau's line was the primary evidence that God loved them.

To the word "love" we now add the antonym "hate" (שָׂנֵא). A careful word study of each of these terms will show that choosing is a major part of the meaning for love, and rejecting (or not choosing) is at the heart of the word for hate. Even Jesus used the word "hate" with this basic meaning when he called for his disciples to hate father and mother, and even their own lives; that is, he called for them to choose to follow him and that often involved a radical break with families (Luke 14:26). It at least required disciples to put Christ first, before anyone. With Jacob and Esau we know that the choice was made for Jacob even before the two boys were born, when the mother was pregnant and sought an oracle about the twins. And that oracle was not just about two boys, but about two nations in her womb (Gen. 25:23). The loving and hating was not personal, but sovereign and providential; it refers to the divine election of one group of people over another for a purpose. That is the nature of God's love for his people.

Paul refers to the same event in Romans 9:13 as a sample of divine election. Thus, he can make the same point for believers in the New Testament: one clear evidence of God's love for them is that he chose them to be his kingdom of priests as well. The point is parallel to the idea that God's love for Jacob was a distinguishing love; it meant that the line from Jacob (i.e., the Israelites) was chosen for a special purpose in the world: to be the channel of blessing to the nations and the source of the Messiah. The Edomites, the descendants of Esau, were not chosen to carry on the covenant and be the primary channel of blessing for the world (even though any individual believer among them could also be such, as all believers are).

The point that Malachi was making to his audience was that their continued existence over the ages as the people of God was the clearest evidence of God's love for them. God chose the Israelites to be his kingdom of priests in the world. He gave them the Scriptures, the temple, the priests, the prophets, the covenants, and ultimately the Messiah. And his love for them was an everlasting love. Even though they failed him again and again, he still retained his covenant with them and chose to gloriously use those who believed in him and were willing to serve him.

III. *God's love for his people is demonstrated in his protective care for them (1:3b–4).*

A. HE HAS PROTECTED THEM IN THE PAST (3B).

Not only did God choose the nation of Israel ("Jacob"), but he also cared for the Israelites whenever they were in trouble, most notably by destroying their enemies. The simple fact was that Israel was protected by God down through the ages, and the Edomites were not. Israel's expectations were being fulfilled; Edom's were not. This also should have told Malachi's audience that the love of God was genuine, for he was always there for help.

The Edomites, mostly descendants of Esau but also a number of aboriginal tribes (see Gen. 36), lived in the region to the south and east of Israel, across the great rift of the Jordan Valley, and south of the Dead Sea. This was called Edom. At one time it was heavily wooded and well-watered. When the Israelites, their cousins, came up from Egypt, the Edomites would not let them pass through their land, but made them go all the way around into the eastern desert. But God would not let the Israelites fight them, for they were relatives. Nevertheless, down through history the Edomites from time to time attacked the people of Israel or supported others who attacked them. And God gave Israel the victory over them many times.

When the Babylonians invaded the land and sacked Jerusalem and carried off the people, Edom proved treacherous. But Edom was left in misery along with the many other little states — their destruction was a part of the prophetic message from God to the region (Obadiah). And even in Babylon the people remembered the way that Edom had dealt treacherously with them (Ps. 137:7). After the exile the Jews were restored to their land, but the Edomites were never again a force in the desert. They were an easy prey for the Persians, and then the Nabateans — Arab bedouin tribes who drove them out of their land so that they moved west. They settled more to the south of Israel, in the region later called Idumaea in the Negev desert, and they became known as the Idumeans. But they were subjugated by the Macedonians, Maccabeans, and finally the Romans. The only sore spot about them for Israel was that in the days of Jesus, the Romans installed on the throne a client king (by a bribe probably) Herod the Great — an Idumean, a descendant of Esau!

In this passage God reminds the nation how the Edomites were ruined by his judgment. He declared through Malachi, "I have made his mountains a waste (שְׁמָמָה) and [left] his heritage to jackals in the desert." The territory of Edom was hill country, identified as Mount Seir; this was their "heritage." At the heart of the land of the Edomites was a city carved out of the cliffs. It was completed later by the Nabataeans and called Petra ("rock"), the entire city accessible through a long narrow canyon that was easily defended. But even that would not protect them, for they were driven out, and their ancient heritage, their land, was occupied by jackals. This was their state after the exile was over — their lands were barren, and they were subjugated.

The Israelites might have been unhappy with what God had been doing for them, but they had to be convinced of his love for them when they considered what happened to these other rival states that God hated.

B. HE PROMISES TO PROTECT THEM IN THE FUTURE (4).

Verse 4 introduces the resolution of the Edomites to rebuild as a conditional clause: "If Edom says, 'We are shattered but we will rebuild the ruins.'" If they begin to do that, then the LORD declares that he will tear it down. "Thus says the LORD of armies, 'They may build, but I shall tear down.'"

And he further declares that when he tears down their building projects, they will become a byword: "and they will be called 'the wicked country' and 'the people with whom the LORD is angry forever.'" The first designation, "the wicked country," is literally "a border of wickedness." "Border" (גְּבוּל) is a metonymy of subject, meaning the people who live in the land of Edom, inside the border. The word "wickedness" is an attributive genitive, a "wicked border" meaning "wicked country," that is of course referring to "wicked people in the country" that make it wicked. Their future judgment will be a perpetual witness to their wickedness.

The reason this will be so is found in the second designation, namely, that they will be a people "with whom the LORD is angry forever." The Edomites will be brought to ruin if they attempt to rebuild to their former greatness, and that devastation will signal to all that God judged them because of their wickedness. The word "angry" (זָעַם) more precisely expresses God's indignation with these people; and it will last forever. The word "anger" is also figurative (metonymy of cause), indicating what the anger will produce: judgment.

Therefore, according to these prophetic oracles God was judging and will be judging the enemies of his people. Here the enemies are the Edomites; for their wickedness, particularly the treachery that they showed to Israel throughout history, they will be judged. God's love for Israel, therefore, is demonstrated not only by the desolation of her enemies, but by her own survival and restoration to the land when all the other states were swept away forever.

IV. *God's judgment on the wicked will inspire the praise of his people (5).*

In the final verse of the passage the prophet declares that the people will see (literally, "your eyes will see") this great judgment — and come to their senses. They will not then challenge God's love for them; rather, they will be filled with praise for his greatness. The words of their praise will be "Great is the LORD beyond the border of Israel," not "Lord" in the sense of sovereign or master, but the holy name Yahweh, Israel's covenant God, the one true and living God of the Bible.

The word "great" is a verb, "he is great" or "he will be great" (יִגְדַּל); and since God already is great, the intended meaning is that people will come to see how great God is and proclaim it publicly. And their description of his greatness will not concern only what he does in Israel. No, it will be evident beyond the borders of Israel. "Yahweh" is not a national God; he is the sovereign God over all the nations. So the prediction is not just that people in the world will turn to God, a god in some way, but to the true God revealed to us in the Bible.

This verse anticipates the themes in this book that speak of the blessings on Israel, the salvation of the Gentiles, and the coming of the Lord to destroy all the wicked. Clearly, not everyone in Malachi's day would see all of this; they would see bits of it. But true to the prophetic style, "you" refers to the people of God in general, and not just the immediate audience.

Expository Idea and Application

Expository Idea

With the public exposition in mind it is necessary to reshape the interpretive wording to form more general, biblical principles — principles that clearly come from this passage. The exegetical summary, therefore, will now be edited and turned into the major idea of the expository presentation. The idea will be written in the form of a timeless truth and just not a statement about ancient Israel. The way this is worded will vary in light of the emphasis of the expositor. My expository idea for this first brief section then can be worded something like this:

> God's love for his people
> is evident in his choosing them and protecting them
> by destroying their enemies to bring them joyful deliverance.

There are other ways to say this, of course, but this statement does capture the theological point of the passage. And that is why it is worded here as a timeless, theological principle, and not merely a description of what he did with Israel.

While this is a theological statement put in sermonic form, we can also see how the theological substance of the material within this passage will fit into the broader arrangement of theology. Clearly the foundational theme here is the love of God displayed in this world. That divine attribute, as well as the greatness of God in the praise section, would form part of the discussion of theology proper, the doctrine of God. But the passage also addresses the doctrine of divine election, and the judgment on the wicked, now and in the age to come. Under the discussion of these doctrines a systematic theology would have to include this passage in Malachi.

Application

For this exposition, the primary application of this passage must be drawn from the meaning of the passage in its context. It was a word of encouragement for the Jews who had been regathered to their land but found that the situation did not fit the promises the prophets had made about the circumstances of their return. And so when they challenged the claim that God loved them, they were reminded that they could have been wiped off the map of human history with the other little states. But God had chosen them, and God had spared them when he judged the nations. The passage should have inspired greater trust, greater confidence, and greater praise in the people.

And as with most prophetic passages dealing with Israel's restoration to the land, there is a near view of the passage and a far view, an "already" and a "not yet." The immediate meaning of the passage to Malachi's audience would be but a preview of the full meaning of it to the Jewish people at the end of the age. How God finally vindicates the remnant by saving them from the judgment will be the greatest display of his everlasting love for Israel.

But we also know that this passage is part of the whole Bible, and therefore God is using this passage to speak to us today as well. What it says to us will have to parallel what it said to ancient Israel. So in a similar way the church can look back over human history and see how the love of God has been demonstrated to them. As he had done with Israel, God has loved us with an everlasting love; he chose us to be his people, to be a kingdom of priests and a light to the world, even before we were born; and he has preserved and protected his saints down through the ages, although so many in the world have tried to destroy the people of God one way or another. The protection he has given to his people has not been complete, because so much persecution has plagued the household of faith. But as with Israel, so in the church do we find that any and every deliverance from our enemies is a preview of the great deliverance that is yet to come. Jesus said that he would not allow the gates of hell to prevail against his church, which means that ultimately the church will have victory over the world, that is, the world system under Satan's dominion. But in the meantime there will be challenges to the faith. Ultimately the "country of wickedness" for all the people of God, Old Testament and New alike, is the kingdom of Satan; only at the end of the age will all that opposition end with great and devastating judgment on the evil one and all who follow in his rebellion against God.

So when believers today begin to doubt God's love for them based on the circumstances of life, they simply have to take stock of what the church is and how it has been preserved and how it has prospered in spite of the circumstances. And as with Malachi's original audience Israel, his current audience, Christians, will be reminded of the abiding love of God. But as with Malachi's original audience, believers today have not appreciated that divine love and have not as a result rejoiced in it nor lived in obedience to God. And so the rest of the messages of this book will be equally applicable to us today.

Key Words

"To Hate"

The verb for "hate" (שָׂנֵא) occurs some 164 times in the Bible. There are very few words that have the same emphasis and range of meanings. The verb can have varying levels of intensity from hate with great hatred to a feeling of aversion to something or someone.

(1) Sometimes "hate" means "to love no longer" (see Judg. 14:16; 15:2). Leah, for example, was "hated" (Gen. 29:31, 33), but meaning less loved or neglected. Many times its distinct force can be measured by the presence of its antonym, "to love" (אָהֵב).

(2) The word is used frequently with God as the subject. Things he hates are many: abominations (Jer. 44:4), hypocritical worship (Isa. 1:14), a series of troubling sins (Prov. 6:16), divorce (Mal. 2:16), and pagan practices (Deut. 16:22). But more than this it can be used for God's sovereign choice. In this category the word "hate" includes the sense of "reject." So we read that he loved Jacob but hated Esau (Mal. 1:3). Two nations were in the womb; God chose the line from Jacob before he was born and so personal feelings were not the issue; he did not choose the line from Esau. Accordingly, most things hated are rejected; whereas things that are loved are chosen. God commands those who love the Lord to hate evil (Ps. 97:10), meaning reject it, but no doubt with feelings of revulsion. The Messiah will hate evil (Ps. 45:7); and the royal charter (Ps. 101) states how he will remove it from his kingdom.

(3) People who reject the Lord and his Law are often said to hate him

(Exod. 20:5). Similarly the psalmist's enemies are often called his "haters," and their hatred may be a mixture of loathing and rejection. Conversely, the people of Israel were warned not to hate their brothers in their hearts (Lev. 19:17).[6]

"To Love"

The word for "love" (אָהַב) occurs in Scripture in a wide array of nuances.

(1) We may consider how it describes the love of humans. The object of their love varies greatly; it could be love for other people, such as a son (Gen. 22:2), or a wife (Gen. 24:67), or a master (Exod. 21:5), all signifying affection and commitment.

The object of the love could also be food (Gen. 27:4), drink (Prov. 21:17), or sleep (Prov. 20:13), all of which show more of a choice based on enjoyment or need than on commitment. The love can also be for knowledge and righteousness and wisdom (Prov. 8:17, 21, and throughout the book). The devout believers love the Law (Ps. 5:12), Jerusalem (Ps. 122:8), and Jerusalem's courts and activities.

The object of the love could also be misplaced. It can be carnal desire based only on physical attraction (2 Sam. 13:1, 4), or it can be used for the love of folly (Ps. 11:5) and of course false gods (Hos. 4:18). Psalm 11 declares the LORD's judgment on those who love violence (v. 5) because he loves righteousness (v. 7).

(2) Love becomes an important covenant word. We find this use even in the political relationships of the countries of the ancient Near East. Hiram of Tyre, for example, loves David, meaning probably that they had a political relationship primarily (1 Kings 5:15). "Love" was also used in Israel to express loyalty to the king (1 Sam. 18:16). So when the people of Israel were commanded to love the LORD their God (Deut. 5:10; 6:5), they were being called to a commitment to keep the covenant based on their devotion to the LORD. That love would also be shown through faithful acts to neighbors and foreigners (Lev. 19:18). These uses reflect love as acts of the will to live as a faithful community. Likewise, Jesus told his disciples and us that if we loved him we would keep his commands (John 14:15).

(3) Covenant love is the proper response to the love of God for his people.

---

6 For further comments, see E. Jenni, "שָׂנֵא *śnʾ* **to hate**," in *The Theological Lexicon of the Old Testament*, ed. Jenni and Westermann, 3:1277–79.

(Malachi 1:1–5)

Malachi reminded his audience that God loved Jacob, but hated Esau. This means that the LORD chose Israel and made a covenant with them so that they would be a holy nation; but he did not make such a covenant with the Edomites. Because the LORD is righteous, he loves righteousness and hates evil (Ps. 11:7; 33:5). And as the anointed king, the Messiah likewise loves righteousness and hates wickedness (Ps. 45:7). Accordingly, those who love the LORD are expected to demonstrate their covenant loyalty by hating, that is, rejecting evil (Ps. 97:10).

2. *Worship That Dishonors God*

(MALACHI 1:6–14)

Introduction

Translation and Textual Notes

6   "A son honors a father, and a servant his master.
      Now if I am a father, where is my honor?
      And if I am a master, where is my respect?"
         says the LORD of armies,
            "to you, O priests, who are despising my name.

But you say, 'Wherein have we despised your name?'

7   By offering defiled food on my altar.

But you say, 'Wherein have we defiled you?'[1]

When you say, 'The LORD's table is to be despised.'

8   Now, when you offer blind animals, is there no evil?
      When you offer crippled or diseased animals, is there no evil?
   Present them to your governor! Will he be pleased with you?[2]
      Or, will he accept you?" says the LORD of armies.

9   "So now, implore God so that he may be gracious to us.
      This is all from your hands. Will he accept you?"
         says the LORD of armies.

1   The Greek translation has the object as "it" and not "you."
2   Some Greek manuscripts and probably the Vulgate read "it" instead of "you."

49

[10] "O that someone among you would shut the doors,
so that you would not light useless fires on my altar!
I am not pleased with you," says the LORD of armies,
"and I will accept no offering from your hands.

[11] For from the rising of the sun to its going down
my name *will be* great among the nations,
and in every place incense and pure offerings
will be offered to my name,
because my name *will be* great among the nations,"
says the LORD of armies.

[12] "But you are profaning it by saying,
'The table of the LORD is defiled, and its food[3] is
contemptible.'
[13] And you say, 'What a drudgery!'
and you sniff at it contemptuously," says the LORD of armies.
"And you bring injured, crippled, or diseased animals
when you bring an offering;
should I accept them from your hands?" says the LORD.[4]

[14] "But cursed is the deceiver who has a male in his flock
but vows and sacrifices a blemished animal to the LORD.[5]
Because I am a great king," says the LORD of armies,
"my name will be feared among the nations."

Context and Composition

Worship was designed to be a celebration of being in covenant fellowship with the holy and sovereign LORD God. It was a time for believers to demonstrate their loyalty and devotion by offering the sacrifice of praise — genuine praise given with sacrifices appropriate for the occasion. In ancient Israel what the people brought to God, and what they said when in the sanctu-

---

3 וְנִיבוֹ is redundant because "its food" is also stated with אָכְלוֹ. The editors suggest that it came by way of dittography with נִבְזֶה. They base this on the Greek and Syriac. If it is retained, the repeated idea would simply emphasize the idea of "its food."

4 A few Hebrew manuscripts, the Greek and Syriac[W] add "armies" to harmonize.

5 The text has לַאדֹנָי but the majority of the manuscripts have לַיהוָה.

ary, revealed whether or not they were truly committed to the worship and service of God.

When the Israelites came up to Jerusalem to worship, they were to bring animals from their flocks, wheat and fruit from their fields, and whatever other gifts of gratitude they wanted to give to God. They had to bring sacrifices every time they entered the sanctuary and for whatever reason. The sacrifices differed in nature, some being for forgiveness and acceptance, and other for dedication and celebration.

We do not know what occasion inspired Malachi's message. He does talk about animals, but he never uses the words "sin offering" or "atonement." That in itself is not a critical issue, for atonement in the Israelite ritual is not the same as the New Testament doctrine; in the Old Testament it is sanctification, but when used of Christ's sacrifice it includes justification. No one in Israel was ever "saved" by bringing the sacrifices; the sacrifices were a means to their maintaining a harmonious relation with the LORD. Neither can we say this was delivered on a particular feast day. Some commentators choose the Day of Atonement for the occasion (without any evidence I would add) perhaps because it makes a better fit to the way they want to focus on the atoning death of Christ. I doubt it was a Day of Atonement, because that had a specific ritual with two goats, one being the scapegoat. And even if the priests disappointed in the sacrifices, they might put the best foot forward on a high holy day, as church services do today. Would it be a Passover? Probably not, because the people would eat the animal, and they would probably bring better animals for that purpose. We simply do not know if it was a festival time or regular worship. This will not change the point of the message. But it would be a mistake to assume a festival and then make that the focus of the exegesis and application, when Malachi does not do that.

When the people came to worship, God did not require a great deal of them in the way of offerings — tokens, really, of their herds and their crops, a handful of grain, or an animal or two for the family. But what they brought had to pass two important tests, and in many cases only they and God would know if they passed them. What they brought had to be the *first* and the *best* — the first of their flock, and the best animal they had. Anything less than this was an insult to God. To bring God an inferior gift would say that one did not think much of God, for the quality of the gift indicates the value the giver places on the one receiving the gift. That is true in a human relationship, and it certainly is true in worship.

But people were (and are) constantly failing to develop and maintain true worship. This is true even of believers who let down, or get carried away with their own needs and interests, and have to be called back again and again because they may have left their first love, as the Lord Jesus said to the Ephesians (Rev. 2:4). And so the prophets came to rebuke, reprove, correct, and exhort the people. In the earlier periods the prophets had to deal with idolatry and pagan corruptions in Israel's worship. After the exile that was no longer a major problem; instead, worship was being corrupted by the indifference and selfishness of people.

Malachi had to address a different set of problems in the nation. His first sermon, directed at the priests but certainly speaking to the worship of the people, deals with their making a mockery out of worship by bringing inferior offerings and treating the whole service as an unpleasant waste of time. God was not pleased with that kind of worship. The primary audience of the oracle is the priests, as the text makes clear. But a closer look at the charges indicates that the people themselves are guilty and therefore being addressed as well. We do not know the spiritual status of all the people being addressed (any more than we can be sure of our audiences today). We would assume that most of them, priests and people, claimed to be believers. If they were unbelievers or pagans, they would not have even made an effort to bring anything. So Malachi is dealing with professing believers, most of whom are probably believers but some are not. They have found a way to make the sacrificial worship less demanding, and in the process did not meet God's standards. The people may have been ignorant of the laws (as 2:1–9 will indicate), but the priests should have known them but diluted them because they showed respect of persons (2:9). We may criticize their violations, but we must also ask how the modern churches change the standards to ensure more people will come.

The flow of the passage is easy to trace. The first three verses form a *rebuke* of the priests' practice of showing contempt for the LORD by offering corrupt animals (vv. 6–8). The next three verses call for the people to *seek God's grace*, a call that would assume repentance by the people and the response of forgiveness by God; and if they refuse, God warns that he will turn to the nations who will respond properly to his greatness (vv. 9–11). In the last three verses he once again addresses their violations and their attitudes, warning that if they persist they will be removed from the place of his blessings and he will *turn to the nations* for fear and honor (vv. 12–14). The first and last sections are parallel in that they rebuke the sins and warn of rejection in favor of the nations; and the middle section offers the clear directive from God. The application must remember this central emphasis, because the very first thing people must do when they realize their worship and service is so deeply flawed is to pray for God's gracious forgiveness, not just spruce up their worship. Sin has been committed, forgiveness is needed.

Exegetical Comments

1:6

"**honors.**"   In verse 6 the verb כָּבֵד means "to be heavy," but in a figurative sense, "to be important." Here the form is יְכַבֵּד, a *piel* imperfect, the *piel* meaning of "honors" being a factitive (causative) or declarative use of the stem, and the imperfect a general truth, that is, the habitual imperfect.

"**my honor.**"   The pronominal suffix "my" on "honor" is a genitive of worth: "the honor that is fitting for/due to me." The same would be the case for the suffix "my" on "fear."

"**Lord.**"   For "and if I am Lord," the text uses אֲדוֹנִים, the ordinary word for "Lord" and not the personal name. But it appears in the plural probably to underscore that this is the sovereign Lord.

"**Despising my name.**"   Those being addressed are the priests, the "despisers of my name," בּוֹזֵי שְׁמִי. The construction is the *qal* active participle, masculine plural, in construct, followed by the word "name," which would here be the objective genitive, that is, they were despising the name. "My" is simply the genitive of possession. In this line the participle is modifying "priests" (the article indicating the vocative) and so may be translated "(O priests) who despise my name."

"**despise.**"   The word "despise," בָּזָה, means "to treat as worthless." A helpful illustration would be Esau in Genesis 25. He sold his birthright for a bowl of lentil soup because he despised the birthright — it had no value to him. He is ever since known as a profane man.

"**name.**"   In the same expression the word "name" is a metonymy of subject. It refers to the nature or the attributes of God, that is, his true nature as it is revealed in his wonderful works. They were treating as worthless everything God revealed himself to be.

"Wherein."   At the end of the verse we have the defiant response of the people. In their challenge is the form בָּזִינוּ, the *qal* perfect, first person common plural, of the same root. The nuance would be a present perfect, indicating something they did that had continuing results: "Wherein have we despised your name?"

1:7

"Offering."   Beginning with verse 7 the charge is explained. The first form מַגִּישִׁים is the *hiphil* participle, masculine plural, from נָגַשׁ, "to draw near," and so here "bring near" or "offer." The participle is a verbal use; the subject "you" is understood from the context: "(you are) offering."

"defiled."   What they were offering was "defiled." The verb גָּאַל, "to defile" (not to be confused with the homonym "to redeem"), is here a *pual* participle, masculine singular. It is an attributive use, modifying "bread."

"(Wherein) have we defiled you?"   Their defiant response has the verb גֵּאַלְנוּךָ, the *piel* perfect, first person common plural, with the second person masculine singular suffix. It should be taken as a present perfect as well: "[wherein] have we defiled you."

"When you say."   The answer uses בֶּאֱמָרְכֶם, the *qal* infinitive construct with a preposition and a second person masculine singular suffix (acting as the subjective genitive): "in the saying of you." But this is to be translated as an adverbial clause of time, "when you say." There is no stated independent clause; that would have to be supplied from the context: "[You have despised his name] when you say . . ."

"The table of the LORD is despised."   They considered the table of the LORD worthless. To call the altar a "table" is figurative, an implied comparison (hypocatastasis). It is a natural comparison to make since the sacrifices offered on it were often communal meals, and what was burned up was said to be "consumed." By making the offerings they did they showed they despised the table. The form נִבְזֶה, a *niphal* participle, would just be translated "despised" since it has a predicate adjective use here: the "table is despised." But the *niphal* is not a simple passive here; rather, it describes the perceived status of the altar.

1:8

"And when you offer."   The charge in response to their defiant challenge is finally explained in verse 8: they were offering worthless animals. תַגִּשׁוּן is the *hiphil* imperfect, second person masculine plural (it has defective writing without *hireq yod* as the parallel clause indicates), from נָגַשׁ again. The nuance would be progressive imperfect: "you offer" or "you are offering."

"is there no evil?"   At the end of each of the first two lines of verse 8 we have the clause אֵין רָע. It should be taken as an interrogative clause, "is there no evil?" or "is that not evil?" A case could be made for reading it as sarcasm based on the next line: "there is no evil!" meaning there is. But the form of a question is preferable. The questions are also rhetorical (erotesis), affirming it is evil.

"Present them."   In verse 8b the challenge is made to the people to try to pay the governor with such worthless things. The verb הַקְרִיבֵהוּ is the *hiphil* imperative from the verb קָרַב, "to be near," and so here "offer."

"Will he take pleasure?"   If they do, the question is "will he take pleasure in you" and "will he lift up your face"? The second question is idiomatic, meaning "will he have respect for you?" These are both rhetorical questions (erotesis) to affirm that he will not.

1:9

"So now, entreat."   Beginning the next section with verse 9 we have the urgency of the prophet's advice. It is expressed by the *piel* imperative חַלּוּ־נָא (from חָלָה), "entreat," and with the introductory "So now."

"that he may be gracious."   The imperative is followed in volitive sequence by וִיחָנֵנוּ, the *qal* jussive or imperfect, third person masculine singular, with the pronominal suffix. The vowel under the prefix was a *qamets,* but reduced by propretonic reduction, and then the *shewa* was lost when the rule of the *shewa* changed וְיְ (*w^{e}y^e*) to the quiescent letter as part of the vowel וִי (*wi*). In sequence it may express the purpose: "in order that he may be gracious to us."

"This was from your hand."   The expression "this was/is from your hand" is

55

(Malachi 1:6–14)

idiomatic, but the original figure was a metonymy of cause, the hands being the instruments for producing the corrupt worship ritual.

1:10

"O that someone"   The apparent question that begins verse 10 is actually a strong wish formula; it literally says, "Who also among you, that he will close the doors," but it means, "O that someone among you would close the doors."

"so you do not light."   The reason for this wish is found in the second clause. The verb is the imperfect tense תָאִירוּ (causative stem of the root אור, "light"), and with its *waw* conjunction shows a purpose or result clause after the preceding clause: "so that you do not light . . ."

1:11

"the nations."   God will turn to the nations for proper worship (v. 11) if his people rebel. Here the idea of burning incense is a figure, a metonymy of adjunct, because incense accompanied the prayers. Prayers will be made as a sweet-smelling aroma, not a stench to God, because of the faith and devotion of the Gentile worshipers.

"will be offered."   מֻגָּשׁ is the *hophal* participle of the same verb we have been seeing for "cause to draw near" or "bring" or "offer." Here it is the predicate: "[will] be offered."

"pure offering."   In every place there will be people offering "a pure offering." The language is Levitical throughout this chapter. An offering (the מִנְחָה of Lev. 2) as well as the sacrifices had to be "pure" or "clean" (טָהוֹר); this is the opposite of "unclean" or "defiled." No one should be allowed in the sanctuary without complete ritual purity.

1:12

"But you."   The last section (vv. 12–14) begins with the disjunctive *waw* to form a contrast with what the nations will do: "But as for you."

"[are] profaning."   מְחַלְלִים is the verb of this clause; it is the *piel* participle, masculine plural, of the verb "to be common, profane." The word is the antonym of "holy." In this causative stem it means they had been making the worship profane; they had been desecrating it. The etymological derivation of the English word "profane," from *pro fanum,* means "outside the temple." It refers to that which is common, not set apart to God.

1:13

"Should I be pleased."   When God asks if he should be pleased with what they were bringing, the question is rhetorical; he is affirming that he will not accept this kind of worship.

1:14a

"the deceiver."   A curse is announced for the "cheat." נוֹכֵל is the participle used as the subject of the clause; אָרוּר is the passive participle used as the predicate. The verb to be supplied could be a jussive, "may the deceiver be cursed," or a simple imperfect, either "is cursed" or "will be cursed." The latter is the strongest for a prophecy. This one (maybe more than one, maybe one is representative) who is cursed tries to deceive everyone by pretending to offer a great sacrifice, but is actually passing off a worthless thing.

"blemished."   What he ends up offering to God is called a מָשְׁחָת, the *hophal* participle from שָׁחַת, used here as the direct object of the two participles. The word is very strong; it was used to describe things like soured milk, or the destruction of Sodom. So the offering is completely worthless because it is a ruined thing.

1:14b

"feared."   In the last line, "feared" is נוֹרָא, the *niphal* participle from יָרֵא, "to be afraid, to fear." It is the predicate adjective use here: "my name [will be] feared among the nations."

Exegetical Outline

Once again we can begin to bring the material together with a fully descriptive outline. Each main idea, verse or clause, is summarized in my words, and then the summaries are grouped and new headings written. Here is my outline, which has gone through a good bit of editing:

I. The LORD rebukes the people for refusing to honor his name and for despising his altar by offering diseased and defiled animals, something they would not even offer to their governor (1:6–8).
  A. He rebukes the priests for despising the name of the LORD (6).
  B. He responds to their challenge by exposing their practice of offering diseased and defiled animals on the altar (7–8a).
  C. He reasons that not even the governor would accept such gifts (8b).
II. The LORD exhorts the people to pray for mercy for their sins, but would rather all worship cease if it is going to be worthless, for he will find true worship among the nations (1:9–11).
  A. He exhorts the people to pray for mercy (9).
  B. He desires that the sanctuary be closed so that vain worship will not take place (10).
  C. He prophesies that if Israel refuses to do so he will be worshiped properly throughout all the nations (11).
III. The LORD rebukes their defilement of and contempt for worship and announces a curse on those who cheat God and lie about their devotion, for he will find true worship among the nations (1:12–14).
  A. He rebukes the people for defiling the altar with corrupt offerings and treating the whole service with contempt (12–13).
  B. He pronounces a curse on hypocritical worshipers who deny God his proper due (14a).
  C. He announces that because he is a great king he will be feared throughout the world if not in Israel (14b).

Exegetical Summary

For this step it simply requires taking the major Roman numeral points of the outline, writing them together as a paragraph, and then editing them to make a one-sentence summary. You have to decide which section is the main part of the passage, then make that point the independent clause, and the others dependent clauses. The wording summarizes the contents of this passage (and no other):

> *Because the people were defiling worship with their corrupt offerings and despising his name with contempt for the ritual, the LORD entreats them to pray for mercy or cease worshiping altogether, for if they continue to cheat God and feign piety he will turn to the Gentiles to find pure and reverential worship.*

The first clause gives the cause for the appeal, the second the appeal (my independent clause), and the third a warning to motivate compliance.

Commentary in Expository Form

I.   *Those who give God worthless things in the name of worship reveal an indifference and inconsideration for the LORD (1:6–8).*

A. GOD DESERVES ADORATION AND REVERENCE (6).

Malachi, always conveying the word of the LORD as is attested by the frequent "says the LORD of armies," begins his message with a couple of affirmations that the people would have agreed with wholeheartedly. But he uses them to lead into his rebuke. He declares, "A son honors a father, and a servant his master." They would have responded, "Yes, this is what the Law says, and this is how things ought to be."

The word "honors" signifies what the son should give his father, and the servant his master — the proper respect and appropriate authority due to their position. That is, they would acknowledge by word and deed their proper weight of authority.

But Malachi follows this with two rhetorical questions from God: Where is my honor? and Where is my reverential fear? These questions are designed to affirm that the people had not been honoring or fearing God, which indicated that they did not treat him as Lord or Father. The expressions form a stinging rebuke; they would have been taken as an insult by the priests who probably thought they were doing everything well enough. But the prophet relays to them the word of the LORD: "'If I am a father, where is my honor; if I am Lord, where is my fear?' says the LORD of armies to you, O priests, who despise my name.'" This rebuke of the priests would also have surprised and overwhelmed the people; they thought the message was going to be on the human relationships he introduced, but he turned it to their spiritual relationship with God. He still had not stated what the actual problem was, but whatever it was it could be summarized that they did not honor the LORD and they did not fear him. And yet they were the priests, and if the priests were in some violation, so were the worshipers!

The prophet turns the rebuke into a direct accusation: they despise his name. This is a further description of what it means not to honor his name — between honoring and despising there is no neutral ground. The message is addressed to the priests directly, but as we shall see, because of their failures, the nation was also guilty of not honoring and fearing the LORD. He said they were also among those "who despise my name." The word "despise" (בָּזָה) essentially means to look down on something as if it is worthless, to treat it with contempt. The use of the participle here stresses that their characteristic nature is being exposed. They did not simply despise the LORD in the way they worshiped; the way they worshiped showed that they were despisers of the LORD. And the specific object of their despising is the very nature of the LORD. Such a violation of worship is an insult to the person of God.

The priests thought they were doing everything right, saying the prayers and the blessings, and making all the right sacrifices. So they responded (Malachi knows how they would respond and so voices their protest): "Wherein have we despised your name?" They use the finite verb now, looking for something they did rather than a general characteristic they revealed. Even if they made a mistake here or there in the service, it did not mean that they despised the name of the LORD, did it? Thus they might have reasoned.

But God said otherwise. There was something seriously wrong in their faith, their attitude toward the LORD. This is a very serious charge even as it stands; but the seriousness is signaled even more by the title used for God, "the LORD of armies" [hosts], a judgment title meaning that God has all the heavenly and earthly armies at his disposal to enforce his will and to judge the people. And so now that Malachi had their attention, he could explain what was happening.

B. OFFERING WORTHLESS GIFTS TO GOD BETRAYS A CONTEMPT FOR GOD (7–8A).

Their answer is defiant: "Wherein have we despised your name?" The answer to their challenge is clear. The LORD says through the prophet that they were offering defiled food on the altar. The altar was the place of sacrifice, of course; and the charge was that what they were offering to God did not measure up to the standards of the Law. The "food" (לֶחֶם) that they brought was defiled or polluted. That the sacrifices were called food was both symbolic and practical. Symbolic because when they were burned on the altar, the table, it was as if God "consumed" them; and practical because some of the sacrifices were to be eaten by the priests and the people as communal meals. But the food they brought was "defiled" (מְגֹאָל). They were supposed to bring sacrifices that were perfect, that is, healthy animals, without any blemish at all.

There were two very important reasons for this. First, the sacrifice was a gift that was to be offered to God. As noted above, the kind of gift that someone gives indicates what he or she thinks of the recipient of the gift (even in our mundane gift-giving this is telling). Second, some of the animals brought were for sin offerings, some for dedication and thanksgiving. In either case the animal had to be perfect. When the animal represented God's provision for the sins of the worshiper, it had to be without blemish itself. This principle came to fulfillment in the sacrifice of Christ on the cross: he was the sinless Lamb of God who gave his life for the sins of the world. If Christ had been defiled, a sinner, his death would have been no better than our own deaths. The only one who could redeem us from sin was the only one who was sinless. But the sacrifice of Christ plays an important part in our sanctification too, for when we confess our sin the blood of Christ goes on cleansing us.[6]

So the indictment that they brought defiled offerings was serious. And they knew it. So they challenged this as well: "Wherein have we defiled you?" Note that in their response the object is made clear — they were not just bringing defiled offerings, they were defiling God. If God is holy, then his sanctuary is holy, his altar is holy, and his sacrifices are to be holy. To bring defiled sacrifices then defiles God.

---

6   This is part of the typology of the Bible. A type is an indirect form of prophecy; it was not clear if it was prophetic until the fulfillment confirmed it. The point is that God legislated the sacrifices the way he did with Christ's sacrifice in mind. But make sure you have it clear in your thinking: atonement in the book of Leviticus is what we would call in the New Testament sanctification — the atoning sacrifices were given by people to maintain a relation they had by faith. They were not saving sacrifices. Now the New Testament will see the fullest meaning in the atoning sacrifices and apply it to Christ's perfect sacrifice. So you have to be careful how you use these words; otherwise you end up saying all the Old Testament people before Christ's sacrifice were not saved.

Malachi answers their challenge again. First, he says ". . . when you say the table of the LORD is contemptible." Not only do they despise the person of God, they think the table, that is, the altar, is worthless. They did not literally "say" this of course, but their actions said that was what they thought, because the people brought defiled gifts they did not think the altar and the ritual was worthwhile. If they thought the altar and the ritual were common, then the logical conclusion would be that they did not think God was special either.

How exactly did they despise the altar and offer defiled things? Here is how: Malachi says, "When you offer the blind for a sacrifice, is that not evil? And when you offer the lame, and the sick, is that not evil?" (v. 8a). He is talking about animals. The people knew they had to bring animal sacrifices to the sanctuary for their worship, and if they did it right that could get expensive. And so they began to cut corners; they brought animals that were diseased, crippled, blind, and worthless, animals they could not sell or use — but they could offer them to God! After all, they were only going to be burned up anyway. This seemed to them a very practical thing to do (so they thought) to not only fulfill the ritual but also to get rid of the worthless livestock at the same time. But the people could only get away with this if priests allowed them to do it, both by their weak teaching and their general acceptance of the gifts.

C. THEY WOULD NOT DARE PAY THEIR TAXES WITH SUCH THINGS (8B).

To make his point clear Malachi reasons further: "'Present them to your governor; will he be pleased with you, or respect you?' says the LORD of armies." Try paying your taxes with worthless things. The questions here are probably rhetorical again — they affirm that the governor will not be pleased. But God is more important than the governor; so why do people think they can give him inferior gifts?

II. *Those who are guilty of offering God worthless things must seek his forgiveness if they are to continue in his favor (1:9–11).*

A. THOSE GUILTY OF CHEAP AND CORRUPT WORSHIP MUST PRAY EARNESTLY FOR GOD'S FORGIVENESS (9).

Now the prophet strongly tells the people what they should do for it is all they can do, but they must do it quickly (the form is an imperative): pray for forgiveness. "Now, entreat the face of God." The expression is bold, but simple: they have to pray for divine favor (the face of God usually represents his favor — see Num. 6:26). Entreating the face is a human expression (anthropomorphic language), signifying something like a child's stroking the face of a parent in order to gain favor. In order to do this they had to admit something they were doing greatly displeased God.

The purpose of this imperative is expressed in the second verb (וִיחָנֵנוּ), "in order that he may be gracious to us." The choice of the word "gracious" (חָנַן) is fitting here; it provides the purpose of the prayer and repeats the main idea of seeking favor. This word means undeserved favor — they are to stroke the face of God in order that he may give them favor they do not deserve, that is, forgiveness by his grace. They would only do this if they were now convinced they had sinned against God.

The reason for the urgent prayer is that the people are guilty: "this is from your hands" is an idiom in the book that means "this is what you have produced." Will God be pleased or will he respect those who do this? The implied answer to the rhetorical questions is that God has no pleasure in or respect for the worshiper who offers to him something that is corrupt, ruined, and therefore worthless.

B. IT WOULD BE BETTER TO STOP VAIN WORSHIP ALTOGETHER (10).

Now the prophet declares the word of the LORD in the form of a strong wish: "O that someone would shut the doors so that you might not kindle fire on my altar in vain." It would be better to lock the doors of the temple and keep the people out. If they continue to worship this way, then the fire they light on the altar will be worthless and their effort in vain. Clearly God would rather they repent and worship correctly; but if not, it is better not to worship at all.

Corrupt worship is another sin. The purpose of shutting the doors would be "so that you do not light my altar in vain." The word "in vain" is the adverbial spelling based on the word "to be gracious" seen above (חִנָּם, from חָנַן). It forms a powerful word play: seek his *grace* or your worship is *gratuitous* (vain). The word "grace" means "undeserved favor," but in this adverbial form it means "for no reason, gratuitously." Their corrupt worship would be pointless, for no good reason, a waste of time. God takes no pleasure in worthless worship; in fact, he rejects it! If people do not worship properly with love and devotion, but only out of compulsion to follow a ritual, their gift will be worthless, and their activities counted as sin.

C. GOD WILL FIND OTHER WORSHIPERS AMONG THE NATIONS WHO WILL HONOR HIM (11).

What would be the outcome of shutting down the temple and keeping false worship out? God would turn to the Gentiles to find people who would honor him. And as we know, this is exactly what happened historically. Verse 11, then, is one of the early predictions of Gentile faith: if the Israelites reject the LORD, the nations will come to the light. So God says, "From the rising of the sun to its setting, my name [will be] great among the nations." The figure (a double merism) means that people everywhere (east to west) all the time (morning to evening) will acknowledge the greatness of God. The people in the world will acknowledge the greatness of the LORD in their praise and in their obedience. Moreover, in every place, he says, "incense and pure offerings will be offered to my name, for my name will be great among the nations." Incense was offered with intercessory prayer, the coals for the altar of incense being taken from the high altar where the pure offering was made. So the nations will acknowledge his greatness by praying to him and by following pure worship. Devout worshipers know that they need God desperately; but the people Malachi addressed apparently had no such understanding.

The prophecy of turning to the Gentiles began to be fulfilled even in Old Testament days, but found its greatest and true fulfillment in New Testament times. The New Testament explains that once the Messiah came, all worship had to be in him, for he is the perfect sacrifice. But when Israel by and large rejected him, then the Lord turned to a people who would bear fruit (see Matt. 21:43; Rom. 11: 11–12). And when the gospel went to all nations, people came to faith in the sacrifice of Christ Jesus. When Paul found Jewish opposition from city to city, he turned to the Gentiles who heard him gladly.

III. *Those whose worship is corrupt must change their attitude or God will take his blessing from them (1:12–14).*

A. WHEN WORSHIP IS WORTHLESS TO GOD THEN PARTICIPATION IN IT BECOMES A DRUDGERY (12–13).

In strong contrast to the prospect of the nations worshiping correctly, Malachi turns back to his audience to reiterate their sin and explain it further. They were "profaning" worship. The word "profane" (חָלַל) means to treat as or make something common, ordinary — the opposite of "holy." Their meal in the sanctuary was not holy; it was profane because they brought unholy or ordinary animals. All of this indicated that they did not treat God as holy — he was nothing special to them, if we judge by how they treated him. So too in the modern world when Christians find church a drudgery (some churches make it so), or do not put the Lord first in their lives, they are in effect also saying the Lord is not that special.

Malachi repeats his charge as he explains they did this when they said the table of the LORD was defiled, and its food corrupt. Of course, they would not literally say this — they were priests, after all, and they had to say the right things in the services. But in the way that they worshiped they were revealing how they saw it.

But even worse, Malachi says they are not even trying to hide their true feelings. In verse 13 he adds that the LORD says, "And you say, 'What a drudgery!' and you sniff at it contemptuously." The ritual had become meaningless, so it was a drudgery to do it; but they had to go through with it anyway. A worship service that becomes empty ritual because the heart is not in it will be drudgery, and sooner or later people will not even go. Then Malachi adds that they sniff at it contemptuously. This is some kind of a gesture or expression of disgust, a loud, quick breathing out through the nose when doing the service. The people would know what the priests thought of all the ritual and liturgy. There was no joy in worship, no delight in serving God, because they did not value him.

This attitude prevails today in so many circles of worship where the ritual has become a routine, then a drudgery. People go through the service, but it is something to endure. And sometimes ministers, for one reason or another, become bored, or indifferent, perhaps burned out. They need to turn the service over to someone else until they can get their spiritual perspective restored. Genuine praise and thanksgiving will go a long way toward bringing life back into the service; but a large part of the problem is going to be concerned with how the word of God is used. And that will be Malachi's next sermon.

Speaking further the word of the LORD, Malachi affirms that all such false worship will be rejected: "When you bring injured, crippled, and diseased animals and bring them as offerings, should I accept them from your hands?" Of course not (is the implied answer to the question). What an insult!

B. DIVINE PUNISHMENT AWAITS THOSE WHO RUIN AND DESPISE THE WORSHIP OF GOD (14A).

The warning concludes with a curse: "Cursed is the deceiver who has in his flock a male [sacrifice], but vows and sacrifices a blemished thing to the LORD." The blemished thing is literally a ruined or corrupt sacrifice. The line could mean that they vow the pure male, but sacrifice the corrupt animal. However, it is more likely that it means they even vow the blemished thing, as if they were making some grand offering. In either case, the one doing this is to be cursed.

This word "cursed" (from אָרַר) basically means to remove from the place of blessing, to banish; essentially it refers to the loss of God's blessing. The blessing jeopardized could be anything, from the temporal blessings, to spiritual blessings, to eternal life. The exposition has to be clear in its meaning here. It will be with this word that Malachi will begin the next sermon: how God curses the blessings of the priests because they do not obey Scripture. So in this passage, based on the usage in the next chapter, the word at least means the priests would be removed from the benefits and service of the priesthood, cut off from God's blessings promised to a righteous and faithful people (like the sons of Eli in 1 Samuel). And if people persisted in this, they would see less and less of the blessings of God on their lives. Now if the guilty were not true believers at all, this curse would be far worse; it would include the removal from the place of divine blessing, both in this world and the world to come.

The principle is very simple: if people keep the best for themselves and offer God the junk, God may take away even the best they have (see Deut. 8), or even their lives, as he did in Acts 5 when Ananias and Sapphira lied to God about what they were giving. So God will not long tolerate false worship; he will get rid of it, or as John warns in Revelation 2 and 3, he will remove the "lampstand," that is, the power and the witness of the congregation.

As we shall see in Malachi, corrupt priests were left in office, but they were made base and low in the eyes of the people — a worthless ministry.

In an exposition we have to state clearly what the warning would mean for believers, for clergy and for worshipers, and then for unbelievers. The impact would be different for all these groups, but essentially have the same meaning of a loss of God's blessing.

C. GOD WILL BE REVERED AMONG THE NATIONS (14B).

As for the people in general if this curse is fulfilled and the deceivers are removed from the place of blessing, the LORD will turn to the nations to find faithful worshipers. And so the text repeats that the LORD's name will be reverenced among the Gentiles because he is a great King. The word "fear" is a worship word; it means reverential fear, that is, adoring, marveling, praising, but shrinking back with a healthy respect and obedience. The LORD

(Yahweh by name) is a great king. These Israelites did not recognize that, but the Gentiles will. As a king, Yahweh has authority to demand allegiance and obedience from his people in what they do, and then to bless and to curse accordingly.

Expository Idea and Application

Expository Idea

The warning to the original audience is a warning to us; so we can adjust the summary message to form an expository idea, the central thesis of the exposition:

> Corrupt and contemptible worship is an insult to God
> and if it is not repented of and corrected
> will lead to God's turning to bless others who will be faithful.

Application

The message of this passage is timeless, even though it is based in a historical setting. The theology of the passage is the same today as it was then, even though the form of worship has changed considerably. Worship of the holy and sovereign God must never be treated as profane, worthless, or a drudgery; if that happens, then worship has been defiled and God's nature despised.

The principle is that in worshiping God people must be spiritual and faithful in all they do and say so that he may be glorified. In John 4 the Lord Jesus Christ told the woman at the well that the Father was seeking worshipers who would worship "in spirit and truth." Worship must be genuine. Worshipers must put their heart into it and it must be spiritual. And they must do it honestly, not deceiving others into thinking they are pious when they are defrauding God. It must be in truth and not hypocrisy. To get to this point they have to grow in the grace and knowledge of the Lord so that they will appreciate more who he is and what he has done. They must know the "name of the Lord," for the greater the experiential knowledge of the object of worship, the greater the worship.

But if people do not venture there in their faith, but live shallow, selfish, and self-indulgent lives, then the worship will be a drudgery and their gifts perfunctory and worthless.

So the applications should be clear. First, people have to have a very good understanding of the nature of the one they claim to worship. If they gain this, they will be overwhelmed in his presence. Second, they have to have a very clear understanding about what they are doing in their rituals of worship. These two call for clear teaching and guidance on these two subjects, two subjects that are often passed over because people assume everyone knows these things. They do not. Then, third, they have to put into practice worship that is honoring to God. This means they will prepare spiritually for worship, they will give the Lord the best they have of their time, their very lives, their talents and spiritual gifts, and their possessions; and they will not pretend to be pillars of the faith if they are not.

It would be well for worshipers to seek God's mercy regularly, knowing that in this life they will not often worship in spirit and in truth. Too many churches never even consider the subject of worship — they just keep doing what they have always done, and it becomes a drudgery. This passage warns of that danger, for if the worship is dead and worthless, God will turn to bless others who will honor his name. This is why there are so many dead churches carrying on as usual, but without divine power.

Key Words

"To Despise"

בָּזָה means "to despise" someone or something in the sense of raising the head loftily and disdainfully, looking down the nose at people or things and treating them with contempt, that is, considering them worthless.

(1) For example, in Psalm 22:7 the suffering Servant is said to be despised by the people, for no one cared whether he lived or not. In Isaiah 53:3 the suffering Servant is despised, because no one esteemed him as the Messiah. They "wrote him off."

(2) The sense remains the same in most of the uses of the verb. Genesis 25:34 has already been mentioned; the story is explained at the end: Esau considered the birthright worthless and so that is why he traded it for a meal. In other uses Malachi accuses the priests of despising the name of the LORD (1:6) because they showed no reverence and made no commitment to obey. They did not value the LORD or the ritual. Their worthless offerings

were the result, for as Malachi indicates, whatever is despised is considered worthless (1:7).

(3) The word is used in Psalm 51:17 in an understatement: God will not despise the broken-hearted penitent. The intended meaning is that God will receive such a person with great rejoicing.

"To Defile"

The word "defile" (II. גָּאַל) is not to be confused with the more frequently used homonym "to redeem." The word is used in the *niphal* stem with the sense of being defiled or polluted, as with hands that are defiled by blood (Isa. 59:30). The active sense is found in the *piel* stem, meaning "to defile"; this is the meaning in Malachi 1:7, in which we read that by bringing diseased animals to the altar they had defiled the altar, meaning, the entire sacrificial ritual and its meaning. They did not simply profane it (make it ordinary or common); they desecrated it. The corresponding *pual* form is used in the same passage for the altar they had defiled. It also appears in Ezra 2:62 for deposed priests, those who were desecrated. The active sense can also be found in the *hiphil* form: "I have polluted/stained all my garment" (Isa. 63:3). And the reflexive meaning is found with the *hithpael,* as when Daniel might defile himself if he ate the foods the Law prohibited (Dan. 1:8).

Other than a cognate noun "defilement" (Neh. 13:29), there are only a couple of other passages where this word or related words appear.

"To Honor"

The word for "honor" or "glory" (כָּבוֹד) is related to the verb "be heavy" (כָּבֵד), which by figurative extension means "important."

(1) In its literal sense the word describes anything that is heavy, such as a man (1 Sam. 4:18) or a rock (Isa. 32:29). But it can also be used figuratively to describe blindness (eyes that are heavy — Gen. 48:10) or unbelief (a heavy or hardened heart — Exod. 9:7).

(2) The related meaning of "important" arises because what has weight is perceived as important (as in our expression of throwing one's weight around). So things and people are said to be important, such as the temple (Hag. 2:3), or robes (Exod. 28:2), or even a forest (Isa. 10:18). The apostle Paul

plays on the meaning of the word when he speaks of the eternal "weight of glory" (2 Cor. 4:17).

(3) In the derived verbal stem the word comes to mean "to treat as important, to honor," such as honoring parents (Exod. 20:12), or the Sabbath (Isa. 58:13), or most importantly, God (Ps. 50:15). If people honor God they will show it by their piety and obedience (Mal. 1:6).

(4) The word "glory" is used for aspects of what we call the "soul" on occasion. As such, it refers to the real person, the essential life (Ps. 30:12). A related noun is "liver," which is also used figuratively for the heart of human life; it was the heaviest organ and considered the most important. The use of "glory" for the essential person is what gives that person "importance." Everyone has this "glory," this inner glory or importance, but the LORD has a quality of it superior to everyone else.[7]

(5) The noun "glory" came to be used for the trappings that reflect the importance or greatness of someone. For example, Joseph told his brothers to tell their father of his glory (NIV "honor" — Gen. 45:13). When this meaning is applied to the LORD, as in "the glory of the LORD," it refers to all the manifestations of his powerful presence, such as the work of creation in Psalm 19. It could also refer to the brilliant, luminous cloud at the sea and in the wilderness (Exod. 14:19–20, 24). Moses saw all that, but still wanted to see God's glory (Exod. 33:18). He wanted to see past the phenomena to the actual person (the Greek version translated "glory" in this verse as "yourself").

(6) When the Bible uses the words "glory" or "glorious" with reference to the LORD, it is basically saying that he is the most important or preeminent person in existence. And when the Bible refers to the glory of God, it is usually referring to all the evidence of God's preeminence and greatness, whether creation, or salvation, or a manifestation of his presence.

"To Fear"

The combination of serving and rejoicing with "fear" may seem to be out of harmony, but an understanding of the word "fear" (יִרְאָה related to the verb "to fear, be afraid," יָרֵא) will clarify its appropriateness here.

(1) One basic meaning of these words is the simple idea of "fear" or "dread," such as the terror of the mariners in the storm (Jonah 1:5), or the sinners

---

7 See further E. Jacob, *The Theology of the Old Testament,* trans. A. W. Heathcote and P. J. Allcock (New York: Harper & Row, 1958), p. 88.

in the garden (Gen. 3:10). There is no reverential element in such passages, only terror of the consequences. At times the word of the LORD seeks to allay such fears, as in the words to Abram after the battle, "Fear not" (Gen. 15:1).

(2) But the word can also be used in a positive sense to describe reverential awe for the LORD (Exod. 34:30; Lev. 19:14; Ps. 66:5). It can be used in this sense for honoring parents (Lev. 19:3) or other things, but it is mostly with reference to God, or the word of God. The devout worshiper is even referred to as a God-fearer; and leaders like the elders were supposed to fear God (Exod. 18:21; see also Josh. 22:25). The English word "revere" includes the ideas of regarding something as sacred or exalted, of holding something in deep and usually affectionate respect, or of venerating. But the religious sense of our word as reverential awe does not eliminate the idea of fear, but turns it into a positive devotion. Like the Israelites at the foot of the fiery mountain, devout believers are drawn to the LORD in adoration and amazement because his power is glorious, but they also shrink back because the powerful presence is overwhelming and therefore frightening. This same tension between adoration and fear occurs with human responses to other things as well, such as dangerous animals, tornadoes, or natural wonders.

So God's presence is both attracting and frightening, which is why people can rejoice in his presence, but with reverential fear (Ps. 2:11). The word includes both aspects; for the believer the aspect of reverence will be uppermost, but for the unbeliever who has every reason to fear God the aspect of fear in the word is uppermost.

(3) Many passages will refer to the activities that result from a believer's fearing the LORD: for example, obedience to God's word and the avoidance of evil (Ps. 34:11–14), as well as pure worship (Ps. 5:7) and praise that honors the LORD (Ps. 118:4).

"To Be Holy"

The adjective "holy" (קָדוֹשׁ) is one of the most important words in Old Testament theology. The related verb means "to be, become holy, set apart"; and related nouns are קֹדֶשׁ, "sacredness, apartness," מִקְדָּשׁ, "sacred place," קֶדֶשׁ, "sanctuary"; and also two forms קָדֵשׁ and קְדֵשָׁה, which mean "cult prostitute" (simply meaning separated from normal marital life for a specific purpose in the pagan temples). These last words illustrate that the common idea of this word group is not holy in the sense of righteous, but simply set apart, different, distinct.

(1) In the Bible this is one of the primary attributes of God. He is the holy one (Isa. 57:15); there is no one like him (Isa. 45:5, 11–13, 19); he is incomparably holy (Isa. 6:3). This means that he is set apart from all others; he is unique. There is no one like him in heaven or on earth. In discussing this attribute of God, we need to survey all the other attributes in order to clarify in what way God is different. For example, God is eternal, and no one else is. Or, God is omniscient, and no one else is. God is righteous, and while we may have moments of righteousness, we are not like him. He is different. God is all powerful, and we are not. This is probably how Psalm 22:3 is using the adjective. To say God is holy in the midst of a lament about unanswered prayer means that God is not indifferent or impotent like the pagan gods — he is different, he has power, and he has a history of answering prayers.

(2) Places are set apart or holy. Mount Zion is holy in Jerusalem (Ps. 2:6) because the place was set apart for the sanctuary. It was a holy mountain because God was there. A holy place had to be set apart to God, that is, sanctified. And other things connected to the sanctuary also had to be sanctified, such as the utensils, the altar, and the tent (Exod. 29:37; 30:29). In fact, the antonym of "holy" is "profane, common, ordinary" (s.v. חָלַל); in English the etymological explanation of profane is "outside the temple."

(3) Times are set apart or holy. God sanctified the Sabbath day (Gen. 2:3), meaning that he set it apart for his own purposes. In Israel under the Law, nothing common or ordinary could be done on the holy day.

(4) People are set apart or sanctified. God established Israel to be a holy nation (Exod. 19:6), a people set apart for the service of the LORD. But religious leaders such as priests were expected to be set apart to service, and in their activities to sanctify the LORD in the eyes of the people (Lev. 10:3). People had to see that this worship was set apart from everything earthy and pagan. Ordinary people would sanctify themselves for all kinds of service, in the sanctuary or elsewhere (e.g., Josh. 7:13). The simple law of Leviticus was, "Be holy, because I the LORD your God am holy" (19:1). God expected his people to be set apart from the world and to him. In this aspect their holiness, their apartness, would have to be characterized by righteousness, truth, justice, morality, and all the other attributes listed in Scripture.

(5) To declare that God is holy is to declare that there is no one like him anywhere; he is set apart from humans, angels, false gods, and everything physical and earthy, in every way imaginable. God's intervention in the affairs of his people demonstrated he was indeed holy. No one else in heaven or on earth could do, or would do, the things that he does. He is unique, distinct, set apart from all others. He is holy!

"To Profane"

The word חִלֵּל is the *piel* of the verb חָלַל III (a third homonym), "to pollute, defile, profane." Its derived noun, חֹל, "profaneness, commonness," is the antonym of the word "holy," קָדוֹשׁ. The verb should not be confused with the verb חָלַל, "to begin," or the verb חָלַל, "to bore, pierce," or חָלַל, "to play the flute." These all are homonyms; whether there was a connection between any of them is debatable.

(1) The verb "to profane" has at its heart the basic meaning of being or making something common, making it lose its distinctiveness (holiness) by the way it is used or violated.

(2) The word can be adapted to many different contexts with the idea of defilement, such as sexual defilement by violating the moral laws of marriage (Gen. 49:4), or the ceremonial laws by defiling the Sabbath and treating it as a common day (Exod. 31:14), or the altar by using common tools and equipment (Exod. 20:25), or the covenant itself by divorcing and marrying pagans (Mal. 2:11).

(3) It can also be used in the simple sense of treating something as common (an idea that lies behind all the uses), such as a vineyard when the vineyard was put to common use (Deut. 20:6), or the name of the LORD by the people who failed to demonstrate God's holiness by the way they were living (Ezek. 36:23). In Ezekiel 36 God assures to fulfill the promises in spite of Israel's sin because of his holy name's sake, that is, he will set aside the punishment to ensure his name is no longer desecrated. Maas defines the word as "desecrate," but he connects it to the idea of "beginning" in the sense of placing something in profane use, such as the beginning of the use of a vineyard at the end of a period of consecration (using Deut. 20:6; 28:30, and Jer. 19:23–25). With regard to the destruction of the temple, the priests and people had already desecrated it by their false worship and rebellions. Since this also meant God himself was desecrated (or treated as common), the judgment on the sanctuary and its people was the necessary result, and so the catastrophe of 587/586 BC is also a desecration.[8]

---

8 See F. Maas, "חלל *hll* pi. **to desecrate**," in *Theological Lexicon of the Old Testament*, ed. Jenni and Westermann, 2:427–30.

3. *Teaching God's Word Faithfully*
(MALACHI 2:1-9)

Introduction

Translation and Textual Notes

¹ "And now, this admonition is for you, O priests:

² If you will not listen and if you will not set it upon your heart
to give honor to my name," says the LORD of armies,
"Then I shall send a curse upon you, and curse your blessings.[1]
Indeed, I have cursed them,[2]
because you are not setting it upon your heart.
³ I am about to rebuke[3] for you the seed;[4]
And I shall spread offal on your faces,
offal from your festal sacrifices,
and you will be carried off with it.[5]

1 The Greek has a singular noun, suggesting בְּרְכַתְכֶם. This no doubt was to harmonize the word with the following verb's suffix "it."

2 The text has "it"; this probably led the Greek version to assume "blessing" was singular. But the more difficult reading would be with the singular pronoun used as a collective.

3 The editors of BHS propose reading גֹרֵעַ, "cut off," based on the Greek text's ἀφορίζω, "I turn (= גרע) [my back on you]." "Rebuking the seed" is very clear and natural; "turning [the back]" on them seems to be an attempt to explain the meaning of the line but does not fit well the next line.

4 The Greek text has τὸν ὦμον, "the back," which may reflect a reading of הַזְּרֹעַ, "the arm," instead of MT's הַזֶּרַע, "the seed." The line according to the Greek (and Aquila and the Vulgate) means that God would turn away the back/arm of the priest. The Hebrew means that God would rebuke the seed, either crops in the field or descendants of the priests. The latter makes the most sense in the passage.

5 The Greek text has the verb in the first person, λήμψομαι, prompting the editors of BHS to read וְנָשָׂאתִי. However, a verb without an expressed subject may be translated as a passive:

⁴ And you will know that I have sent you this admonition
   so that my covenant with the Levites⁶ may continue,"
      says the LORD of armies.

⁵ "My covenant was with them,
      one of life and peace;
   and I gave them to them *for* fear,
      and they feared me and stood in awe of my name.
⁶ True instruction was in their mouths
      and nothing false was found on their lips.
   They walked with me in peace and uprightness,
      and turned many from iniquity.
⁷ For the lips of the priest must preserve knowledge,
      and from his mouth people should seek instruction —
         for he is the messenger of the LORD of armies.

⁸ But you have turned from the way
      and by your teaching have caused many to stumble;
   you have ruined the covenant with the Levites,"
      says the LORD of armies.
⁹ "So I have made you despised and humiliated
      before all the people,
         because you are not keeping my ways
         but are showing partiality in your instruction."

Context and Composition

Malachi had to deal with a variety of sins among the clergy and the people. In chapter 1 he focused on their "cheap" worship and contempt for the

---

"one will take you away" means "you will be taken away." The Greek finishes the line with "at
the same time" rather than "unto it" in the MT. The editors propose continuing the idea of
the first person by reading "from me."

6   The text has singular "Levi." Levi, of course, was never a priest. The text means the
tribe from Levi, the Levites (the figure of speech is a metonymy of cause, the name put for the
tribe that came from him). This is common in the Bible. For example, we have the scepter not
departing from "Judah," meaning the tribe. So I have changed the translation for clarity. This
means, though, that the references to follow had to be put into the plural, whereas the MT
continues with "him," referring to singular Levi.

ritual; and in the second half of this chapter he will address the problem of divorce and marriage to pagans. Whenever there are such violations, it almost always is connected to corrupt teaching. Somehow the people had the idea that these things were not serious sins, or that they could do them and get away with them. Malachi turns in this passage therefore to lay the blame where it belongs: with the priests and their false teaching. Blaming the priests for the problems in no way let the guilty off the hook; they too were responsible for their sins even if they were unaware of what Scripture said about it — ignorance is never an excuse for breaking the Law. But the guilt was greater for those who by their false teaching caused people to stumble.

The short message breaks down into three parts: the condemnation (vv. 1–4), the covenant standard (vv. 5–7), and the charge (vv. 8–9). It is constructed for the greatest rhetorical effect. First, he condemns the priests for their failure in ministry — this would have grabbed their attention, but also sparked their interest to see what he was so upset about. Second, he lays out the standard for the ministry so they would know what they failed to do. And finally he states explicitly what they have done wrong in the light of that standard.

Exegetical Comments

2:1

"admonition." The word is מִצְוָה, which is normally to be translated "commandment" but often includes more. Here it includes a rebuke, a warning, and an instruction from the Lord through the prophet.

2:2

"If you will not listen." The conditional clauses are powerful. The first, "if you will not listen" (אִם־לֹא תִשְׁמְעוּ), means "if you will not obey" (not just listen); and the second, "if you will not take it to heart" (set it on the heart, וְאִם־לֹא תָשִׂימוּ עַל־לֵב), stresses the intention to take heed. The implication is that they have no intention of obeying to give God the glory.

"then I shall send." וְשִׁלַּחְתִּי is the *piel* perfect, first person common singular, with a *waw* consecutive (note the accent shift to the suffix): "then/and I shall send." This clause continues the sequence begun with the conditional clauses.

"a curse."   The form has an article, "the curse," but it simply heightens the meaning of the word. The verb and the noun "curse" are prominent in this passage. The play on the words with "blessing" helps the expositor to stress the distinction. A "blessing" is essentially an enrichment, a gift, a benefit from God, and one that includes enablement. A "curse" will destroy or remove the blessing; the verb may have the sense of "banish." Here the privileges of the priesthood were blessings; but with a curse God could take them all away.

"And I shall curse."   The form וְאָרוֹתִי is the *qal* perfect, first person common singular from the geminate root, with a *waw* consecutive (note again the accent shift) to put it into the future. Not only will the LORD send a curse, he will even curse their blessings.

"And also I have cursed it."   The form now is the *qal* perfect without a *waw*, and so it will be understand in the past tense — here the present perfect: "I have (already) cursed it." Recall the textual problem with the singular suffix "it" referring to the plural noun "blessings."

"you are not setting it upon your heart."   Instead of the conditional clause, the construction changes now to the *qal* active participle, masculine plural, to stress the durative sense of the verb, "you are not setting. . . ." The subject is the suffix on אֵין: "there is not you setting" means "you are not setting it upon [your] heart." They not only had no intention of obeying, but they were even now disobedient.

This same failure in other leaders can be illustrated easily. In Numbers 20 when the people murmured against God because there was no water, God told Moses to *speak* to the rock in the presence of the people so that water would come out for them. But Moses lost his temper. He said, "Listen, you rebels, must we bring you water from this rock?" And he *struck* the rock twice and water came out. Because of that, Moses was not allowed to lead the Israelites into the Promised Land. What did Moses do wrong? He was angry and impatient, he took credit for the mission ("we"), and he disobeyed the word of God in the presence of the people. This was not the picture of God that he was to convey. And so God made sure he was sanctified in the eyes of the people by punishing Moses. As God said when the sons of the priests offered strange fire on the altar (Lev. 10), "I must be sanctified by those who draw near to me (i.e., priests), and before all the people I must be glorified." Those who are called to represent God must be sure to represent him. If by their words or their works they bring down God's reputation or character, they fail to glorify his name. And God will not let anyone destroy his reputation.

2:3

"I am about to rebuke." The imminent future is stressed by הִנְנִי (with a suffix) and the active participle. It says, "Here I am rebuking," and means "Look, I am about to rebuke," that is, it could happen any time.

The verb "rebuke" (גָּעַר) is a strong word. It is often much more than a criticism or a reproach. If God rebukes something, it means he stops it (such as Christ's rebuking the wind and the sea). The verb is used in Zechariah 3 for the LORD's rebuking Satan. The adversary Satan was there to accuse ("satanize") Joshua the high priest, but when the LORD rebuked Satan, he stopped immediately.

"the seed." Assuming this to be a reference to the priest's descendants and not the seed planted in the fields, the word would be figurative, a metonymy of cause. The "seed" is what is stated in the text, but the intended effect is that the descendants are meant, that is, what the seed produced.

If the reading of "arm" were accepted, it might mean that the priest could not offer sacrifices on the altar, or could not lift his arm to give the priestly blessing, or that he was physically incapacitated in some way so that he was no longer qualified to be the priest (priests, according to Lev. 21 and 22, had to be healthy and whole with no broken bones or any physical defects at all, because they were conveying to the people the ideal). In that case "arm" would represent the whole person who would be disqualified.

"And I will spread [offal]." וְזֵרִיתִי is the *piel* perfect, first person common singular, from זָרָה with the *waw* consecutive. The word means "to scatter, throw, winnow," and so here "throw" would fit fairly well. The object is "offal," the unclean parts of the animal. The LORD will not literally do this, so it is an implied comparison. It means that the priests will be unclean in God's sight and so removed from the holy place, as if they were smeared with offal from their festivals.

"and you will be carried off with it." The text literally says "and he/one will carry you unto it." Because there is no expressed subject, we may make the verb a passive: "you will be carried away." There is a textual difficulty on the prepositional phrase, and the editors propose going with the change. We would expect "with it," but we have "unto it," either to the dung heap or to the unclean parts that will be carried away.

2:4
_____

"that [my covenant] may continue." The line begins with the *qal* infinitive construct of הָיָה—לִהְיוֹת; the preposition with the infinitive would give a sense of purpose or result: "that [my covenant] be" with Levi. But it should be interpreted to mean "continue to be" or "remain" because the priesthood was already in existence.

The central focus of the ministry of the Levitical priesthood is expressed in Deuteronomy 33:9–10. First, they were to teach Israel the Law. Second, they were to make intercessory prayers (stated as burning incense). Third, they were to keep the provision of atonement through the burnt offering always available to people.

2:5
_____

"[one of] life and peace." The definite article ("the life" and "the peace") is often used to underscore an abstract idea and need not be translated. This line is probably also elliptical, because "life and peace" refer to what the covenant was like, that is, what it was designed to do. So the word "covenant" may be repeated for clarity: "my covenant was with them, a covenant of life and peace."

"And I gave them to him [them]." וָאֶתְּנֵם is the *qal* preterite, first person common singular, from נָתַן, with a *waw* consecutive and a third person masculine plural pronominal suffix: "and I gave them [life and peace] to him [the Levites]."

"[for] fear." מוֹרָא is the noun "fear." The word seems to be placed between the clauses with no clearly expressed connection. So it is to be classified as an adverbial accusative expressing the product or intended result of giving them spiritual life and peace. God gave them life and peace "for fear," meaning, so that they would fear. And the next clause confirms this: "and they (lit. "he") feared me."

"and stood in awe." נִחַת is the *niphal* perfect, third person masculine singular, of חָתַת, which actually means "be shattered, dismayed," and so is stronger than "stood in awe." The early priests were overcome by the presence of the power and glory of God and were afraid in the proper and healthy sense.

2:6

"true instruction." The word "true" is literally "truth," אֱמֶת. It designates what was taught as reliable, that is, they taught the truth, God's word, and their teaching was faithful to that revelation. The teaching would guide people through life, as the word "instruction" (תּוֹרָה) signifies a pointing in the right direction.

"mouths" and "lips." These two words are figures of speech, metonymies of cause. This means that the instruments (of speech) are stated, but what is meant is the effect, what is taught.

"false." The word "righteous" basically means to conform to the standard. The standard is God and his revealed will, the Word of God. To fail to obey the Word is to fail to measure up to the standard, and so would be unrighteousness. Teaching anything different would be false teaching because it would go against the standard of Scripture.

"and turned." הֵשִׁיב is the *hiphil* perfect, third person masculine singular, of שׁוּב. שׁוּב means "to turn, return"; but it is often used for "repent," that is, turning back to the LORD. This is probably the meaning here, but since the verb is causative (*hiphil*), it was the ministry of the priests that accomplished this: "he [Levi, i.e., the priests] turned many" or "caused many to turn/repent."

2:7

"must preserve." The imperfect tense here should be given the modal nuance of obligation because this is the expected and standard obligation of the priests — they must do this! They must preserve knowledge, that is, the knowledge of God's revelation, by studying it, memorizing it, and teaching it.

"should seek." The imperfect tense is third person common plural, "they should seek"; but since there is no expressed subject, we may either supply one ("people") or render the clause in the passive voice. Parallel to the first verb in the verse, this one also expresses the standard: it is what people should do, or better, should be able to do.

2:8
___

"But you." This *waw* disjunctive with the pronoun is adversative: "But as for you" signals a shift in the argument of the passage, that is, in contrast to what the faithful priests did, the failures of this group will now be detailed.

"you have turned." סַרְתֶּם is the *qal* perfect, second person masculine plural, from סוּר, "to turn aside." The form should be given a present perfect translation — the priests turned aside and have remained alienated from the right course of the ministry ("the way"). The defection was deliberate and continued. They still were not following the way.

"and [by your teaching] you have caused [many] to stumble." The verb in this clause also has a present perfect nuance, here of the *hiphil* perfect, second person masculine plural, from כָּשַׁל — "you have caused to stumble." The figure of stumbling is an idiom (it is an implied comparison between stumbling and falling into sin, which by frequent use became an idiom). It follows in line with the use of "the way" for an obedient course of action. The priests turned aside from the way, and in practice caused others to sin.

"you have ruined." The verb שִׁחַתֶּם is the *piel* perfect, second person masculine plural, from שָׁחַת. It also will have the present perfect nuance, because what they did had ruined the covenant, and it was still in ruins. Their unfaithfulness and disobedience destroyed the ministry, for it no longer caused people to turn from sin to righteousness.

2:9
___

"[So I have made you] despised and humiliated." The first word is נִבְזִים, the *niphal* participle of the verb בָּזָה, "to despise, treat as worthless." God exposed the corruption of the priests here and as a result people had no respect for the priests at all. To this is added שְׁפָלִים, "low." By exposing and condemning the priests God brought them down; he made them the lowest in the eyes of the people. They would be left in office, but in the opinion of the congregation, they were contemptible and base.

(Malachi 2:1–9)

"because you are not keeping my ways." Here we have the active participle שֹׁמְרִים following the negative with a suffix אֵינְכֶם — the suffix "you" becomes the subject of the participle (used as a predicate, with a durative sense): "because there is not you keeping." The divine punishment will continue because they persist in disobedience.

"but are showing partiality." The expression in the text is the participle וְנֹשְׂאִים followed by the object, "faces." "Lifting up faces" indicates preferment, that is, they were favoring some people by their [your] instruction (תּוֹרָה). This usually occurs when wealthy and powerful people are given special treatment in the application of the Law.

Exegetical Outline

I.   The LORD announced that because the priests had not honored his name he was about to curse them so that they could no longer minister as part of the Levitical priesthood (2:1–4).
   A.   The admonition was for the priests who treated God with contempt (1).
   B.   The LORD announced the curse:
      1.   He would take away the privileges and power of their ministry, which he had already begun to do (2).
      2.   He would make them so disqualified that they would be removed ingloriously from the sanctuary (3).
   C.   This purging of corrupt priests would ensure that the Levitical priesthood would remain useful to God (4).
II.   After reviewing how the early priests communicated life and peace to people by their reverence, teaching, obedience, and influence, the LORD reminded the current priests that they were to be faithful messengers (5–7).
   A.   The ministry of the priests was designed to communicate life and peace so that in faith people would fear the LORD (5).
   B.   The early priests feared the LORD; they faithfully taught the word, obeyed it, and turned many to righteousness (6).
   C.   Because the priests were the messengers of the LORD, they were to preserve knowledge and guide the people into truth (7).

III. The LORD condemned the disobedient priests to an ignominious existence because they had departed from the ministry and caused many to stumble in their false and preferential teaching (8–9).
   A. The priests had abandoned the true ministry and by their teaching caused many to stumble in their faith (8a).
   B. The LORD made them base and low in the estimation of the people (9a).
   C. The priests had been showing favoritism to some people in the way they conducted the ministry (9b).

Exegetical Summary

Because the priesthood was supposed to communicate life and peace in the fear of the LORD, and because the priests were to be faithful teachers, obedient examples, and effective messengers in bringing people to the LORD, the LORD announced that he would remove the glory and power of ministry from those priests who brought dishonor to his name by their corrupt teaching and favoritism.

Commentary in Expository Form

I. *God will remove his blessing from ministers who refuse to give glory to his name (2:1–4).*

A. GOD WARNS UNFAITHFUL MINISTERS OF HIS DISCIPLINE (1–2).

Malachi's sermon begins with the bold, direct confrontation: "This instruction is for you, O priests." One can only envision the temple filled with priests, Levites, and people — and all of a sudden the prophet stood up to speak and spoke directly and bluntly to the spiritual leaders. They might have anticipated that he would be critical of something, as prophets were, but they were not sure how critical.

The message was that God would send a curse on them if they did not give glory to his name, that is, treat the LORD (Yahweh) himself with honor and reverence. The priests no doubt thought they were giving God the glory because they were saying and doing all the right things in the ritual, but their heart was not in it to do it in a way that honored and exalted God. And so God announced that he would send the curse on them. The word "curse" (מְאֵרָה) is related to the verb (אָרַר), which is also used in the context. It essentially means to remove or banish from the place of blessing. In this text God made it clear that he would curse their blessings, an interesting word play given the meanings of the two words: "I will curse (remove from the place of blessing) your priestly blessings" (ministry and its privileges).

The word for "blessing" (בְּרָכָה along with its related verb בָּרַךְ) means an enrichment — physical, spiritual, and/or material. A blessing is a gift from God, but it is a gift that comes with a certain amount of empowerment or enablement. So what blessings had God given them? In addition to the normal blessings for the nation (rain, good crops, peace in their time, good health, and all that), there were the blessings or benefits and entitlements of the priesthood. As priests they were entitled and empowered to lead the people in worship, teach the word of God, announce God's forgiveness of sin and full atonement, eat from the holy offerings, dwell safely in the sanctuaries or the priestly cities, and have the respect of the congregation. It was a wonderful life because God had given them so much. But they could be easily disqualified from such benefits; and any removal of priestly privileges would be considered a curse. If God cursed their blessings, it meant that he would render them unfit for ministry, or they would have no effective ministry even though they might remain in office. In fact, this passage ends with God's making them contemptible and base in the opinion of the people (v. 9). And this is so true of the household of faith in all ages — because of sin the blessing of God is removed, even though the organization may continue to grind on.

The text adds that this cursing of their blessings had already begun: "and also I have cursed it [them] because you are not taking it to heart." The priests had heard the word of God concerning their ministry, but they did not pay attention to it and so made no decision to obey it. They were disqualified from ministering in his name because they were not glorifying his name.

They failed "to give glory" to the "name of the Lord." The name in the text is Yahweh, and so "the name of Yahweh" has to refer to something other than Yahweh. It means who he is — the "name" referring to his nature and his works. Because God is already full of glory, the only way humans can glorify him is by extending and expanding the knowledge of God in the world, by causing him to be seen in everything that is done. If people sin, or fail to do what God wants them to do in worship and service, they do not glorify him but give the congregation the wrong impression about God. And this is what these priests were doing.

Malachi has not yet stated what the priests were doing wrong. But whatever it was that they were doing was ruining the understanding that people had of God and of his sanctuary.

B. GOD EXPLAINS WHAT HIS JUDGMENT WILL BE (3–4).

Now the word from the LORD announces what this curse on the priests will be: "I am about to rebuke for you the seed." For God to rebuke something means to change it, stop it, or replace it (see Zech. 3). What God was about to rebuke in this passage was "the seed" (הַזֶּרַע). This is a difficult word to interpret, as the textual problem addressed earlier attests. The word "seed" could mean the seed sown in the fields for the crops. Haggai actually discussed how God punished the nation a little earlier by bringing a blight on their crops. But since this message is addressed primarily to priests, "your seed" would most likely refer to their descendants.

Because of the sins of these priests, their family line would be stopped from being priests. This happened in the beginning days of Samuel when God removed Eli and his corrupt sons from the priesthood and chose another line. This interpretation would either mean that the sons of the priests were already as bad as their fathers, or that such a curse on the fathers would be severely felt by the descendants who would be put out of ministry because of the sins of their fathers.

There is no ambiguity in the second half of the verse; it is graphically clear. God said to the priests, "I will throw offal on your faces, the offal of your feasts, and you shall be carried away with it." The vivid language is figurative because God will not literally throw the unclean parts of the animals on the faces of the priests. It is hyperbole, but also an implied comparison (hypocatastasis), for they were to be treated the same as the intestines and dung of the sacrificial animals. In other words, they were spiritually unclean, as symbolized by the offal, and so unfit for the sanctuary. Zechariah used the same harsh language to describe the sins of the nation in the figure of the high priest; in chapter 3 he portrayed the high priest as being clothed with "excrement be-spattered garments."

These post-exilic prophets did not mince words. The background of Malachi's image is that in the ritual the priests would sacrifice the animals, cut out the internal unclean parts, and carry them outside the camp and burn them. God was saying that since the priests were unclean they deserved to be carried out with the offal to the rubbish heap. Their ministry was over! This announcement would have absolutely overwhelmed Malachi's priestly audience, probably present in clean white garments. They thought they were doing everything correctly, as their frequent protests indicate. But God was saying they were unclean, disqualified, and not welcome in the holy place because they were now cursed by God.

Why was God going to do this? Verse 4 says that one reason for removing corrupt priests was that when it happened they would know (by experience) that this message was from God. Their rejection and disgrace would be the sure evidence that the message was not just the raving of some prophet, but a clear word from God.

But verse 4 gives another purpose of the judgment on this generation: that his covenant would remain with Levi. There is no specific covenant laid out in the Bible with Levi; Levi was a son of Jacob and not a priest. But because God chose the tribe of Levi to be the priestly tribe, that choice with all the promises and stipulations formed a covenant, which was sealed with a sacrifice (see Lev. 8 and 9). The covenant of Levi was the ministry of the priests.

II. *God reminds his messengers that they must teach and live the truth (2:5–7).*

A. THE ESSENCE OF THE COVENANT: IT IS A MINISTRY OF LIFE AND PEACE (5).

Now the prophet reminded the priests of the calling that they received. First, he set forth the nature of the covenant: "[the] life and peace," (הַחַיִּים וְהַשָּׁלוֹם)), or "[it was one of] life and peace." The nouns "life and peace" modify the covenant, either as predicates after a supplied "it was," or a genitive after an implied repetition of covenant. In either case they state what the covenant (the ministry) was designed to produce. If the priests were faithfully serving in the sanctuary, speaking the truth, offering the sacrifices for atonement, praying for the people, then the worshipers would find life and peace with God. This is what any form of ministry is about. "Peace" signifies well-being, and peace with God can only be enjoyed through forgiveness and atonement. And "life" signifies all the physical, spiritual, and eternal life of God's blessing and provision. When the temple was functioning correctly, people left the sanctuary knowing they had been blessed with life because they were at peace with God. It should be the same in any service.

God reminded these rebellious folk that the earlier priests not only accepted the ministry and understood what an awesome task it was, but they also were given life and peace. It was critical for them — and for ministers today — to live the spiritual life and enjoy God's peace so that they could easily communicate them to others. The statement that God gave them these indicates that those early priests truly believed in the LORD and walked in righteousness.

God gave life and peace "[for] fear," meaning, "[so that they would] fear." And his plan achieved its purpose: "and they feared me, and stood in awe before my name (i.e., before me)." If people receive such a position as priest, minister, pastor, spiritual director, teacher without it striking the fear of the LORD in them, then they have missed the fundamental meaning of serving the LORD. It has to be service because he is the Lord God.

B. THE MEANS OF THE COVENANT: IT IS A MINISTRY OF THE WORD (6–7).

And what was the evidence that they feared God? Their faithful and effective ministry! The text first describes their faithful teaching ministry as "the law of truth was in his [their] mouth." This expression (תּוֹרַת אֱמֶת) could be interpreted either as "instruction of truth" (for "law" can mean "instruction," and "truth" may be taken as an objective genitive, meaning that the content of the instruction was true, i.e., biblical); or as "faithful instruction" (because "truth" is related to the basic idea of what is reliable, or dependable; and the genitive could be an attributive genitive). Probably the first is intended, given the context of this message; but that would also include the second, because if people teach the truth, then their teaching is faithful.

The correlation to this is that "unrighteousness was not found in their lips" — this is the same point but clarifying it by stating what they did not teach. The early priests did not say things that did not conform to the standard of the Torah. They did not teach in such a way as to condone evil — that came later as false prophets called good evil, and evil good. They taught the truth, and that was their primary task (see Deut. 33:10).

Besides their faithful teaching, the text states that they lived the truth they taught: they walked with God in peace and uprightness. "To walk" is an idiom, an implied comparison (hypocatastasis) for the conduct of life. To walk with God means to live one's life in accordance with the will of God, and that would be characterized by "peace" and "uprightness." To walk with

God one has to be at peace with God; and to be at peace with God one has to follow a life of obedience, meaning upright. To walk with God is to go where he is going, to stay close to him, and to commune with him along the way. This common biblical idiom contains even more nuances that believers should appreciate.

And finally, their faithful teaching and obedient living caused many people to turn away from iniquity. Their ministry had results. People turned from iniquity to righteousness as they trusted in the LORD. In the words of the apostle Paul, those who turned by faith to follow the Lord were the letters of commendation for the ministry.

All of this is still the pattern of effective spiritual leadership: demonstrate reverential fear of God, teach the word of God faithfully, live in obedience to it, and bring people to repentance and faith in the Lord. So Malachi reminds ministers of the primary function of ministry: "The lips of the priest must preserve knowledge, and instruction should be sought from his mouth." The "knowledge" must be spiritual knowledge, that is, understanding doctrine and righteousness, because of the point of the context, and because of the parallelism with "law" (or "instruction"). Ministers must not neglect this primary responsibility. Why? Because it is the word of God that redeems and guides believers into truth and righteousness.

There is still a more basic reason why this aspect cannot be neglected: because ministers are the messengers of the LORD of armies. This word "messenger" (מַלְאָךְ) is the key theme of the book. "Malachi" means "my messenger." But here ministers are also God's messengers. That means essentially they are to carry the message of God to the people.

The point of Malachi's principle is based on the blessing of Moses for Levi in Deuteronomy 33:10. There were three basic duties the priests were to perform: teach the Law of God, burn incense (which was done when priests made intercessory prayer), and make the atoning sacrifices (i.e., always be ready to help people get to God through the provision of atonement).

But first and foremost, they were teachers. This they did year round. And whatever else might be said about teaching, the teacher must have knowledge (here the knowledge of God's word). There is no place in ministry for ignorant ministers, for ministers who do not have biblical and theological knowledge, for ministers who will not study or do not use the word of God much in their messages. People in the congregation must feel confident that their ministers know what God said and what it means, and that they can go to them with their questions and some minister will answer them. This is central to ministry, to the faith itself. If there is no solid teaching, worship becomes a meaningless ritual (chapter 1), and the standards of righteousness irrelevant or unknown (chapters 2 and 3). Those who speak for God must remember that the message is not theirs, no matter how clever they might be. It is God's message.

III. *God treats those ministers with contempt who do not comply with the standard of spiritual service (2:8–9).*

Verse 8 starts with "But you," a sharp contrast to the standard in verse 7. That is an ominous way to begin when the ideal has just been set forth. "But you have turned aside out of the way." They had deliberately changed the course of their service — they did not study, they did not tell people the truth, they did not live out the faith before the people, they made no converts. Divine service did not change; they changed. They turned away. They may have thought that they were making practical innovations, perhaps making it easier for people to bring animal sacrifices by lowering the standards, but they were corrupting God's plan.

Moreover, by their teaching they had caused many to stumble. The image of stumbling (a hypocatastasis) refers to faltering and failing in their faith and in their life of obedience. It is in contrast to the idiom of walking for living by faith. This no doubt refers to things like the first chapter where the priests were allowing corrupt gifts to be brought, and to the next oracle, which is concerned with permitting divorce and marriage to pagans.

The last line of this sermon gives us the basis for the problem and an idea of how this worked — they were showing respect of persons (lifting up the face) over the (teaching of the) Law. They applied the biblical instruction differently to different people, perhaps more leniently with the rich and powerful, the same kind of favoritism that James decried in his epistle to the church (2:1–7). It is evil to approve of sin through such teaching, but this approval had a shrewd motive. To show favoritism through it means simply not applying the standard to some people, so they will sin under the false understanding they are free to do so. If there were powerful and influential people, the priests would wink at their sins, as often happened when a country was governed by a powerful aristocracy. They were privileged. But ordinary people were held accountable for their sins and crimes.

The conclusion of the prophet concerning their ministry was that they had ruined the covenant. The verb "ruin" (שָׁחַת) means "to destroy, corrupt, ruin"; it is a strong word as evidenced by its use for the destruction of the cities of the plain (Gen. 19). Here, again, the perfect tense would indicate the nuance of present perfect — they ruined the covenant and it now continued to be in complete disarray.

Now comes the announcement of divine judgment — the explication of cursing their blessings. They dishonored God in their ministry; God will now dishonor them. This verse also begins with a sharp contrast: "But I [for my part] also have made you despised and base to all the people." The verb "despise" plays off the charge that they had been despising the name of the LORD; in their lofty arrogance they had also challenged God's authority, and so now they would be brought low in public opinion (especially in the eyes of people they tried to favor). God would leave them to themselves and their office powerless without God's enablement and blessing — and humiliated now that they had been exposed. Everyone would know that they were base and low; they would be without respect and placement, just living out their lives as failed ministers. How horrible to try to be a minister in the sanctuary with everyone knowing that you are corrupt and unfaithful, a pleaser of people and not God, and that as a result there would be no evidence that God was in this ministry. Today people could leave the church, but in Israel there was only one sanctuary and the priests served on their rounds.

Malachi closes with the theme with which he started: God will do this because these people were not keeping God's ways but were showing favoritism. That could change, of course, if they repented and renewed their commitment. But no prospect of that happening is held out in this passage.

Expository Idea and Application

Expository Idea

Now that we have the exegetical content clearly in mind we can write the expository idea, which will be the central thesis statement of the message to be delivered. It must be worded carefully to express the message from the LORD through this passage of Scripture.

As we have seen, the passage addresses the problem of corrupt, disqualifying ministry, but it does so with many theological ideas that form the heart of the message. Taking these theological ideas, we are ready to formulate the homiletical idea, already anticipated, of course, with the expository outline included in the commentary. This was a sermon addressed to the priests, and the central part of the message concerns the knowledge and use of Scripture in ministry. The writing of the central idea could be slanted toward the rebuke and warning side of the passage:

> The LORD will remove respect and success from ministers
> who dishonor him by failing to teach and live the truth
> so that people remain in their sins.

I could use "honor" instead of "respect," because the book of Exodus speaks of all the blessings of the priesthood as their honor (or glory) and beauty, all the benefits and trappings. But "respect" might be clearer to the modern audience. I used "success" because the ministry was to turn people to righteousness, but if the priests were made base and low, they would be ineffectual, powerless, and so ruined.

Or the expository idea could be worded on the positive side:

> The messengers of the LORD must know, teach, and obey his word,
> so that they bring honor to him and life and peace to the people.

Wording a central idea for the message will keep the expositor connected to the core of the text and give clarity to the presentation. You do not just expound this idea and fix it up with stories and illustrations. No, you clearly expound the entire passage so that people can understand how this idea emerges from the passage. They have to see that it is in there. The message of this passage is pretty obvious and will not take a lot of convincing. The principles set forth here certainly apply directly to people who are fully active in ministry today — pastors, teachers, counselors, and the like. How they handle the Word is critical; they dare not make mistakes. James said that it was a dangerous thing to teach. Perhaps people rush into ministry too eagerly, or stand up to preach too casually, not realizing how serious a matter it is to speak for God.

Application

To whom, then, do we deliver this message? The closest correlation would be to ministers, pastors and teachers, spiritual advisers, and the like. A clergy conference or denominational congress would be an ideal setting for the message. But the message can also apply, perhaps as a secondary application, to the whole congregation. The congregation should know this passage too so that (1) they can hold their pastors to it, and so that (2) they too would be faithful in their ministry. As with Israel, so in the church, all believers are a kingdom of priests (Exod. 19:6; 1 Peter 2:9). What the priests were to the people, the people were supposed to be to the world — teachers of God's word, living in peace and uprightness, and turning people into faithful believers. Christians, especially if they have been Christians for some time, must know the word of God and be able to teach it and live it so that they may influence people toward righteousness (Heb. 5:2; 2 Tim. 3:14–17). It is a wonderful, but solemn obligation.

The passage focused on the priests themselves, but also spoke to the guilty members of the congregation to remind them that no matter what the priests said in their teaching, they were to obey Scripture. Jesus in his day had to remind the people that when the Pharisees sat in Moses' seat, reading and teaching Scripture (Matt. 23:2–3a), they had to listen to them. But then Jesus also said to beware of their false teachings, their leaven, and be careful not to do what they do. So the laity must know the word of God well enough to discern when the teacher or preacher gets it wrong. And all these applications remain today, even though Malachi preached about 2,400 years ago. Those who minister, that is, those who teach the Bible, whether pastors, teachers, missionaries, or any others, must be very careful how they interpret and apply Scripture. And those who hear the Scripture taught must study it to know if the message or lesson is true or not.

KEY WORDS

"To Bless"

The word "bless" in this passage is בָּרַךְ; the related noun "blessing" is בְּרָכָה. These words are not to be confused with the homonym, "kneel down," and its noun "knee," בֶּרֶךְ, even though older dictionaries lumped the two roots together. The verb "bless" is used primarily in the *piel* verbal system, but it does occur in the *qal* passive participle in the form of praise, בָּרוּךְ יהוה, "blessed [be] the LORD," and related expressions.

(1) The basic meaning of the verb "bless" is "to enrich" in some way — physically, materially, or spiritually; and the noun "blessing" can even mean a "gift" (Gen. 33:11).

(2) The enrichment that comes from the LORD often included the divine enablement to achieve the blessing, such as the initial blessing for Adam and

Eve to be fruitful and multiply. Such declarations of divine blessing often fell to the theocratic administrators who spoke for God, such as the high priest who announced the blessing on the people (Num. 6:22–27; see also Gen. 14:19 for Melchizedek; and Deut. 33:1 for Moses). In many cases the expressed desire for the LORD's blessing on someone serves as a favorable greeting on arrival or departure (Gen. 24:60).

(3) The blessing from the LORD on people would bring any number of benefits to those blessed, such as children, victory, fruitful crops in the field, rain, privileges of the priesthood, and peace. But the LORD also blessed things, such as the Sabbath day (Gen. 2:3), which apparently enriched that day as a special time, especially when it says he also sanctified it.

(4) When people blessed the LORD, the meaning was essentially "praise." In what way can people enrich the LORD or make him more blessed than he is? After all, he is blessed forever above all that is imaginable. But in offering praise, one enriches the reputation of the LORD in the mind of the congregation. It is here that the expression "Blessed be the LORD" finds its specific meaning. Moreover, giving praise to the LORD is giving a gift to him, and so "bless" does fit well.[7]

"To Curse"

The word "curse" (אָרַר) and its related noun form the antonyms of bless and its noun blessing. The essential meaning of curse is to remove or ban someone or something from the blessing, or the place of blessing. Its synonym (from the verb "to be light," קָלַל), on the other hand, means to curse in the sense of treating something lightly or of no importance.

(1) The result of the curse as the opposite of the blessing has the effect of covering someone or something with misfortune and affliction. But if the person cursed is covered with such disaster or disability, it is only by the power of God and not by any pronouncement of a curse. It is God who makes people and things cursed, so the announcement of the curse by those who speak for God is the announcement of a divine oracle. And in the

---

7 For further information, see A. Murtonen, "The Use and Meaning of the Words *L*ᵉ*barek* and *B*ᵉ*rakah* in the Old Testament," *Vetus Testamentum* 9 (1959):166–68; and especially Claus Westermann, *Blessing in the Bible and the Life of the Church,* trans. Keith Crim (Philadelphia: Fortress Press, 1968).

passages, the extent of the disaster or the nature of the banishment is determined by God.[8]

(2) Malachi puts the words "bless" and "curse" together for maximum effect: "I will curse your blessings." All of the privileges and entitlements that the priests enjoyed were about to be removed. The usage of the word illustrates this meaning very well. The ground in Genesis 3 will be cursed, and as a result no longer produce in abundance. Cain in Genesis 4 will be the first human cursed; he will be banished from the land, the fertile soil, to be a ceaseless wanderer in the "world." Those who treat Abraham and his new covenant with contempt will of necessity be removed from the blessing (Gen. 12:1–3). And those who disobey God's word will be cursed (Ps. 119:21). So in this passage in Malachi the individual who has the proper animal but tries to pass off a ruined thing as something vowed to the LORD will be "cursed." It was bad enough to bring a worthless gift; but to try to make it seem like a spiritual act was contemptible.

"To Hear, Obey"

The verb שָׁמַע, "to hear," is very common in the Bible (occurring more than 1,100 times); and although it has a wide range of uses it often means to respond to what is heard. There are many related words: שֵׁמַע is a "sound," parallel to the blowing of trumpets in Psalm 150:5; שֵׁמַע is a report, some good news (e.g., about Jacob in Gen. 29:13); שֹׁמַע is also a "report" (Josh. 6:27) as is שְׁמוּעָה ("Who has believed our report" in Isa. 53:1); מִשְׁמָע is a "thing heard"; and מִשְׁמַעַת is a word for bodyguard, an obedient band of men.

(1) The verb in the *qal* system has a number of similar but distinct meanings. One category of meanings is the simple idea of "hear" (Gen. 3:10; Deut. 4:33). The negative of this affirms that idols do not hear, even though they have ears (Ps. 115:6); however, this passage may have the stronger sense of responding to prayer.

(2) Another meaning is "to hear with interest" or to give attention to something (e.g., hearing a case — Deut. 1:17).

(3) A third category has the idea of "understand" (they could hear sounds but could not "hear" — Gen. 11:7 after the confusion of languages).

(4) A fourth category means "agree, consent," with the sense of obeying.

---

8 For a more thorough discussion, see C. A. Keller, under "ארר, *'rr* to curse," in *Theological Lexicon of the Old Testament,* ed. Jenni and Westermann, 1:179–82.

Here in Malachi the prophet accused the people of not hearing, meaning, not responding by obeying what the word said (2:2). The idea of obey is often found in the expression "listen to the voice of" (Gen. 3:17; also Exod. 15:26 as a requirement to obey; cf. Isa. 1:19).

This meaning of responding appropriately to what is heard is clear in passages where the LORD is the subject. When the LORD heard the cries of distress he did something about them (Gen. 16:11; 21:7). In this sense it is used for his answering prayer, as when he hears from heaven (1 Kings 8:28) or hears a prayer (Ps. 6:9). And so frequently in the Psalms we find people praying for God to hear them (Ps. 4:1), or praising him because he heard (Ps. 22:24).

(5) In the *hiphil* system the word has the meaning "cause to hear." It can be used in the sense of declaring or making proclamation (1 Kings 15:22) as well as informing (Deut. 30:12). It also is used in a musical context for sounding aloud (1 Chron. 15:19), which may have something to do with sounding time in the music.

"Peace, Well-being, Wholeness"

The word for "peace" is שָׁלוֹם. The main verb שָׁלֵם means "to be complete, sound" in the *qal* stem, and "to complete, requite" in the *piel*. There are several related nouns: the most common is our word שָׁלוֹם, which can mean "completeness, soundness, welfare," and of course "peace"; then there is שָׁלֵם, "complete, safe, at peace"; and שֶׁלֶם, "peace offering."

(1) The verb occurs a few times in the *qal*. It describes something as complete, or ended, such as the temple (1 Kings 7:51); or it means someone is sound or uninjured (Job 9:14).

(2) It has a wider range of meanings in the *piel/pual* system. Here, it can have the basic causative idea for something being made complete, that is, "to complete" something (e.g., the temple — 1 Kings 9:25).

(3) Another category of the causative has the meaning "to make whole, restore." It is used in this sense in Leviticus 24:18 for making compensation; and in 2 Kings 4:7 for paying a debt.

(4) Another category is that of paying vows, or making good on vows (e.g., Pss. 50:14; 55:13). Then, it can also be used with the meaning "reward, requite, recompense." It is used this way in Ruth 2:12 in the desire that the LORD reward Ruth's faithfulness. The reward is a response to works done (2 Sam. 3:39; Ps. 31:24); but on occasion the good seems to be "rewarded" with evil (Gen. 44:4; Pss. 35:12; 38:20).

(5) The *hiphil* meaning is "complete, perform." In Isaiah 38:12 and 13, King Hezekiah laments that in his suffering the LORD was making an end of him.

(6) The noun שָׁלוֹם has a similar range of meanings. First, it can mean "completeness," as in referring to Judah being completely carried captive (Jer. 13:19). Second, it can mean "soundness," as in Psalm 38:3, but also in Isaiah 38:17 and in Job 5:24 with the additional sense of safety. Third, it can mean "health," as when someone asks about a person's welfare (Gen. 43:27), or similarly "prosperity" (Ps. 122:6). And fourth, it can mean "peace." This may refer to tranquility in life (Gen. 15:15). It may be used in reference to a relationship, such as a man of peace, meaning a friend. More significantly, it is used with God in the covenant (Num. 6:26; Mal. 2:5; Isa. 54:10). It may, of course, refer to peace from war (Isa. 9:5; Micah 5:4; Josh. 9:15). But within the covenant relationship peace is often paralleled with righteousness (Isa. 53:5; Ps. 125:5); peace and righteousness both refer to right order (Ps. 72:3, 7).

(7) In the Bible, especially the psalms, שָׁלוֹם has a wide range of meanings: security (4:8), calmness or tranquility (29:11; 35:27), possession and enjoyment of the land (37:11), health (38:3), freedom from the threat of enemies (55:18), prosperity (73:3), protection from misfortunes (119:165), and in general, the heart of divine blessing (147:14). In general, the term defines the relationship between God and man, linking heaven and earth, and portrays the outworking of that connection in many spheres of existence.[9]

"Instruction, Law"

The word "instruction" (*tôrâ*, תּוֹרָה) is probably related to the verb (יָרָה) that seems to mean "to show, point, direct."

(1) The verb may be related in the *qal* stem with the meaning of shooting, as with arrows (Ps. 64:5), or rain shooting down (Hos. 6:3); but this may be another word entirely, a homonym.

(2) The verb does appear in the *hiphil* stem with the meaning of pointing or instructing, such as the way to Goshen (Gen. 46:28), pointing out a tree that would sweeten the bitter waters (Exod. 15:25), as well as the duty of the priests to teach the laws of God (Deut. 33:10). The Hebrews made a clear connection between the noun "law, instruction" and the verb that meant "guide, instruct, teach."

---

9   See further F. J. Stendebach, "*šālôm*," in *Theological Dictionary of the Old Testament*, ed. G. J. Botterweck, H. Ringgren, and Heinz-Josef Fabry, 15:13–48.

(3) The noun "law" (תּוֹרָה) would then refer to any instruction or author-itative direction. It could be used for any specific teaching or collection of teachings in general, such as the instruction in wisdom given to children by their parents (Prov. 1:8; 3:1; 4:4). It was also used for traditional customs handed down to be followed (2 Sam. 7:19) and for the training of people in a skill, such as for the construction of the sanctuary (Exod. 35:34).

But most of the uses of the noun refer to teaching that comes from the holy books. It basically refers to divine revelation recorded in Scripture (Josh. 24:26); but how much of Scripture was included in a reference to the "Law of the LORD" is difficult to say. In general, it probably refers to the entire law code, that is, the books of the law that were available (see Ps. 19:7 as well as Ps. 1:2). It could refer to specific instructions in the code, such as concerning unleavened bread (Exod. 13:9), or to the heart of the code, the command-ments and decisions (Exod. 24:12, which may refer to the contents of Exod. 20–23). Deuteronomy is also called the law of the LORD (Deut. 1:5), and de-pending on one's conclusions about the dating of the books of the law, these books of the law or their contents would have been available to the pre-exilic community. The word can refer to decisions that were made in judging civil cases (Exod. 18:16), instruction that came through the servants of the LORD (Isa. 30:9), collections of prophetic books (Isa. 42:21, 24), or the teachings about the ritual that the Levites were to be doing (Mal. 2:7). So any divine instruction from a single teaching to all of Scripture could be included in a reference to the "law," but the most likely understanding is that it would refer to the instructions of the Law itself.

"Truth"

The word for "truth" (אֱמֶת) is related to the verb "to be firm, support" (אָמַן) and its various other derivatives. A survey of the usage of these words will not only help clarify the word "truth," but will be valuable for the other re-lated words when they appear.

(1) The dictionaries usually define the verb as "confirm, support, be firm, steady, trustworthy." The verb does not occur often in the *qal* verbal systems; but the participle is used for "foster-mother" (Ruth 4:16) and "guardian" or "trustee" (Esth. 2:7). The relationship of a trustee to the idea of trustworthy, dependable, is obvious.

(2) In the *niphal* system the verb carries the ideas of "steadfast, secure." For example, it describes a lasting river (Isa. 33:16) or the moon as a lasting

witness (Ps. 89:37). The house of David was to be "established" (2 Sam. 7:16); and the priesthood would have a "sure" house (1 Sam. 2:35). But the *niphal* also is used for that which is "faithful, reliable." God said he would raise up a "faithful" priest (1 Sam. 2:35). Nehemiah uses it to describe "faithful" people in charge of the storehouses (13:13). Of course, God is "faithful" (Deut. 7:9). And Psalm 111:7 says his works are "truth and justice" (taken as a hendiadys, meaning dependably just), and his precepts are "sure." And the prayer of Solomon asks that the promises be fulfilled, that God would be "faithful" to them (2 Chron. 1:9).

(3) The *hiphil* is a little less obvious; it means "believe." This could be explained as a declarative use, that is, considering something reliable or sure, and acting on it. There are other, less convincing suggestions. Its common translation is simply "believe." It could refer to various things: the queen of Sheba did not believe what she had heard (1 Kings 10:6–7); Gedaliah did not believe the report about the threat on his life (Jer. 40:13, 14); Moses was afraid people would not believe him (Exod. 4:8); and on the positive side, Achish came around to believe David (1 Sam. 27:12). But most importantly it refers to believing in God (the elders in Exod. 4:31; the men of Nineveh in Jon. 3:5; and Abram in Gen. 15:6–for which faith he was credited with righteousness).

(4) The common idea in the verbal uses seems to be reliable, dependable — something that can be counted on. A number of related words have this emphasis as well: the noun "master workman," אָמוֹן (Prov. 8:30), a participle-noun "doorposts," אֹמְנוֹת (2 Kings 18:16), the word "amen, truly," אָמֵן (Neh. 5:13; Ps. 106:48), a noun "faithfulness, firmness," אֱמוּנָה (Exod. 17:12 for making Moses' hands steady; Hab. 2:4 for the righteous living by his faith), and a number of other related words that appear less frequently.

(5) The most common derivative is the noun אֱמֶת, "truth, firmness, faithfulness." What is true is reliable, that is, it can be trusted, depended on, believed. The word can be used for truth in general or faithfulness. The word often shows up in a hendiadys: "truth and peace," for example, would mean a "lasting peace" or a "reliable peace" (Isa. 39:8; Jer. 14:13); likewise "loyal love and truth" would mean "faithful love."

So then, if people speak truth, then what they say is reliable and dependable. There is no such idea in biblical usage that one person's truth may differ from another's truth; that is what may be called Aaron's spiritual nonsense (see Exod. 32:24). The truth is from God, and there is no other truth and no alteration of God's truth that has the quality of reliability or that can demand obedience.

"Injustice, Wrong, Unrighteousness"

עַוְלָה means "injustice, wrong, unrighteousness." It has basically three main categories of meanings, although there may be some overlap.

(1) First, it means violent deeds of injustice. In the Davidic covenant God promised that no unjust man would oppress the servant of the LORD (2 Sam. 7:10). People who unjustly oppress others are called "sons of the unjust" (Ps. 89:22).

The word is also a designation for the wicked who plan unjust acts in their hearts (Ps. 58:2). The pilgrim-psalmist affirms that wicked government will not be so severe and influential as to cause the righteous to get involved in such unrighteousness (Ps. 125:3). An unjust man such as is mentioned in Psalm 43:1 is essentially a lawless person.

(2) A second category focuses on unjust speech. Malachi tells how the original priests taught the truth and not unjust things, probably false teachings that would show respect of persons and allow people to set aside the Law, thus making the Law unfair and unjust and causing people to stumble (Mal. 2:6). Isaiah also speaks of the tongue that utters wicked things (59:3); but Psalm 107:42 anticipates how these unjust people will shut their mouths.

(3) A third category is the meaning of injustice in general. Psalm 64:6 refers to people who plot injustice, but this does not say much about the exact meaning. More helpful is Job 6:29, where Job tells his friends to stop being unjust — what they were saying was not right because it did not apply to him. Ezekiel 28 refers to the anointed cherub who was perfect in all his ways until evil (עַוְלָתָה) was found in him (v. 15).

(4) There are other related words that help clarify the meaning. The noun עַוָּל is an "unjust one." It describes oppressive rulers by contrasting the LORD's reign that will have no wrong or injustice (Zeph. 3:5). The noun עָוֶל refers to injustice, for example, the miscarriage of justice by unjust judges in Psalm 82:2. Psalm 7:3 uses this word in the protestation of innocence where the psalmist claims there is no injustice in his hands.

So these words refer to wicked acts and words that are simply wrong and therefore unjust. An unjust person is not harmless — he oppresses people and perverts justice. Leviticus 19:15 warns: "do not do injustice" (עָוֶל). And unjust teaching is not harmless either, because it allows people to live in violation of God's word and therefore be guilty.

(Malachi 2:1–9)

"To Ruin"

The verb "to ruin" (שָׁחַת) is a very strong one; it means "to ruin suddenly, spoil, or corrupt."

(1) We find one group of passages that refer to destruction in warfare (2 Sam. 11:1). The (*hiphil*) participle becomes at times a technical military term for the "slayer" (1 Sam. 13:17; 14:15; 2 Sam. 24:16). Marauding bands also could ruin the crop (Judg. 6:4).

(2) It can also refer to ruining things within the community, such as ruining the covenant with Levi by corrupt teaching (Mal. 2:9), or marring an inheritance by marrying a Moabitess (Ruth 4:6). It is even used for willingly wasting seed during intercourse (Gen. 38:9). It is also possible to ruin someone's life by careless words (Prov. 11:9). Even more astounding is how to the point is its use on the moral and spiritual level, such as when the word describes the corruption of Israel in making the golden calf (Exod. 32:7).

(3) Sinfulness is described as corruption and perversion with this word. It was the assessment of the LORD that the human race had become corrupt morally and needed to be removed (Gen. 6:12; this is much the same theme that Ps. 14:1 has). Isaiah described the wicked, hypocritical people of his day as having "acted corruptly" (Isa. 1:4). And the diseased and defiled animals the Israelites tried to offer to God are called ruined or corrupted (Mal. 1:14).

(4) The word is therefore used of God's judgment on the corrupt human race (Gen. 9:11, 15; Exod. 8:20). It is used in Genesis 13:10 and 19:13 for the complete ruin of Sodom and Gomorrah (and see the intercession in Gen. 18:28). And in Egypt if the people did not put blood on the doorposts, the angel of "destruction" would enter (Exod. 12:23).

Related to this theme of judgment is the prophecy in Isaiah 52:14 that describes the suffering servant as "disfigured."

4. *Profaning the Holy Covenant of Marriage*

(MALACHI 2:10–16)

Introduction

Translation and Textual Notes

¹⁰ Do we not all have one Father?
    Has not one God created us?
    Why [then] does a man deal treacherously[1] against his brother
        so that *they* profane the covenant of our fathers?
¹¹ Judah has dealt treacherously
    and an abomination has been done
        in Israel and in Jerusalem;
    for Judah has profaned the holiness[2] of the LORD
        which he loves,
    and married the daughter of a foreign god.[3]
¹² May the LORD cut off the man who does this
    from the tents of Jacob
        — the one waking, and the one answering,[4]

---

   1 The MT has "Why do we deal treacherously [נִבְגַּד], a man against his brother?" The Greek version interprets with ἐγκατελίπετε, "[why] have you forsaken?" The editors of BHS propose correcting the reading to נִבְגַּד.

   2 The word "holiness" could refer to a holy thing, a holy place, the holy one, or holiness in general.

   3 The Moabites are called sons and daughters of Chemosh in Numbers 21:29; and the Israelites are called sons and daughters of Yahweh in Deuteronomy 32:19.

   4 The two words are participles. The expression may very well refer to the sentries or watchmen at each end of the settlement, and so refer to everyone there.

> even one who presents[5] a dedication offering
> to the Lord of armies.

13 And this second thing you do:
> covering[6] the altar of the Lord with tears,
> with weeping and groaning,
> so that[7] there is no longer any regard for the offering
> to receive it with pleasure from your hand.

14 And you say, "Why?"
> Because the Lord was witness between you
> and the wife of your earlier lifetime,
> against whom you have dealt treacherously,
> even though she is your partner
> and the wife of your covenant.

15 And did he not make one?[8] —
> and yet he had the residue of the Spirit!
> Why the one? —
> seeking a godly seed.
> So take heed in your spirit
> and do not deal treacherously[9] with the wife of your youth.

16 For I hate putting away,[10] says the Lord, the God of Israel,

---

5   The Greek version apparently attempted to harmonize the expression with the preceding and has "and from among those who offer," representing possibly וּמִמַּגִּישֵׁי.

6   The Greek translation has the verb ἐκαλύπτετε, "you cover," and the editors of BHS propose the reading תְּכַסּוּ. This Greek form may not actually be a textual problem; it may simply be a translator's choice to interpret the infinitive construct. The infinitive is functioning either epexegetically ("by covering"), or perhaps better, as a noun, either in apposition to "this" ("you do this, covering") or adverbially ("covering"). The NIV 1984 followed the BHS proposal after the Greek, but the MT preserves the harder reading, accounting for the attempt to smooth it out.

7   Some interpret this as "because (he will not regard . . .)," to harmonize the line with the idea that the men were the ones who were weeping at the altar.

8   The Greek reads "did he not do well?"

9   The MT has the third person masculine form, "may he not deal treacherously," even though the pronominal suffixes are second person masculine singular. Some Masoretic manuscripts, the Greek, Targum, and Vulgate, have the second person masculine singular verb, as if it were תִּבְגֹּד, which is how everyone translates it. It makes little sense to read "May he not deal treacherously against the wife of your youth." If we assume the second person masculine singular form is correct, then the negative with it would give a jussive force: "stop dealing treacherously."

10   The form "hate," שָׂנֵא, in the line is problematic. As it stands, it is the *qal* perfect, 3msg

and [whoever] covers his clothing with violence,
  says the LORD of armies,
Take heed in your spirit, and do not act treacherously.

Context and Composition

Marriage is an institution of God. It accords with the divine plan and the dictates of nature. And as it was intended to be an integral ingredient in the bliss of Eden (Gen. 2:23), so should it be in a healthy society. But even more importantly, marriage was designed as a social blessing to continue the race, to develop people spiritually and emotionally and intellectually, to soothe and sustain them amidst the depressing and difficult circumstances of life, and to enable people to function as the image of God, especially now in a sinful world (Gen. 1:27–28).

Unfortunately, people have introduced conflict and pain into their relationships and attempted to change God's institution of marriage to suit their desires. The divine plan was simple and clear: one man and one woman becoming one united life (one flesh) throughout their earthly lives, to fulfill God's plan for his creation, significantly, to produce a godly seed. But the human race embraced every form of profane and vile activity; and so formally or informally, marriages were ruined and dissolved because of sin (Matt. 19:8).

So Malachi addressed the problem directly. Nowhere in the Bible do we find a more powerful presentation of the effects of the violation of marriage — what it does to the plan of God, what pain it causes, and what the

---

of the verb. In some stative verbs the participle would be spelled this way, but the participle of this verb appears to be regular, שָׂנֵא. This problem has led to several proposals. It could be translated as it stands: "for he (Yahweh) hates divorce." But that is a little awkward when followed by "says Yahweh." It could be treated as an elliptical clause: "for (the LORD) says, 'I hate divorce,'" being the equivalent of "he hates divorce." "I hate divorce" is the traditional translation because it says what the passage means. But this explanation is difficult to sustain. Rudolph says that the form is a verbal adjective with the force of a participle, meaning "[I] am hating" (W. Rudolph, "Zu Malachi 2:10–16," *Zeitschrift für die alttestamentliche Wissenschaft* [1981]:85–90, see p. 85). The Greek (B) has "If you hate your wife and put her away . . . then ungodliness will cover your thoughts." It clearly had trouble with the first verb and offered a paraphrase for the line.

The second verb, שַׁלַּח, is the *piel* infinitive construct, used here as a noun, the object of the verb "hate": "[I] hate putting away," meaning divorce (as it means in Deut. 21:14).

divine response to it is. And we find no better description in the Bible of the value of marriage either.

Malachi's ministry overlapped on this message with those of Ezra and Nehemiah, but he alone focused on the pain all this caused, and he alone announced simply that God hates divorce. In 454 BC Ezra discovered that many of the people, especially priests and Levites, had married foreign women and mingled the holy race with pagans (9:2). He was appalled; and after his initial response he prayed, confessing the sins of the people to God. The people also wept bitterly (10:1); they wanted to make a new vow to send away the foreign wives and their children and so offered all their support to Ezra. When the people appealed that it would take time, Ezra appointed overseers to hear each case. Ezra 10 lists the names of the guilty priests and Levites.

About a decade later, 444 BC, Nehemiah came back to the land and began his building program and reforms. In response to Nehemiah's ministry the people vowed not to marry pagan women (10:30). Nehemiah was called away for a short time, and when he returned he found serious violations of the Law, as if the people had ignored the earlier instruction of Ezra. One of the violations Nehemiah discovered was that they had married pagan women (13:23–31). He denounced the sin and cursed the guilty. Nehemiah rebuked them for being unfaithful by marrying foreign women and made them take an oath to retain the purity of the faith through holy marriages. How long this reform lasted we do not know; Ezra's reforms for this issue clearly did not last more than a few years — if that long. This matter as well as Nehemiah's other reforms match Malachi's messages and indicate the time of Malachi's preaching was close to Nehemiah's reforms.

This message by Malachi falls into two parts, which are two accusations. The first part denounced the people for marrying women who were devotees of false gods. The second part revealed how the men who did this were causing grief and suffering by putting away their true wives, something that ruined worship completely. And so God declared through the prophet that he hated this practice.

Exegetical Comments

2:10

"one Father." The expression might suggest that Malachi is speaking about original creation — we all have one Father (implied metaphor for Creator) and one God who created us. But in this context he is using these words in reference to the covenant. God formed the people into the nation at Sinai; thus he is their Father. Certainly the daughters of strange gods in this passage do not have the same father.

"deal treacherously."   The form נִבְגַּד is the *qal* imperfect, first person common plural, "(why) do we deal treacherously (each man against his brother)?" A progressive imperfect category fits well because the treachery is ongoing.

There is a related noun בֶּגֶד that means "garment." It is possible that the idea of treachery grew out of a custom of seizing the garment of someone.

"a man against his brother."   The text literally has "a man against his brother," but the idiom means "with each other."

"so that [they] profane."   לְחַלֵּל is the *piel* infinitive construct. If it is interpreted epexegetically, it would say "by profaning" the covenant, explaining how the treachery was done. It may be better to take this as the result: in committing this treachery they profaned the covenant.

2:11

"Judah."   The word is used figuratively, as a metonymy of either cause (the ancestor for the descendants) or better, subject (the region where the tribe of Judah lives). The classification has to work with Jerusalem as well as Judah.

"holiness."   The word used is the noun קֹדֶשׁ, "the holiness (of the LORD)." The word could be used for the sanctuary (they did ruin worship there), the covenant of marriage, or the nature of the LORD himself. All three fit the context well and make good sense. It may be that all three were profaned by the people.

A word study of "holy" should be reviewed for this passage, noting that "profane" is its antonym. These words should be contrasted in this passage, showing that their practice and God's design are poles apart. Here Judah "profaned" the holiness of the LORD. The verb is the *piel* perfect; it covers all the related sins.

"he loves."   The form אָהֵב describes the LORD's abiding love for his holiness. That he loves his holiness may indicate that either the sanctuary or marriage is in view here. Since the verb describes what is always true we use the English present tense.

"and has married."   The verb is בָּעַל, later elsewhere connected to the idea of lordship and also to the name of the pagan god Baal. Here the verb is present perfect — they married the women and are presently married to them.

"daughter of a foreign god."   Because such a woman (collective for women) was not a literal daughter of a god, the word forms an implied comparison (hypocatastasis) between family relationships and spiritual alliances (as we in the church refer to fellow believers as brothers and sisters). The word implies a strong covenant association with the god, here a foreign god. These women were not merely foreigners; they were active devotees of another god and another religion.

Myers suggests that this might include marrying Samaritans in order to reclaim lands that had been abandoned.[11]

It was not illegal to marry a foreign woman if she became a part of Israel's faith (like Ruth). But if she remained loyal to her own gods (like Jezebel), then the Law prohibited this because there would be serious complications for the faith. Even if the marriage was permissible, it would likely be viewed with suspicion by people.

2:12

"May [the Lord] cut off."   יַכְרֵת is the *hiphil* jussive; since the prophet was speaking on behalf of God, this is probably stronger than a wish or prayer from Malachi. It would be closer to an oracle, as in the blessing given by Isaac to Jacob. Such an oracle would certainly come to pass eventually — the speaker is simply asking God to do soon what he knows will be done. In the New Testament we have things like, "Come quickly, Lord Jesus."

"who does this."   The verb is an imperfect tense, but must refer to what was presently happening. The nuance of progressive imperfect fits well: it is still going on, but the verb implies nothing of the future.

"the one waking and the one answering."   The Hebrew is very cryptic, leading to many suggestions: עֵר וְעֹנֶה. These are two active participles, a hollow verb and then a III *he'* verb; the first means "waking" or "waker" and the second "answering" or "answerer." One suggestion is that it refers to "teacher

---

11 J. M. Myers, *The World of the Restoration* (Englewood Cliffs, NJ: Prentice-Hall, 1968), p. 98.

and student," which is far from this context. It more likely refers to the watchmen of the city, as we have just had a reference to the "tents of Jacob." The watchmen were often priests, awakening people to the early morning prayers. The idea is that one would call to the other at the ends of the settlements. Whether this was the intended meaning or not is uncertain. But what we can say is that the two words form a merism: two opposites meaning the totality. So the entire population was under scrutiny, and whoever was doing this would be cut off.

The reference to Jacob may seem strange at first since Malachi has used Judah, Israel, and Jerusalem. It may be that the name Jacob is used to underscore that this generation, like early Jacob, does not deserve the blessing but needs divine grace.

"presents." The form in the text is מַגִּישׁ, the *hiphil* participle from the *I nun* verb. It has the meaning of bringing something near, here bringing the offering to the sanctuary. Since the prophet is listing the types of people who may be guilty, then this would be hypocritical worshipers. If an individual has violated the Law, no ritual would be acceptable to God.

"dedication offering." This type of offering is the meal offering or the first fruits offering (Lev. 2). It was a thank offering as well as a dedication offering that accompanied the animal sacrifice. One must not miss the irony here — individuals were living in open sin in violation of the Law and yet bringing a dedication offering to the LORD! Any and every act of dedication to God is nullified by sin.

2:13

"second thing." שֵׁנִית is the adverbial accusative use of the number "second." The verb וּתַעֲשׂוּ is the *qal* imperfect of עָשָׂה; it should be classified as a progressive imperfect in that their activity is ongoing: "you are doing this second thing." The verb makes it clear that this too is a horrible sin that the men are committing. It introduces a second charge against them.

"covering." The form is rather easy: כַּסּוֹת is the *piel* infinitive construct of the *III he'* verb "to cover." But the syntax is more difficult. Here it could be an epexegetical use (explaining the verb), but that would leave unanswered in the sentence the object of the verb "you do," that is, "you do (something) by covering." The infinitive may instead be taken as a noun use, perhaps in apposition to "second thing," that is, "you do this second thing, covering . . ."

"[with] tear[s] . . . weeping and groaning."   The nouns are adverbial accusatives, explaining how or with what they were covering the altar. The point is not to be taken literally — people would not be on or over the altar crying.

The exegesis will have to explain who is doing this. The men are charged with covering the altar with tears. It is unlikely to refer to their own tears of remorse; rather, it refers to the pain that they have caused the women. We are dealing with a figure of speech; it is a figure of substitution. Covering the altar with tears is hyperbolic to be sure, but also a metonymy of effect, the cause being their treachery. There was a lot of weeping and groaning at the altar, so much so that the altar was less noticeable. The fact that tears and weeping and groaning are mentioned goes beyond any description of feigned piety.

"the altar."   What was being put on the altar? Not tears, literally, but the offering they brought. And yet, the prophet interprets that they thought they were bringing a sacrifice, but what they were really doing was covering over all that with the signs of their sin.

"so that there is no longer any regard."   The second thing they were doing — covering the altar with tears — rendered their sacrifice unacceptable. Some take it that the guilty men were weeping *because* their offering was rejected. But there is no hint in the passage that they repented. And this is still part of the charge: "this second thing you are doing." The word מֵאֵין is rendered here "so that there is not" in Brown, Driver, and Briggs.[12] The result of the crying is that the sacrifices they offered were not accepted.

"regard."   פְּנוֹת is the *qal* infinitive construct from the *III he'* verb, "to turn [the face]." It is functioning nominally: there is no longer a turning. The idea of the verb is "look on favorably, pay attention to, or have regard for." So the meaning would be: "[so that] there is no longer a turning to [your] offering." God was no longer responding to their attempts to worship.

"nor to receive."   This infinitive construct לָקַחַת could function here as a

---

12 *A Hebrew and English Lexicon of the Old Testament* (Oxford: Oxford University Press, 1907), p. 35.

result or purpose clause of the preceding clause: God was not regarding their offering to receive it. It could also be seen as parallel to the first infinitive: there is "no longer a regarding . . . nor a receiving . . ."

If the men had been offering a sin offering, then the case for their weeping over being rejected might be stronger. But they are bringing the dedicatory offering (the מִנְחָה).

"pleasure."   The noun "pleasure," רָצוֹן, is an adverbial accusative: "with pleasure." It explains that God is not pleased to accept the dedicatory offering, an understatement. He strongly rejects it.

2:14

"Why?"   Their question reveals their heart. They did not know why God was no longer accepting their offerings, and so the prophet will have to explain their sin more clearly.

"was witness."   הֵעִיד is the *hiphil* perfect of the hollow root: "for the LORD was witness between you and the wife of your youth." If it is not taken as a simple past, it could be given either a present perfect translation ("the LORD has witnessed — and still does witness") or gnomic perfect ("the LORD remains a witness"). The expression will be part of the point that marriage was a covenant because they took an oath; and God witnessed it, and in doing so he gave his approval to the marriage. He certainly would not give his approval to its dissolution, for the covenant he witnessed would be broken. This will be stated fully at the end of the verse: "she is the wife of your covenant," or, "your covenant wife." To end that marriage is to break a covenant. And therein is the treachery.

"the wife of your youth."   "Your youth" is נְעוּרֶיךָ, the plural form of the noun with a suffix. This special use of the plural includes all that went on in the early years of their married life. The plural is often used to include many aspects.

"against whom you have dealt treacherously."   אֲשֶׁר אַתָּה בָּגַדְתָּה בָּהּ is a classic example of a relative clause, which includes the following: relative pronoun, subject, verb, preposition with a resumptive pronoun. So the translation is "who you have dealt treacherously (against) whom." The pronoun "her" is joined to the relative "who" and written "whom."

"And did he not make one?" The Hebrew is simply וְלֹא־אֶחָד עָשָׂה. There is no formal indication this is a question, but that is the only interpretation in the context: he made "one." And why did he make "one"? To translate it "He did not make one" would make no sense here. The NIV (1995) adds the subject and a pronoun: "Has not the LORD made them one?"

"and yet he had the residue of the Spirit." The Hebrew expression is simple, but difficult to interpret: וּשְׁאָר רוּחַ לוֹ. Literally it means "and the residue of the Spirit to him." The simplest way to render it is with the possessive: "yet he had the residue of the Spirit." The residue is the remnant, what is left. The idea may be that he had other resources and options, but he chose to make one. In other words, he could have done anything he wanted — he was not limited. But he chose to make one. In this passage, which is about divorce and remarriage, the one probably refers to the wife that he made for the man in Genesis 2.

"And why the one?" The form at first sight is "what?" But that does not make a smooth translation without adding a few words. Another look in the dictionary shows this can mean "why?" as well. *Why* did he make one?

"seeking." The form is the *piel* participle, מְבַקֵּשׁ, "seeking." It will function here as the predicate, but a pronoun will be implied: "he was seeking."

"a godly seed." The expression is "a seed of God." The genitive "God" is normally taken as an attributive genitive modifying seed. "God" could also signify the source, that is, a "seed of/from God." And seed is another sample of a metonymy of cause, meaning children from the seed. The figure is metonymy because there literally was a human seed, but here it means more.

The point seems to be saying more than a marriage of one man and one woman will produce godly children, for that is not true for most of the people. The emphasis would be on the fact that God made that man and that woman in the way that they would produce godly children. And so in Malachi it will be a holy marriage within the covenant that would do that, not a marriage to a pagan. This point is implied in the words of Jesus: "What God has joined together . . ."

For an illustration of the worst type, King Ahab married Jezebel, a zealot of Baal worship. She proceeded to kill the true prophets and replace them with her own in an effort to change the state religion. Then there was Athaliah who married the king of Judah and tried to exterminate the Davidic line. The marriage was made worse in these cases because the women (at times it would be the men) were devoted to their false gods.

"So take heed."   The form וְנִשְׁמַרְתֶּם is a perfect tense, and so the *waw* is consecutive; in the context of rebuke and instruction, this form will have the force of an imperative or an imperfect of instruction, even though no clear verb form precedes.

2:16

"I hate."   The form שָׂנֵא appears to be a *qal* perfect, third masculine singular. Since this is a quote from the LORD, that is, the understood subject is first common singular "I," the line would have to be explained as an elliptical clause to get the translation: "[I] hate." Some commentators have translated it as "he hates" (says the LORD), and while that would fit the form, it would require the whole line to be reworked. Rudolph suggested it was a verbal adjectival form, which would allow the traditional view to stand without alteration of the text.

"putting away."   The form שַׁלַּח is the *piel* infinitive construct. It functions here as the direct object (even without the preposition) of the verb, completing the statement with what it was God hated. It cannot be translated as an imperfect or a jussive the way it is; but in ancient manuscripts without vocalization it could have been taken as a perfect tense and made to fit with the first form ("he hates . . . he puts away," yielding the idea, "the one who hates his wife puts her away and covers with violence"). But it is vocalized as an infinitive in the Masoretic Text, and to get the other reading the text would have to be changed. There is no reason to do this.

"and covers."   The construction simply has וְכִסָּה, the *piel* perfect, third person masculine singular, with the conjunction: "and he covers" (if we take the perfect tense as characteristic perfect). To make a smooth translation we would add a clarifying subject: "and *the one who* covers," or, "and *him who* covers."

"with violence."   The older translation, "who covers violence with his garments," will not work syntactically; עַל with the verb determines what is covered. The expression is figurative, of course. The appearance of the type of clothing a person wore indicated his nature or character — clothed with white raiment means they are pure, clothed with filthy garments means they are sinful. Here violence covers their clothes; one can only see the evil they do and never get beyond that.

"do not act treacherously."   The verb is a third person jussive, which makes no sense here (= "and let him not deal treacherously"). Many Hebrew manuscripts and the major versions have a second person form, which goes with the negative jussive. This simply must be an error in transcription.

Exegetical Outline

I.   The prophet announced that marrying pagans was a treacherous and abominable sin that destroyed the holy covenant the LORD made with Israel and incurred the judgment of God on all the guilty (2:10–12).
   A.   He declared that the people had committed a great treachery that had profaned the covenant of the LORD (10).
   B.   He clarified that their abominable sin that had destroyed the holiness the LORD loved was their marriage to pagans (11).
   C.   He called on the LORD to cut off everyone who was guilty, even if they were pretending to be worshipers (12).
II. The prophet announced that because their treachery against the marriage covenant that God witnessed caused great suffering, their worship was nullified and protests rejected (2:13–14).
   A.   He declared that because their treachery also caused great pain to their abandoned spouses, it nullified their worship (13).
   B.   He rejected their self-righteous protests because the LORD was witness to the covenant of marriage they violated and because their sin undermined everything that made up the marriage (14).
III. The prophet warned everyone to guard their marriages so that they would fulfill the divine plan of producing godly children, explaining that the LORD hates divorce and the violence it causes (2:15–16).

A. He exhorted the people to guard against this treachery
because God designed marriage to produce a holy seed (15).
B. He exhorted the people to guard against this treachery
because God hates divorce and the violence it causes (16).

Exegetical Summary

Malachi strongly exhorted the people to guard against the treachery of destroying a holy marriage for a profane marriage to a pagan, because such treachery broke a covenant that God witnessed, destroyed the purpose of marriage to produce a godly seed, caused great pain and violence in society, and nullified any further efforts to worship, all of which was hateful to God and would be judged by him.

Commentary in Expository Form

I. *Those who willfully violate the covenant of marriage face the punishment of God (2:10–12).*

A. THE WILLFUL DESTRUCTION OF A MARRIAGE IS A TREACHEROUS SIN (10).

Malachi begins his message by laying down a principle: Israel was created as a covenant people by one Father, God. Nevertheless, they were now guilty of treachery against that covenant. The first statement affirms the principle by rhetorical question that they all had one Father, one God who created them. The use of Father is a figurative description of God; the word signifies that he is the sovereign creator of all things, that he has made a covenant with Israel, and that he has made himself known to his people in a personal way. And the verb "created" (בָּרָא) in this context refers to God's forming them into a nation by making a covenant with them at Mount Sinai, because otherwise we would be saying the whole human race has this same Father; "one Creator" would be fine, but "Father" is a covenant term. The language of creation used for the Sinai event makes a clear parallel between the two works of God. And concerning the main topic of this passage, we may note that both in the original creation and in the creating of Israel as a covenant people God had a clear plan for marriage.

Malachi's reference to their Creator as Father recalls the language of Malachi 1:6, "Is not God our Father?" The term "Father" (an implied comparison) is used in covenant relationships, notably here to signify the covenant relationship that God established in Egypt and confirmed at Sinai ("let my son [Israel] go"; see Exod. 4:22; Deut. 32:18; Isa. 1:2; and Jer. 3:9). Spiritual unity should have existed because they had a close relationship with God and with one another by means of the covenant with Abraham, activated by the covenant at Sinai. But more to the point, because loyalty to the covenant was paramount, the Law strictly prohibited intermarriage with the pagans (see Exod. 34:11 and Deut. 7:1–4), unless, of course, the pagan came to faith in Yahweh. Corrupt marriages would destroy worship and divide the covenant community (as the experience of Solomon so clearly shows). To do this, then, was to dishonor God and the covenant.

And this is the point of the second half of the verse. It too uses a rhetorical question to express the prophet's amazement and rebuke (although a case could be made for taking it as an actual question, calling for the people to explain why they are violating the plan of God). "Why do we deal treacherously with one another?" The verb (בָּגַד) signifies a willful betrayal of trust or of truth. One who is treacherous is a traitor, unreliable, and disloyal; and a traitor is dangerous because his word, even under oath, means nothing.

The result of the treachery was "that [they] profane the covenant," or more simply "so that the covenant is profaned." And that covenant is designated as the "covenant of our fathers," the patriarchs being known as the fathers, although the reference might include other ancestors as well.

The word rendered "profane" (חָלַל) means to treat something as common or ordinary; it is the antonym of "holy," which refers to something set apart to God and therefore distinct. The covenant was holy, but they made it commonplace; matrimony was supposed to be holy, but they made it profane — no different than marriages in the world.

The prophet at this beginning of the message was speaking in general terms to get the people's attention; when he had it, he narrowed the focus to the actual sins involved. As we shall see, Malachi was condemning marrying pagan women, more so because those intermarriages were the cause of the divorces. And since the message begins with the affirmation of the sovereignty of God, then the message is that unfaithfulness to the marriage covenant is also disloyalty to God. The principle is well summarized by Hengstenberg, who said that the one who annulled the distinction between an Israelite and a heathen woman proved by this very action that he had already annihilated the distinction between the God of

Israel and the idols of the heathen, that he no longer had the theocratic consciousness of God.[13]

B. MARRYING DEVOTEES OF FALSE GODS PROFANES GOD'S HOLINESS (11).

From the general description of treachery the prophet now identifies the exact problem: illegal and dangerous marriages. The culprits are simply referred to as Judah, Israel, and Jerusalem, all of which are figures of speech (metonymies of subject) for the people in these regions who had sinned. Israel was mentioned because it was the name of the country, and so refers to the whole nation; Judah and Jerusalem draw our attention to the immediately relevant section of the country, the religious center of the nation. On the one hand, then, the guilty were throughout the land; but on the other hand, the identification with these important places heightened the boldness of the sin. It was not a problem in remote areas where people had little knowledge and therefore little religious instruction; it was in the very center of the religious and political community. Ezra had listed guilty priests and Levites (Ezra 10).

The seriousness of the sin is expressed well enough by the word "treachery"; but the parallel word "abomination" (תּוֹעֵבָה) emphasizes that it was something that God loathes, something that is repugnant to him, and therefore taboo. The verse explains why it was so repugnant: "Judah has profaned the holiness of the LORD, which he loves, and has married the daughter of a foreign god." Malachi was not simply talking about illegitimate marriages, but about bringing devoted idol-worshiping women into the community of Israel by marriage!

The statement that they "profaned the holiness" of the LORD is powerful because it plays on words that are antonyms: "holiness" (קֹדֶשׁ) refers to something that is distinct, set apart, separate to God; and "profane" (חָלַל, a *piel* verb) means to make something common, defiled, separated from the sanctuary. Those who were dealing treacherously were reversing the process of sanctification and so were undermining the faith.

But what did Malachi mean by "the holiness" of the LORD? It could refer to the temple, of course. The idea would be that some Israelites were bringing active pagan idolaters into the house of the LORD and therefore profaning it. Support for this view comes from passages that affirm that the LORD loves

---

13 E. W. Hengstenberg, *Christology of the Old Testament* (1847; reprint, Grand Rapids: Kregel, 1970), 3:381.

Zion (Pss. 78:68; 87:2) and prohibits idolatry in the sanctuary. Support could also come from the context, which will say that God rejects their worship when they try to make sacrifices.

But the word "holiness" could also refer to the people of the covenant, the nation itself. The support for this view is a little more convincing, although not much. First, Israel is called a holy nation (Deut. 7:6) and God's sanctuary (Ps. 114:2). Second, the immediate context is based on the fact that God made them one nation (if that interpretation of the first verse is accepted); and the word "profaned" has already been used for their violation of the covenant of the fathers. Third, Malachi begins his book with the fact that God loves Israel. And fourth, intermarriage with pagans profaned the holy seed (Ezra 9:2; Jer. 2:3; Deut. 14:2). God established the marriage laws (Lev. 21:14, 15; Neh. 13:29) for the people he loved (i.e., chose) in order that they might be set apart to him. Now, however, Israelites had profaned that holiness and made themselves common, no different than the other nations. So the holiness may very well refer to the covenant people themselves, the nation — here the people in their marriages.

There is yet another possible interpretation: closely related to this second view is the idea that holiness refers to the proper marriage. Here it says God loves this holiness, and in contrast at the end of the passage we will read that God hates divorce. But it is hard to distinguish one of these over the others because the covenant people, their holy marriages, and the holy place are interrelated. Their sin has defiled all of these; they defiled the plan of God for them.

The last clause explains how they defiled all this: "and married the daughter of a foreign god (בַּת־אֵל נֵכָר)." The reference to "daughter of a foreign god" we know from Jeremiah 2:27 and other places means a devoted worshiper of a strange or foreign deity. The text uses the singular "daughter" to harmonize with the collective "Judah," and so it means the practice was a widespread sin in the land, not just one daughter. The serious sin, therefore, was that many men were marrying women who were committed worshipers of other deities. Bringing them into Israelite families would destroy the spiritual life of the nation, which was how it all started with Solomon.

C. INTRODUCING IDOLATRY INTO THE FAMILY OF GOD WARRANTS THE THREAT OF A CURSE FROM HIM (12).

The grave sin brought a clear rebuke from the prophet because a violation of the covenant had been committed — intermarriage with a committed pagan (not a convert from paganism). Malachi says, "May Yahweh cut off. . . ." This is not an announcement of doom; it is the expressed desire of the prophet that God judge the guilty. But coming from a prophet the expression would be ominous. Such an expressed imprecation from the prophet was warning enough that if this sin was not stopped it would bring the severest penalty.

The idea of being "cut off" (כָּרַת) has several levels of meaning. In its uses in the Law for divine punishment the verb could call for the death penalty at the hands of the people, or for premature death at the hand of God, or for excommunication by the religious community, depending on the nature of the violation. The community seldom put people to death (only a couple of times we have on record) because it was hard to get a conviction. So one of the latter two is probably in the mind of the prophet; that is, God would deal with this matter if the righteous in the land did not.

Who stood to be "cut off" by God? The answer, through some poetic expressions, indicates that none of the guilty is excluded from this ominous oracle. The general statement is given first: "the man who does this." Whoever was doing it, without exception, was under an expressed curse, and could expect divine punishment sooner or later. Then with an obscure expression Malachi declared that the punishment was all-inclusive: "from the waker and the answerer." There are a number of suggestions for this difficult phrase, but perhaps the best interpretation may be that it refers to watchmen in the camps, watchmen at either end of the settlement, one calling out and the other answering. In any case, it is a figure to express the totality of the people (a merism), meaning everyone, from one extreme to the other (opposite).

And then to get to the even more important qualification, Malachi asserts that not even a worshiper was exempt: "even the one offering a gift (מִנְחָה) to the LORD of armies." The point is that judgment would fall on such covenant violators, even if they *appeared* to be generous and devout. To give this type of offering or gift along with the blood sacrifice would be the way to indicate gratitude for God's provision and express dedication of life to his service.

But here the outward sign of dedication was betrayed by the treachery of uniting with paganism in marriage. Such dedication is a delusion. God could fulfill the curse of Malachi by bringing premature death on them, or by having them banished from the sanctuary. It would be a decisive act of God should it happen. What the eternal destiny of the culprits was is impossible to say; that is another issue entirely. Divine judgment could fall on any who were guilty, whether actual believers going astray or make-believers who never were faithful.

11.   *The LORD rejects participation in worship by those who violate the marriage covenant and bring pain to their spouses (2:13–14).*

A. THE PAIN CAUSED BY SIN NULLIFIES ANY ATTEMPTS TO WORSHIP (13).

A second but related sin was uncovered by the prophet: "And this second thing you do," or, "and again you do this." This second sin grew out of the first, for in finding and marrying pagan women they put away their primary wives by divorce. So the prophet turns his attention now to the treachery on the personal level: marrying an idolatrous woman was one thing; but treachery against a faithful wife is equally serious, for it caused great pain to the women who were put away and it ruined any chance of acceptable worship.

The text simply says, "covering the altar of the LORD with tears, with weeping and with groaning." The infinitive "covering" serves to explain this second thing they were doing, and the full clause envisions the impact of their sin: they had caused their wives so much pain that it was as if they were covering the altar with tears, weeping, and groaning. God did not pay attention to their sacrifices, only the pain they caused.

But the line has been taken in different ways. First, some interpret it to mean that the guilty men were filled with remorse and were weeping at the altar because God no longer paid attention to their sacrifices (see NIV 1995). Their remorse would have to have been insincere if God was not responding to them. The difficulty with this view is that there is no indication at all that these people were repenting or even feigning repentance; in fact, they would not have known that the LORD no longer regarded their sacrifices if Malachi had not told them. And it was because of the sin and the pain it caused that God no longer regarded their offerings. In Malachi the guilty are always belligerent and challenging the accusation of the prophet. Covering the altar with tears and groaning is presented as a second sin they were doing, not a change of heart, and the description fits the idea of their treachery very well. They were not repenting, or feigning remorse.

So the second view fits the context better. It says that the verse vividly reports the painful effect of their sin as the abandoned wives were weeping and groaning at the altar. This was the pain that the men caused. And because of this heartless sin, God was no longer regarding their offering to receive it with pleasure from their hands. When they made an offering, all God could see was the pain they caused by their treachery.

One argument often raised against this view is that nowhere in the Bible do we read about women approaching the altar. But the statement would not require that the women actually approached the altar with their weeping, or were even in the sanctuary for that matter. It simply describes in figurative terms the effect of their sin. It reports in effect what the men were actually presenting to the LORD — the pain of their sin and not their sacrifices.

The picture is painted dramatically. The wives who had been put away were in great anguish — they now had nothing, no marriage, no security, no hope. When the women prayed, their tears flowed freely and intermingled with their prayers. Their anguish rose up to God with such intensity that God refused to regard (give attention to) the dedicatory offerings brought by the men. So in God's sight the men were not putting a legitimate offering on the altar; rather, they were covering the altar with tears and sighing, not their tears, for they were cavalier about it all and thought God was pleased with their gifts, but with their wives' tears, because by causing the pain the men were actually making their sacrifices of no effect. That is what their hand produced, as Malachi would put it. And all such hard-hearted and hypocritical worship is completely rejected.

Here were men, calloused and disloyal to the historic faith, coming to the sanctuary with their gifts of dedication and thanksgiving. It was the Law! But over to the side were their unfortunate wives, now abandoned, crying and groaning. Their tears were what God saw, not the offerings of their husbands. There is scarcely a thought more solemn and searching than the thought that few, if any, of our prayers go up to God unqualified and unchecked. We pray for something, but our sins cry out for something else, and the prayer is hindered. After all, Peter reminded all Christian men to treat their wives with respect as joint heirs of the covenant "so that nothing will hinder [their] prayers" (1 Peter 3:7).

B. SELF-RIGHTEOUS PROTESTING OF GOD'S WORD WILL NOT WORK FOR GOD WITNESSED THE MARRIAGE AND THE TREACHERY (14).

The response of the men was again to challenge the word of the prophet: "Why?" "Why was God not accepting our sacrifices?" There was a cold defiance in these words, a defiance that came from rationalized sin. When they were told by the prophet that God was rejecting their worship, their response was not conviction and guilty fear. They thought that if they did the worship routine well enough and gave to the sanctuary they would be highly favored. Well, God not only did not need their gifts; he did not want them.

So this passage is instructive for what we are seeing today, people entering all kinds of religious worship and service with similarly unlawful and questionable marriages, never having acknowledged their guilt in destroying the covenant of marriage or bringing pain to the family, let alone even admitting that there might have been a violation of God's word.

Malachi's answer to the culprits' challenging question was a sharp rebuke based on the divine plan for marriage: they had violated the covenant of marriage, a covenant that God himself witnessed. Malachi begins by stating that the LORD witnessed their marriage, indicating that it was a sacred oath, duly witnessed and sealed by Almighty God in heaven. So their treachery was basically breaking their oaths, and that would have carried a death penalty. To agree to live together as man and wife is a covenant and God is the witness; to dissolve the marriage is to break the covenant — and God witnesses that too.

Several passages use covenant language for marriage: Proverbs 2:17; Ezekiel 16:7 (applying it to God and the nation); Ruth 4:11 (witnessed by the community); and Genesis 24:60 (based on love and faithfulness). The covenant agreement of a marriage is to be based on loyal love, characterized by the protection and care of the partners, and dedicated to producing righteous, believing children that God may provide (Ps. 127). As a covenant, it was to be a picture of the covenant that God made with his people, Israel, his wife.

Malachi intensifies the description of the treachery by the way he describes the marriage relationship (this is also good counseling method to remind the individual what he had in his marriage). First, he calls the wife the "wife of your youth (time)." The word "youth" can refer to ages up to the age of thirty or forty even, but usually a woman would have been younger when married. The use of the plural, "youths" (נְעוּרֶיךָ), is intended to recall all the times and events of the early years of their marriage when they were full of love and devotion and ambition and plans, beginning their family and their life together. She was the wife of his youth — the time of his vigor and industry. She was the one who had his first affections when they were the strongest, the one who gave him children, the one who brought up the children, and the one who had lived through it all with him. Now in a treacherous change he broke faith with her and their vows; she had become the scorn and loathing of his later years. So the prophet inserts the relative clause to heighten this betrayal: "against whom you have dealt treacherously." The word "treachery" now appears for the third time in the oracle — it was against women like this that the treachery was committed.

Malachi also says that she was his "companion" (חֲבֶרֶת). The word comes from a verb "to unite"; the verb and its nouns are used for close associates, partners, worshipers, armies, all of which are bound as a unit and share the same characteristics and goals. She was not just the wife of his early years, and not a servant–she was a partner, a companion. The marriage meant that they were bound together as one in the eyes of God. They shared everything together, griefs and joys, successes and failures, hard times and good times. But now, these women were being cast aside like an old garment for something new and fresh and exciting, but thoroughly worldly. Whatever had been there as *holy matrimony* was now being replaced by *profane fornication.*

Finally, he returns to the theme of covenant: "and the wife of your covenant." He essentially says, "You made a covenant with your wife." This was the binding oath that was witnessed by the LORD. But that covenant is now being abandoned in violation of the Law. Here is the warning for all who dissolve a marriage, even if they think they have reason to do so: it is covenant breaking.

All of these qualifications of marriage are piled up by the prophet to convey how treacherous this all was. God planned that a man and a woman would become one flesh, be partners, share everything, build a life together, and together seek to please God. Their personal blessing depended on preserving this covenant; and the well-being of the nation depended on the marriages doing what they were supposed to do. When one of the partners broke the marriage vow, not simply in a sin that should not have happened, but a deliberate nullification of the marriage and a pursuit of an illegal marriage to another, that person was seen as a traitor because his or her words could never again be believed, even if made with an oath.

III. *Believers must be on guard against treachery in marriage because it thwarts God's plans for marriage (15–16).*

A. BECAUSE GOD DESIGNED A HOLY MARRIAGE TO PRODUCE A GODLY SEED, PEOPLE MUST PROTECT THEIR MARRIAGES (15).

Malachi is not yet through. The final section is clearly set off as a warning for those who are in a marriage. They must understand its purpose if they are going to preserve it.

Basic to this section is the difficult verse 15. It begins with, "Did he not make one?" For the meaning of "one," some suggest the reference is to Abraham, and the warning comes from the fact that Abram turned from Sarai to have a child with Hagar, and that did not produce a godly seed. So take heed.

But the view just does not stand up with the details of the text. Abraham is never called "one" or "the one." He did not divorce Sarai and marry Hagar. And the question of the "residue of the Spirit" is not accounted for in the interpretation. It is rather forced to see verse 15 as a reference to Abram's failure as a warning to this generation.

A second view takes the "one" back to the creation of Eve for Adam. God could have done it differently: "he had the residue (or remainder) of the Spirit," that is, he had all the resources and options that the Spirit of God could provide. But he chose to make one wife for one man. A difficulty of this view is that monogamy does not guarantee godly children would be produced. The two would have to be committed to the faith and to the training of children in it.

Another view is that the "one" refers to the nation of Israel, the covenant people. This view fits well in Malachi, which presents the nation as the creation of God. Why did God make one nation, Israel? To produce a godly seed in the earth. Pagan intermarriage and the dissolution of good marriages would ruin the chance to do this. God wanted a nation. He could have chosen and worked with others, or more. But by focusing on one that he created as the means of bringing blessing to the world, he would form a righteous people on earth. This too has the drawback that God's preparing a nation would not necessarily produce a godly seed. If they were the covenant people, living under the Law, worshiping in the sanctuary as the covenant people, it would then be likely that they would produce righteous children. But they did not always live up to that.

The second view remains the best choice if we take it to refer to "one flesh" and not simply to one wife. After all, Genesis clearly says that the two of them will be *one* flesh, that is, united in mind and spirit, sharing the faith, and serving the LORD (see also Matt. 19:4–6; Mark 10:7–8). It was the purpose of the LORD that they should be so united, because then they could extend the faith to the next generation.

This next clause is also difficult. The Hebrew has "and/yet he had the residue/remainder of the Spirit/spirit" (וּשְׁאָר רוּחַ לוֹ). It cannot be arranged to mean that he gave them the Spirit, as some commentaries suggest; for that would have been easy to say if that was the point. Rather, it says that the "remnant of the Spirit" belonged to him. Neither should we be too quick to change the text to obtain a desired emphasis. Some commentators (and the NIV 1995) suggest changing the vowel of the first word from שְׁאָר to שְׁאֵר, to get "flesh," and then translate it "in flesh and spirit they are his." That is forced into the text and without manuscript support; even the Greek has "residue." Some writers propose turning the word into a causative form (a *hiphil* preterite), "and he spared/caused to remain"; but that changes the text even more. The clause probably is meant to say that God had (it was "to him") all the resources of the Spirit, that is, he had much more at his disposal and could have done much more or many other things, but he had this singular purpose in mind that required unified marriages.

The purpose of a proper marriage was "seeking a godly seed." It was God's purpose, and it should be the purpose of the couple. There was little or no chance at all to produce godly children if the marriage was to loyal worshipers of pagan deities — the best that one could hope for was competition for the faith. But if the parents were both devout believers and faithful to the covenant, their children would most likely be influenced properly to be godly.

Therefore Malachi warns them to take heed in their spirit (note the word play with God's Spirit) not to deal treacherously against the wife of their youth. The verb "take heed" means "to watch carefully" (here in the *niphal*, "take heed to yourselves," "watch yourselves"). It calls for constant vigilance and concern, like a night watchman watching the city. The husband (and the wife) must be careful and alert to protect the marriage covenant from any treachery, by himself or from outside.

B. BECAUSE GOD HATES DIVORCE, PEOPLE MUST SAFEGUARD
THEIR MARRIAGES (16).

The next line completes the message in a most powerful way: the LORD gives the reason for all this rebuke and warning by exclaiming: "I hate putting away." Some of the ancient versions, the Greek primarily, interpreted the line to say, "if a man hates his wife and puts her away. . . ." What Malachi is doing is offering the quintessential reason for trying to keep a marriage together come what may: God hates divorce (as opposed to the sanctity of marriage and the covenant, which earlier we read, "he loves").

What does it mean when it says God hates it? When hate is used in contrast to love in passages, as it is here in Malachi, it conveys the sense of rejection along with intense feelings, whereas love would convey the sense of choosing with different feelings (see comments in chapter 1). Here the word is not used in such a contrast, although he has already said that God loves the holiness that they were defiling; this passage adds to the idea of rejection the feeling of detesting, abhorring. We can see from this that God is emotionally involved in the lives of his people. He hates it when they destroy their marriages, because he knows the pain that will cause, and the effect that will have on the faith for the future. If God hates divorce, then he loves faithful marriages.

The text adds something else as the object of his hatred: "when people cover their garments with violence." This word for "violence" (חָמָס) is used often for social injustice. Not only had their sins covered the altar with the tears of their wives, but now also their sins covered them with violence (an implied comparison with clothing). Their replacing of their vows of love and devotion to their wives with acts of social abuse and emotional and even physical violence God hated as well. Divorcing their wives was violence against their wives; it created havoc with their lives, as well as with society, and spoiled the covenant God loved.

The prophet repeats the warning at the end: "Take heed to yourselves in your spirits and do not act treacherously." The people are called on to guard their hearts and minds and attitudes in this matter so that they would not be guilty of such treachery.

Expository Idea and Application

Expository Idea

The main thrust of the passage is a rebuke and a warning for the treachery of breaking up holy marriages and marrying devoted idolaters. The treachery is seen in the fact that this violates the sanctity of marriage, frustrates its purpose, causes great pain and violence to the people involved, and breaks a covenant that God witnessed. The consequences of such an abomination include the rejection of their worship now, and divine discipline later if they did not repent.

The theological ideas of this passage are clear. The focus on God concerns his acts mostly: he created one flesh, male and female, to serve him; he made a covenant with Israel and formed the nation into one people to be a godly seed; and he witnessed the marriages. He hates divorce, treachery, and violence; and he will judge those who are guilty, their hypocritical offerings accounting for nothing.

The focus on the people in this passage is primarily on the guilty but also their victims. They acted treacherously, breaking the marriage covenant and therefore the Law; they profaned everything God has declared sacred; they were calloused and indifferent to the rebuke, continuing to worship as if nothing was wrong, even though they caused their true wives great pain.

There are different ways that an expository idea of this passage could be worded (and the wording does depend to some degree on the audience and the occasion or purpose of the message). It could be stated strongly and fully:

> Those who willfully destroy a marriage to marry another, a pagan,
> will find rejection of their worship and punishment from God
> because they betrayed their partners, broke their covenant,
> caused pain and violence, and nullified the purpose of marriage.

This is certainly complete, but a bit too long for a spoken exposition that the people only hear. So it could be simplified, even though this full statement will be a good concluding summary of the main message and the main reasons for it. A shorter, more positively worded expository idea could be stated this way:

> God's people must protect their marriages,
> so that they remain faithful to their sacred vows,
> fulfill the purpose of a marriage, and please God in their worship.

Application

When a principle like this is developed to convey the central message of the exposition, it will be easier to make the applications. The clearest application in the text is to take heed and not to act treacherously, or, to be always on guard against such unfaithfulness to the marriage. This involves two very important considerations: knowing and carrying out the covenant God has made for his people, and knowing and maintaining what God planned for the marriage. To fulfill the first part, one must be committed to worshiping and serving God in holiness and righteousness. To fulfill the second part, one must know that the marriage is a covenant confirmed by God and the spouse is a lifelong partner.

To motivate diligence in the care for the marriage, Malachi included three warnings: (1) divorce and remarriage (especially to a devotee of a false god) destroys worship; (2) divorce and remarriage (especially to such an idolater) hinders producing godly children; and (3) divorcing a legitimate wife is hated by God. So the message to the household of faith is urgent: if you truly see how the marriage covenant fits the covenant God has made with his people, then you will marry within the faith and you will give all diligence to preserve that marriage, come what may.

No marriage is perfect. In marriages there will be many failures to measure up to the ideal; the marriage may be strained and thinned by friction, or marred and sullied by violations against its moral meaning. But the failures and abuses do not destroy the ideal. And we are always called back to the ideal, to the standard of God. For marriage to be *holy* matrimony, it must be pleasing to God. And to develop this there must be a real commitment to the will of God, so that the husband and wife truly see their marriage as service to God. Malachi says, "Take heed not to deal treacherously." That is, do everything in your power to remain faithful to the covenant of marriage. And it will take such diligence because the way of the world is so different.

Additional Applications

Jesus placed a holy grandeur around this particular relationship of a man and a woman. To him it was a blessed estate, and so he presented it with honor and sublimity. He ratified its contract, guarded its obligations, and expounded its laws (Matt. 19:1–6). He graced its celebration with his presence; in fact, the first sign that his hands performed was at the bridal festival where he turned the water into wine for the joyous celebrations to continue (John 2:1–11).

The apostles carried forward the ideas of the Lord, recognizing marriage as also a type of the substantial, invisible, and everlasting union existing between Christ and his bride, the church (e.g., 2 Cor. 11:1–3; Eph. 5:22–33; and Rev. 19:7–8). Accordingly, it is portrayed ideally as the most intimate and enduring of human relationships on earth, and one that has the greatest influence.

But in the modern world the dissolution or perversion of a marriage is rarely considered a sin; rather, it is an option. Of course divorce is regarded as a painful experience, and a failure on some level. But a sin? Or even an embarrassment? Only in the strictest of religious settings. To God divorce is a failure to meet the standard of the will of God—and therefore a sin. It is the breaking of a covenant and thus a serious and painful complication of life that seems never to go away. For those who willfully destroy a marriage, the Bible has the strongest condemnation. But to add to this violation the error of marrying someone devoted to a false religion or no religion, or living in a union that the Bible prohibits, creates great problems for those involved and for the standard of holiness that the church must be following. The church must, therefore, distinguish holy matrimony from the world's misuse of so-called marriage with a clear teaching on it within the covenant by faithful believers (as opposed to those who claim to be Christians but reject Scripture to justify unlawful marriages and lifestyles). And individual believers must renew their commitments to their spouses so that they will not be guilty of such treachery.

Key Words

"To Create"

The verb "create" (בָּרָא) means "shape, create, fashion."

(1) It is used, of course, for the creation of the universe and all its contents. This is the most common use. Isaiah states that the LORD created the heavens (Isa. 42:5), the stars (Isa. 40:26), and the ends of the earth (Isa. 40:28). And for the creation of living creatures three times the verb is used in Genesis 1:27; then in the same sense it is repeated in Genesis 5:1, 2; 6:7; and in Deuteronomy 4:32.

(2) A second category of meaning refers to the establishment of the nation of Israel. God says to Israel, "I am the LORD, your Holy One, the Creator of Israel, your king" (Isa. 43:15). The same meaning appears to be the point of Malachi 2:10, but determining the reference is difficult, whether it is to creation in general (as above) or to formation of the nation. Malachi asks, "Has not one God created us?" It appears that the verb describes the formation of the nation; but it would also mean the inclusion of individual believers within it: "Everyone that is called by my name, for I have created him for my glory" (Isa. 43:7). Here there is an emphasis on transformation, producing something fresh, new, and perfect, because God formed the nation out of people.

(3) A third category of meaning is clearly transformation or renewal. That the action is the transformation of something that already exists can be seen from each of the contexts. Isaiah records, "I create new heavens and a new earth" (Isa. 65:17). In the same context he adds, "I am about to create Jerusalem as a rejoicing, and her people as a joy" (Isa. 65:18).

(4) Finally, the word can also be used for individual spiritual renewal. Psalm 51:10 fits here, for the word "create" is actually paralleled with "renew": "create in me a clean heart // renew in me a steadfast spirit." A similar use is

found in Isaiah 57:19, which says, "I create the fruit of the lips." The point is that when the LORD heals someone he inspires praise once again.

The word "create" is used in the Bible exclusively for the activity of God in which he fashions something new and pristine. The word could be used in sentences affirming that God created something out of nothing, but that emphasis must come from the context and not from the meaning of this word. The word often refers to transforming and changing something with the result that what is created is perfect and complete.

"To Deal Treacherously"

The word "to act" or "to deal treacherously" (בָּגַד) does not have a great number of uses — 49 in all. But the idea of acting treacherously, deceitfully, or faithlessly is the constant meaning. It describes unfaithfulness (usually to the covenant), meaning that the people went back on their word.

(1) The use of the word in Malachi 2 with regard to the marriage covenant may prove the most helpful illustration for the word's use elsewhere. Here we have the accusation that the men had dealt treacherously with their wives, the ones with whom they had a (marriage) covenant that was witnessed by God. The simple meaning is that they broke their marriage vows.

(2) Another illustration comes from Job 6:15, which refers to the words of the people as deceitful as a brook. One might expect water in the brook, but if it is a seasonal stream, those looking for water may be disappointed. Isaiah provides the most emphatic use of the words with word plays: "the treacherous have dealt treacherously, yea, in treachery have the treacherous dealt treacherously" (24:16).

"To Make Abominable"

The verb "to make abominable" (תָּעַב) and the noun "abomination" (תּוֹעֵבָה) must be studied in their uses and by their synonyms. In general, they describe something that is seriously incompatible with God and his order of life, things that are dangerous, grotesque, out of place, and repulsive. It is hard to find a translation that works for all uses.

(1) There are places where the emphasis is simply that things do not fit (somewhat of a neutral use). For example, the Egyptians thought it an abomination to eat with Semites (Gen. 43:32). Certain types of people or condi-

tions just do not fit together (such as the righteous and the wicked, Prov. 29:27; fools and turning from evil, Prov. 13:19; or kings and wrong-doers, Prov. 16:12).

(2) Naturally, then, things that are totally incompatible with the divine nature are designated as abominations. In the social world, dishonest weights are taboo (Prov. 11:11; 20:10), as are evil judges (Prov. 17:15) and liars (Prov. 12:22).

(3) Perhaps in a group by themselves are passages about false worship which is an abomination to the LORD (Isa. 1:13) as serious as deceit, discord, and murder (Prov. 6:16–19). Idolatry and despicably pagan practices are abominations (Ezek. 5:9; 11:7; Deut. 7:25; 17:1) along with pagan cultic practices like prostitution (Deut. 23:19), sexual rites (Deut. 22:11), and any relations with pagan idolaters.

Things that are abominations are taboo, loathsome to God. Parallel terms draw this out: "reject" (מָאַס), "hate" (שָׂנֵא), and "abhor as cultically unclean" (שָׁקֵץ), as well as several other words for "harmful adulteration, taboo, unclean, abhorrent (excretion), shameful," and the like. What is described as abominable is not only incompatible with the divine nature, but it is so bad that it is repulsive to God and people alike.

"To Take Heed, Guard, Watch"

The verb rendered "take heed" (usually a *hithpael* from שָׁמַר) is commonly used with reference to God's protective care but also for humans in a wide array of capacities; the basic meaning is "observe, keep, preserve." Verbal forms are used for a number of things, from devotion, that is, meticulously observing religion practices (Jonah 2:9), to retaining someone in custody (Gen. 37:11), to night watchmen (Ps. 130:6). Related nouns illustrate these ideas: a "prison" (מִשְׁמָר), "a guard, watch" (מִשְׁמֶרֶת), a "watch," referring to a period of time (אַשְׁמֹרֶת), and the "eye-lid" (שְׁמֻרָה). This word "eye-lid" may provide the best illustration, for the eye-lid naturally and constantly protects the eye. But the categories of meanings for the verb give us the range of the word.

(1) The first category of meaning is "observe" (with the eye). Here the use of the participle for night watchmen would apply (Ps. 130:6). Watching often involves waiting (Jer. 20:10).

(2) A second and closely related category has the meaning of "preserve by observing," that is, keeping laws and customs. Here we find expressions

about keeping a covenant (Ezek. 17:14). This usage may include the ideas of meticulous keeping of laws, vows, holy days, and the faith (see Deut. 5:12; 23:24; Jer. 35:18; Gen. 18:19; Neh. 13:14). Meticulously observing religious practices would be part of this idea (Jonah 2:9). But it was also used for keeping something in memory (Gen. 37:11), or storing up food (Gen. 41:35).

(3) A third category means "protect." This meaning may be expressed with a translation "guard" or "protect," but the objects are very different. It is used for the cherubim guarding the way to the tree of life (Gen. 3:24); the LORD guarding a city (Ps. 127:1); and Amasa, we are told, not on guard (the *niphal*) against Joab's sword (2 Sam. 20:10). The guarding or protecting could have the connotation of restraining something, such as an ox from harming others (Exod. 21:36), or the mouth from harming others (Prov. 22:23). In a spiritual context, Malachi warns the people to take heed, watch themselves carefully so that they do not deal treacherously (Mal. 2:15 and 16).

(4) The idea of "protect" ("keep" or "guard") is used for the LORD's protection of his people as well (see the priestly benediction in Num. 6:24). The LORD is known as "the keeper of Israel," the result of which is protection from harm for pilgrims on a holy mission (Ps. 121). God may do this by assigning angels to guard his people (Ps. 91:11); or he himself may protect his people from all dangers, as he did through the wilderness years (Josh. 24:17).

5. *God's Justice and Faithfulness*

(MALACHI 2:17 – 3:5)

Introduction

Translation and Textual Notes

¹⁷ You have wearied¹ the LORD with your words.
But you say, "Wherein have we wearied [him]?"
When you say,
"Everyone who does evil is good
in the sight of the LORD,
and he delights in them."
Or [by asking],
"Where is the God of justice?"

¹ "Behold, I am about to send my messenger
and he will prepare the way before me;
And the Lord whom you seek will suddenly come to his temple,
even the messenger of the covenant whom you desire.²
He is coming," says the LORD of armies.
² But who can endure the day of his coming,
and who can stand when he appears?
For he³ [will be] like a refiner's fire and like fullers' soap.
³ And he will sit as a refiner and purifier of silver;

1   On the basis of some Greek manuscripts and other ancient versions, the editors of BHS propose changing the verb to הוֹגַעֲנֻהוּ, "we have wearied him," probably to match the verb in their response. But this change does not fit the style of the oracle.

2   The editors of BHS suggest that this whole line was a later addition. But there is no evidence for that, and the presence of the line forms an effective parallelism.

3   The Greek adds the verb εἰσπορεύεται (the equivalent of בָּא), "he comes." This is a

>   and he will purify the sons of Levi
>   and refine them like gold and silver,
>   and they will bring offerings in righteousness to the LORD.
> ⁴   Then the offering of Judah and Jerusalem
>   will be pleasing to the LORD
>   as in the days of old and as in former years.

> ⁵   "Then I will draw near to you for judgment.
>   And I will be a swift witness
>   against the sorcerers, and against the adulterers,
>   and against those who swear falsely,⁴
>   and against those who oppress the hired worker in his wages,
>   the widow and the fatherless,
>   and those who thrust aside the alien,
>   and do not fear me,"
>   says the LORD of armies.

Context and Composition

The prophet Malachi had to deal with a different kind of situation now be-cause people were wondering why God was not doing something to correct the sins and the corruption in the land. The only answer that they could come up with was that God was not just, that he was unwilling to judge sin. The prophet came down hard on this kind of shallow thinking; he made it very clear that if they really wanted the justice of God to be meted out, no one would stand! The individual who understands doctrine will always de-sire divine grace over divine justice. And we who live in the New Testament age understand this very well: what the justice of God demanded for our sins, the grace of God provided in the death of Christ on our behalf. And for those who are in Christ by faith, there is no condemnation (Rom. 8:1).

In this prophetic message, the promise of justice (or judgment) is tied to the coming of the Messiah. And so here we get into Malachi's eschatology (the study of last things). In anticipation of the material in this chapter we

---

clarification based on the context, the kind of clarification scribes made. It is to be rejected as secondary.

4   A large number of Masoretic manuscripts and the old Greek translation witness to an additional בִּשְׁמִי, "by my name." This reading also is the kind of additional clarification a scribe would make. Had it been part of the original, it is hard to explain why it would have been lost.

need to be reminded of a couple of things. Most informed Christians know that the word "Messiah" (a passive adjective מָשִׁיחַ from the verb מָשַׁח, "to anoint") means "anointed one," that is, the anointed king who is to come. The word was translated into Greek as "the Christ" (ὁ χριστός). Every king who came to the throne of David was *anointed* and so a *messiah*, but as time passed the prophets began to write of the great coming king, *The Messiah*. And his kingdom, or the age that he would usher in, is called the *Messianic Age*. This hope was the desire of the nation, as Malachi 3:1 says.

But that golden age to come would begin with judgment on the world, for the Messiah would come and judge the wicked before establishing universal righteousness and peace. They knew the facts about the Messiah, but they did not have the time sequence of the events of the Messiah. They did not know that there was going to be a second coming of the Messiah; it appeared that there would be only one. When they spoke about the coming of the Messiah, they could not quite understand how he could be born into the family of David as the heir to the throne and also come in the clouds with power and glory. But Scripture said he would do both.

We, of course, can look back to the prophecies with the New Testament in hand and realize that what was promised was a first and a second coming. But they did not know that. And this is what we must keep in mind in this little passage.

Here we also have the theme of Malachi developed prophetically. As noted before, the name "Malachi" means "my messenger." But in this passage it does not apply to Malachi, but to John the Baptist. He will fulfill the meaning of *my messenger,* preparing the way of the Lord. But then the Lord also is called a messenger here, "the messenger of the covenant," and he also will come.

Exegetical Notes

2:17

"You have wearied."   The form is the *hiphil* perfect, second person masculine plural, from יָגַע; here it has the present perfect nuance: "you have wearied," action in the past with continuing results. God does not get weary, but from our human perspective such challenges to God are wearying (hence, written in human terms it is an anthropomorphism). It is a way of saying that their endless complaints and charges are tiresome.

"When you say." The word בְּאֶמָרְכֶם is a *qal* infinitive construct with a preposition and a pronominal suffix, forming a temporal clause, "when you say." That is how they wearied God.

"Everyone who does evil." The line reads: כָּל־עֹשֵׂה רָע, literally, "every doer of evil." The *qal* active participle is in construct, so "evil" is an objective genitive.

"the God of justice." The word "justice" is a genitive after the construct. It could be an attributive adjective use, "the God characterized by justice." The emphasis may also be on the God who executes justice. The question is rhetorical; they are not asking for the location. The question is their way of asserting that he is not available or active in meting out justice.

3:1

"Behold, I am about to send." The construction is הִנְנִי שֹׁלֵחַ; this particle preceding an active participle emphasizes the imminent future: "I am about to send," almost "here I am sending." Here the LORD is sending his messenger.

"and he shall prepare the way before me." "Way" has become an idiom; but it was originally an implied comparison between a road or way and one's conduct in life, that is, the habits and practices. To prepare the way in this passage would mean preparing the hearts of people so that they would be living in the expectation of the coming of the LORD. John did this by calling for repentance. In the parallel description in Isaiah 40, crooked places are sins, and valleys are omissions so that the way has to be straightened and leveled. It will be a ministry calling for repentance (i.e., change) and spiritual renewal.

"before me." The LORD (i.e., Yahweh) is the speaker. This messenger will prepare people before the LORD. Here we begin to see something of the mystery of the Godhead. We know from the New Testament that John the Baptist is this messenger, and he was preparing the way for Christ. But from what we know from Malachi at this point, preparing the way for Christ Jesus is preparing the way for the LORD (Yahweh), either because Jesus will do the work of the LORD, or Jesus and the LORD are one and the same. The rest of the passage will shed more light on the subject.

"he will come."   The verb is the *qal* imperfect, for the specific future. There is not an expressed subject for the verb — not yet at least. The subject is in the next phrase.

"the Lord."   The Hebrew is "the Lord whom you seek." הָאָדוֹן is the expression; it is general enough to mean a lord or master, human or divine. First, the previous clause gives a detail that indicates that he is divine: he will come to his temple. The temple, or the house of the LORD, belonged to God. But here the one they desired comes to his temple. Second, he is the "messenger of the covenant." The conjunction on the word should be translated "even," for the Lord is this messenger. That they are the same person is indicated by the repeated note of the desire of the people: "the Lord, whom you seek . . . the messenger of the covenant, whom you desire."

"the messenger of the covenant."   The word "messenger" is in the construct, so that "covenant" is the genitive. This genitive is not a simple possession; it probably indicates that this messenger carries the covenant. From the historical perspective, since this is an oracle about John the Baptist preparing people for Jesus the Messiah, then the covenant must be the new covenant that Christ inaugurated in the upper room and sealed with his blood at the cross.

It is partial because we must look at this prophecy as having a double fulfillment. It would have a partial fulfillment in the first advent of Christ when he came and cleansed the temple. But ultimately it will be fulfilled at the second coming when he comes to his holy place to judge the world. This makes full use of the theme of *the coming day*. But typical of Old Testament prophecies, the text does not distinguish two comings.

"Behold, he comes."   Here again we have the particle and the active participle.

The repetition is meant to affirm the answer to their question. They wanted to know where the God of justice was, and the answer to their concern is a forceful, repeated announcement, "Look (behold), he is coming."

3:2

"But who can endure?"   The verb is מְכַלְכֵּל, the *pilpel* participle from כּוּל. The word "endure" is then paralleled with the word "stand," the *qal* participle הָעֹמֵד. The image of standing in this parallel construction must mean "remain standing" or "survive" (see Ps. 1:5–6). The questions are rhetorical, for the answer is that no one can survive the time of judgment.

"The day." This expression is a metonymy of subject; the word "day" is put for the details of what happens on that day — judgment. And it is further modified by "the day *of his coming*," that is, the coming to judge. The expression with the *qal* infinitive construct, בּוֹא, is paralleled with "when he appears," בְּהֵרָאוֹתוֹ, the *niphal* infinitive construct in a temporal clause: "in the appearing of him," or "when he appears." The desire of the people will change to fear when they learn that the Messiah is coming to judge the world — and no one can endure that day.

"he will be like a refiner's fire." The causal clause first uses the *piel* participle מְצָרֵף, "refiner"; it is a genitive after "fire." He will be like a fire, specifically, a fire that refines. The refiner's fire does not consume everything; it only removes impurities. The second simile is "like fullers' (washermens') soap," again, a *piel* participle מְכַבְּסִים serves as the genitive modifying "soap." These two similes illustrate how the Lord will purge sin out of the people, soap recalling the washing process, and fire the refining. In both cases the element is purged of imperfections and spots, but not destroyed.

3:3

"He will sit as a refiner and a purifier of silver." Another participle is added here, מְטַהֵר, a Levitical term "to be clean," but in the *piel*, "make clean, purify." These participles function adverbially. And the idea of his sitting indicates sovereign authority.

"the sons of Levi." The Levites will be purified and refined. Different interpretations are made for this section. The reference to Levi could be taken literally, in the restrictive sense, that is, only the actual tribe of Levi will be purged and once again made useful. Or it could be interpreted more widely, the sons of Levi meaning priestly nation, especially its spiritual leaders. There is support for this in the vision of restoring the high priest to service after the exile in Zechariah 3. There the high priest represented the priests and the priests represented the priestly nation, for the prophecy interpreted the cleansing of the priest by saying that the sins of all the people would be removed in one day. So this could be using the Levites as representative of the people of God who are to serve as a royal priesthood. They are believers who will not be destroyed, but purified.

Here too there is a near view and a far view for the fulfillment; the near view was the cleansing at the return from the exile so they could once again minister, but that group was to be a sign of the regathering and purification at the end of the age.

"And they will bring offerings in righteousness to the Lord." The point of the line is that they will become faithful worshipers. Literally it reads: "And they will become to the Lord offerers of (מַגִּישֵׁי, the *hiphil* participle in construct) offerings (מִנְחָה, a gift, dedicatory offering; used collectively) in righteousness." The word "righteousness" (צְדָקָה) means that their worship will correspond to the standard, in both the letter and the spirit.

3:4

"Then the offering of Judah and Jerusalem will be pleasing." Their worship and service will then be acceptable to God (וְעָרְבָה, the *waw* consecutive on the perfect stressing the sequence). "Judah" and "Jerusalem" are metonymical, referring to the people in those regions who make the offerings.

"as in the days of old." The reference is to an earlier time in Israel's history when the worship was done correctly, but no specific period is mentioned. The word "old" is עוֹלָם, which can mean "ever, forever." Its range is much like these words in English, for the context determines the extent of meaning. Here the parallel with former years restricts its meaning to an earlier historical period.

3:5

"Then I will draw near." The verb is the *qal* perfect with the *waw* consecutive, וְקָרַבְתִּי. The Lord, who is sending the forerunner and the Messiah, is the speaker.

"for judgment." The word מִשְׁפָּט has a wide range of uses, but here it is surely condemnation — judgment in the common understanding of the term. The verse is no longer talking about purifying people so that they will worship in righteousness, but condemning people for their sins. Here those to be judged are said not to fear the LORD, meaning that they are not believers.

Somewhere in this exposition, perhaps here briefly in passing, it will be necessary to say that the believer's place in judgment is different. The New Testament teaches that believers must appear before the Lord, not for condemnation, but for rewards or loss of rewards based on their lives of service and faithfulness. But when the LORD comes to judge the world at the end of the age, it will be unbelievers who will be judged. To explain these things clearly will require a good deal of additional study into the passages.

"a swift witness." The text reads עֵד מְמַהֵר, the *piel* participle functioning adjectivally with the word for "witness." The LORD himself will be the witness against them for their sins, and there will be no delay.

"against the sorcerers." Those judged are sorcerers, adulterers, false swearers, oppressors, and those who thrust away the alien. These are a series of participles, each functioning nominally as objects of the preposition "against." The emphasis of the participle is on the nature or character of the person.

The focus on the oppressors is on their mistreatment of hired people in their wages, the widows and the fatherless — those who are most vulnerable in society. This list often appears in passages about the test of true righteousness.

"and they do not fear me." וְלֹא יְרֵאוּנִי is the perfect tense, now with a suffix. After a list of grievous sins, this statement summarizes the character of the guilty: they do not fear the LORD. The theme has appeared before in Malachi; those who fear the LORD are the faithful believers, but those who do not are outside the faith. This will appear again in Malachi's final picture in 4:2 (3:20 in the Masoretic Text).

Exegetical Outline

I. The prophet rebuked the people for their tiresome challenges to God's integrity over the way he deals patiently with the unrighteous (2:17).

II. God announced that he was about to send his messenger and the messenger of the covenant whom they desired (3:1).

      A. The messenger would come and prepare the way before the Lord.

      B. The messenger of the covenant, the Lord whom the people desired, would come to his temple.

  III. God warned everyone that his coming would be a day of refining for his people but a day of judgment for the unbelievers (3:2–5).

      A. Everyone will be held accountable for what they have done (2a).

      B. When the Lord comes he will purify the people of God so that they will be righteous worshipers (2b–4).

      C. The Lord will draw near to condemn the guilty sinners who do not fear him (5).

Exegetical Summary

The summary of this message can now be written using the three major points of the outline. It will be a full sentence because the passage, though short, has a lot of important ideas in it:

> *In response to the presumptuous charges of the people that he was not just, God announces that he is sending a messenger to prepare the way for the Lord of the covenant who is coming to his temple and who will purify his people so that they may worship in righteousness, but destroy the wicked who do not fear him.*

Commentary in Expository Form

I.   *Criticism of God's justice is presumptuous and tiresome (2:17).*

The passage opens with another imagined short exchange between the people and the prophet. But this is more than rhetoric for this exchange must have occurred frequently enough for Malachi to turn it into a prophetic message about their presumption. There were those who came to the conclusion that because God was not dealing with all the sin that was present, he must not be just. This is tremendously presumptuous; they concluded that God was somehow to blame for the fact that sin was rampant.

And so Malachi began by affirming that their challenges and questions wearied God (הוֹגַעְתֶּם). The expression uses human language for the effect of their words on the LORD, and so it is figurative (an anthropomorphism). Their endless complaints and charges were tiresome. It is as if God was tired of their words, as if he was fed up with these people, and did not want to hear any more of it. But God does not get tired. The text uses this language to communicate God's response in terms we can understand, how we find persistent argumentation tiresome.

The prophet's charge was met immediately with the belligerent reply: "Wherein have we wearied [him]?" They thought everything they said was accurate and helpful, but they were corrected by the prophet's reply. First, they were saying, or at least implying, that everyone who was doing evil was good in the opinion of the LORD. The statement was meant to be hyperbolic; it seemed to them that God must be approving the evil that people were doing because he was not judging it.

There are a number of reasons why God would delay judgment, apart from the fact that he is slow to anger. God often postponed judgments to give people a better chance to put their lives in order — meaning, to repent and prepare spiritually. We also read in the Bible that our Lord has other sheep to bring from other sheep folds, and he must bring them. Thus, judgment is delayed. But also, in the divine plan of redemption, the Messiah had to come and pay for the sins of the world so that judgment would be poured out on him on behalf of people. We know now that he would not come to judge in the days of Malachi, but in his own time.

But the prophet told his audience that their request was presumptuous. If they really wanted the justice of God then they too would be in trouble, for no one could stand up under divine scrutiny. Everyone was accountable.

II.   *When the LORD sends the messenger to prepare the way, the Lord,*
       whom the people desire, will also suddenly come to his temple (3:1).

The entire section through the judgment of verse 5 could be one major point, divided into sub-points. But it seems clearer and simpler to make verse 1 a separate point announcing the coming, and then the next two sections explaining what that means, to the people of God, and then to the wicked unbelievers.

Verse 1 has two people in mind, two messengers. The first will prove to be John the Baptist and the second the Messiah himself. The LORD announces,

> "Behold, I am about to send my messenger
> and he will prepare the way before me."

The grammatical formula "Behold" (הִנְנִי) plus the participle (literally, "here I am sending") is a way to express the imminent future. It is what God is about to do, even though four hundred years off. Then, in Matthew 11 Jesus made it clear that this was a prophecy of John the Baptist. As the messenger of the LORD, John was to prepare the way before the coming of the Lord. That was to involve a spiritual preparation, repentance, and renewed commitment to the faith. Isaiah 40 also prophesied that the voice (John the Baptist) would cry out to prepare the way of the LORD; every valley would be filled, and the crooked places made straight, so that the LORD would have direct access to them. The imagery of building a super highway refers to spiritual preparation — the crooked places in the heart had to be straight, and the things missing had to be supplied, so that people would be spiritually prepared to receive the Messiah and his sacrifice, for he was introduced as the Lamb of God. John came preaching repentance so that they would be in the right place spiritually for the sins to be removed by the sacrificial Lamb of God.

Jesus does something very significant in his use of Malachi. He changes the pronoun from "my face" to "your face." In Malachi the LORD (Yahweh) was speaking, saying "I (Yahweh) am sending my messenger before my (Yahweh's) face." Then, when the Son of God spoke of John, he wanted to make clear that if John who introduced him and preached repentance was this forerunner in Malachi, then he, Jesus, was Yahweh. The "my face" in Malachi is interpreted to be "your face" in Matthew by Jesus. It was a not-so-veiled claim of deity.

The second person in Malachi's prophecy is also called a messenger, but he is called "the messenger of the covenant," that is, the one who was going to bring in the covenant. This must refer to the new covenant prophesied in Isaiah 54, Jeremiah 31, and Ezekiel 36 because it is the covenant that the messenger, Jesus, would bring.

Two things are said about this messenger. First, he is the one that they all strongly desired, so he is the Messiah for whom the people had been longing. Second, he would come to "his temple." In the Old Testament the temple is called "the house of Yahweh." Here this messenger will come to "his temple." This is another revelation that the longed-for Messiah would be divine — he is Yahweh, God in the flesh. So this second messenger is Jesus the Messiah, who is divine.

"Suddenly" he will come. This does not mean quickly, but surprisingly.

And yet, the prophecy of Daniel 9 helped the diligent students of the Bible in those days, especially at Qumran, to determine the time of the appearance of Messiah on earth. And even then his appearance took people by surprise. But when he entered into the temple and cleansed it, then this part of this prophecy found fulfillment.

Note, then, that we have God the sender, and God the one being sent. We can read this from the New Testament and see the hint of the Trinity, as in other Old Testament passages. But in the Old Testament times it would have been confusing; people would not have thought of the Messiah as divine, only certainly pre-existent (according to Dan. 7:13–14), for he was in heaven and given the kingdom before he appeared on earth. And even though he was born in Bethlehem, his goings were from everlasting (Micah 5:2). People could not imagine that a descendant of David would be God, and so most of them concluded that the Messiah was the first creation of God and would come to earth in some way.

But with the full revelation of the New Testament we know that Jesus is indeed the Son of God, the second person of the Trinity, and we can now understand so many Old Testament passages that either hinted or spoke of this, but needed confirmation by further revelation. In Christ we have that confirming revelation — God the Father sent God the Son into the world, and he, God the Son, came to his temple.

III. *Everyone will be accountable before the Lord, some to be purified of sin and some to be judged for sin (3:2–5).*

A. EVERYONE WILL BE ACCOUNTABLE FOR SIN (2A).

This section begins with the rhetorical question, "Who can endure the day of his coming?" The meaning is that no one can survive divine judgment, no one can stand secure on individual merits.

The first scene is that on the day of his coming he will be like a refiner's fire and laundrymen's soap. This, of course, did not happen when Jesus was here on earth. His first coming was to establish who he is and so to pay for the sins of the world; it will be at his second appearing that through fire and judgment he will bring to fulfillment all things. John the Baptist already made this clear in Matthew 3, prior to the baptism of Jesus. He announced that Jesus would baptize with the Spirit and with fire. In that context "fire" is mentioned twice, in the sense of judgment; it is an unquenchable fire that will burn up the chaff. The baptism of (identification with) the Spirit was established by the first coming. But the second coming will bring the judgment by fire. Similarly, when Jesus read the scroll of Isaiah in the synagogue in Luke 4, he read the prophecy about his ministry, but he stopped halfway through the passage and said that what he had read was fulfilled in their presence. But the next line, which he did not read, announced the time of God's wrath.

B. SOME HE WILL PURIFY AND MAKE THEM FIT FOR
RIGHTEOUS SERVICE (2B–4).

The focus of the appearance will first be on purifying the Levites, so that the LORD will have purified servants to worship in righteousness. It is a frequent theme in biblical prophecy that the LORD will purify his priestly people from sin so that they will by faith in the Messiah be a holy nation and a kingdom of priests. This purifying of people has been going on since Christ began building his church, but the judgments at the end of the age will be designed to bring Israel to repentance and faith in its Messiah as well. The reference in Malachi is not limited to any time that the LORD purifies people; it will ultimately be fulfilled in the coming day at the end of the age.

C. THE GUILTY SINNERS WHO HAVE NEVER FEARED THE LORD WILL BE
CONDEMNED AND DESTROYED IN THE JUDGMENT (5).

Then, in verse 5, we read that the LORD is coming for judgment and he will be a swift witness against the great sinners of the people for judgment will be immediate. God himself will be the witness and the judge of those who are characterized by sorcery; adultery; false-swearing; oppressing workers, widows and orphans; and depriving foreigners of justice. The judgment is not simply for these sins, but for those characterized by them because they are not believers. They do not fear the LORD. The expression "fear me" means to worship and obey the LORD. The judgment will fall on unbelievers, people who have no such reverential fear of the LORD, no matter who they are. That judgment will be for their sins.

The sins that the prophet listed here covered a wide array of crimes, from the gross violations of the moral code to the breakdown of social justice. Not caring for the poor and needy and the foreigner were serious matters in Israel. Psalm 72 makes it clear that the ideal king must champion these people; and James reminds us that this is at the heart of pure religion. And so Malachi's messages continued to convict the so-called good people of his day, as well as today. Such people think God should come and judge sinners, punishing them for their failure to do works of righteousness. They have looked out and seen things they think God should punish. But ironically they did not look within to see their own sins that must be dealt with — and will be in the final analysis.

Expository Idea and Application

Expository Idea

Developing the expository idea of this passage will take more time because of the complexity of the prophecy, what Malachi said, and how it fits into the whole biblical scene of prophecy. But one may be expressed this way:

> The God of justice will send the Lord of the covenant and his messenger
> to purify his people for spiritual service,
> and to judge unbelievers for their sins.

This statement captures the main points of the passage. It does not do much with verse 17, except to affirm that God is just. It is worded to reflect the whole passage, so that the expositor will have to discuss the details of the text more fully, using the clarity in the New Testament that verse 1 is fulfilled in the first coming, but verses 2–5 will await the second coming. In the first coming the Bible makes it clear that the Lord made the atoning sacrifice for sins, which gives him the right to judge.

To fill out the details of the times and circumstances of this prophecy, the expositor will have to bring in other prophetic passages. For example, how and when will the Lord purge his people with fire? The purifying of the people at the end of the age prepares them for service in his kingdom. While there are other applications of the LORD's purging his people, this prophecy ultimately concerns the people of God at the second coming of the Lord, for the prophets and the New Testament speak about the time of "Jacob's trouble" when Israel endures great tribulation prior to the appearance of the Lord, in whom they will believe when they look on him whom they have pierced (read Zech. 9–14). But the discussion will have to be succinct, for there is so much material to discuss once eschatology is brought up. However, the point is that when the Lord comes he will judge the world and destroy unrepentant ("who do not fear") sinners. Then the righteous will be delivered from this sinful world.

Application

The message would be just as applicable on the practical level today as it was to Malachi's audience. If people who claim to be believers are not doing what verse 5 said — helping people in need, championing justice for the oppressed and the stranger, fearing the LORD, and avoiding sin — then they had better think twice about calling for the God of justice to step in, and they better look within themselves to make sure there is genuine faith.

Second, God also will purge believers of their sin, certainly at the end of the age, but even now to make them more useful to him. And since Malachi calls people to order their lives aright in view of the coming of the LORD, we too would do well to heed that call so that we would be useful now and found faithful at his coming.

And a third application would be this: we find ourselves in the same place and calling as John the Baptist, to prepare the way of the Lord who is surely coming. This, for him was the first coming, but for us it is now the second. This means calling the believers to live righteously and the unbelievers to repentance.

Key Words

"To Send"

The verb "to send," שָׁלַח, is a very common word in the Bible, occurring some 847 times.

(1) It can be used in all the normal contexts of sending people or things, such as messengers, gifts, cattle, and even idiomatically for sending one's hand, that is, reaching out (some 70 times). And in Malachi 2:16 the word is used for divorce, sending a wife away.

(2) Our interest here, though, is when God sends someone. It is similar to uses where people send individuals on a mission. But when God sends an individual on a mission, whether an official messenger like a prophet or a king or an ordinary person, the purpose of the mission is usually higher, and the authority behind the sending is the LORD himself. Sometimes the

sending is added to the call to go in order to emphasize that the person is going with the authority of God.

(3) God is said to send other things as well, and they will fulfill the divine purpose in sending them. God sends angels at times (Exod. 23:20 and 33:2), plagues (Exod. 9:14), the sword (Jer. 25:16, 17), signs and wonders (Ps. 135:9), and food (Ps. 78:25).

Whatever is "sent" by God will be part of the working out of the divine will on earth because it carries the power and authority of heaven with it.

"To Purify"

The verb "to purify" is טָהֵר, a Levitical term predominantly.

(1) The basic word in the *qal* stem means "to be pure, clean." It can refer to being clean physically (2 Kings 5:10), morally (Lev. 16:30), or purifying ceremonially (Lev. 15:13).

(2) In the *piel* stem it means "to purify, make clean." It can be used for purifying metals (Mal. 3:3), or purifying ceremonially (Lev. 16:19), or morally (Ps. 51:2).

(3) The ideas of clean and unclean in the Bible are hard for people to understand. What caused a person to be declared unclean in the ceremonial sense could be sin; but it could also be contamination and disease without any sin involved, such as the process of childbirth (Lev. 12) or skin diseases (Lev. 13–14). The classification unclean simply meant that the person or thing so designated was not permitted in the holy place. Whatever was sinful, diseased, contaminated, or too earthy was simply incompatible with the holiness and perfection of the LORD.

(4) The whole purifying sanctuary ritual was designed to transfer the person from the category unclean to that of clean by washing, and to the category of holy by atonement. But none of this was effectual if the individual did not believe in the LORD, confess his sin and sinful condition, and receive forgiveness from the LORD. Then the offerings that were brought could be called "pure" offerings.[5]

---

5 For further discussion of the idea of purity and purification, see my work on Leviticus, *Holiness to the LORD: A Guide to the Exposition of the Book of Leviticus* (Grand Rapids: Baker, 2002), pp. 243–49.

"Righteousness"

The word for "righteousness," צְדָקָה, is related to the verb צָדַק and other words such as צַדִּיק, the "righteous" (as opposed to the "wicked"). The emphases of the words "righteousness" and "righteous" are similar in their meanings.

(1) As a description of the people of God, the words would emphasize their relationship to God through the covenant and their way of living in obedience to that covenant.

(2) One helpful way to summarize the meaning is "to conform to the standard." Deuteronomy 25:13–15 provides a clear illustration of the meaning in a non-theological context. People were not to have diverse weights and measurements in the market place; they were to have *righteous* weights, that is, they had to conform to the standard.

In the religious contexts the standard is God himself and his revealed will. So the term "the righteous" came to describe people who believed in the LORD and were declared righteous by God (Gen. 15:6). God reckoned righteousness to those who believed in him. This we call imputed righteousness.

(3) But these words also describe the way the righteous are to live to please God. The activities of those who were in the covenant were to be right, to correspond to the will of God revealed to them. Here we find that righteousness is often linked to truthfulness, meaning what is trustworthy and dependable (Isa. 48:1; Jer. 4:2). In general, it means to do what is right (Ps. 45:7; Prov. 11:6; 21:3).

(4) Along with this emphasis on personal righteousness there is also the use of the words for justice in the courts, decisions that are right (Prov. 16:12; Amos 5:7; 6:12). The decisions are to be right, because the Judge of the whole world always does right (Gen. 18:25).

(5) In fact, righteousness is one of the main descriptions of God in the Bible — one of his attributes. He is just and right in everything he does because it is his nature; he loves righteousness and hates wickedness (Ps. 11:5–7).

(6) There are a number of passages where righteousness is used figuratively for what righteousness produces (so they are metonymies of cause). For example, Psalm 24:5 seems to use the word to mean salvation. Likewise, if God reveals his righteousness in battle, it must also refer to the proper outcome of the war (Ps. 98:2).

C. A. Briggs in the commentary on *The Book of Psalms* (1:110) captures the related ideas for this term: (1) God is the standard of righteousness; (2) people are called righteous because they are justified and vindicated by God;

(Malachi 2:17 – 3:5)

(3) people are then known as the righteous because of their zeal for God and the righteousness of his Law; (4) and they are called righteous because their conduct and character are most often in line with the Law.

6. God's Faithfulness to the Faithful

(MALACHI 3:6–12)

Introduction

Translation and Textual Notes

6   "Because I, the LORD, do not change,
      you, O descendants of Jacob, are not destroyed.
7   Ever since the time of your forefathers
      you have turned away from my decrees and have not kept them.
  Return to me, and I will return to you," says the LORD of armies.

  "But you say, 'How should we return?'

8   Will a man rob[1] God? Yet you are robbing[2] me.

  But you say, 'How do we rob you?'[3]

  In tithes and offerings.[4]

---

1   The Greek has πτερνιεῖ "will he insult?" This may represent a confusion of letters, reading הַיַעֲקֹב instead of MT's הֲיִקְבַּע. The name "Jacob" was already in the text in verse 6; this may have suggested the idea.

2   The Greek version follows consistently with its translation "you insult" (πτερνίζετέ).

3   Here too the Greek has the same idea: ἐπτερνίκαμέν σε.

4   The Syriac, Targum, and Vulgate, as well as most modern English translations, render these two words using a preposition: "in tithes and in offerings." The Greek adds μεθ' ὑμῶν εἰσιν, giving the sense "in that the tithes and the offerings are [still] with you."

⁹   You are cursed with a curse⁵ — the whole nation of you —
     because you are robbing⁶ me.

¹⁰ Bring the whole tithe into the storehouse,
        that there may be food in my house.
     Prove me in this," says the LORD of armies,
          "and see if I will not throw open the floodgates of heaven
             and pour out so much blessing
                that you will not have room enough for it.
¹¹ I will rebuke the devouring pests
        and they will not ruin for you the fruit of the field,
        and the vines in your fields will not cast their fruit,"
           says the LORD of armies.
¹² "Then all the nations will call you blessed,
        for yours will be a delightful land,"
           says the LORD of armies.

Context and Composition

The focus in this passage is on the people's failure to bring to God their tithes and offerings. These were not voluntary gifts to the sanctuary; they were tithes that were due. It was a sin to refuse to bring them — here equated with robbing God. Behind this refusal, though, was a bigger problem: the lack of faith. Like so many before and after them, they would give if and when they were able and willing to do so. But the passage will make it clear that it is an act of faith; they should give, believing that the LORD would provide. Then they would see the blessing of God in their harvests.

The passage falls into three major parts: the rebuke of the people for their unfaithfulness and a call for them to repent (vv. 6–7), the accusation that they were robbing God by not bringing tithes and the explanation that they were being cursed for it (vv. 8–9), and a challenge to prove the promises of God's blessing by bringing the tithes to him by faith (vv. 10–12).

---

5   One ancient Greek manuscript (B) has a different reading altogether: καὶ ἀποβλέποντες ὑμεῖς ἀποβλέπετε ("and you surely look off from me"). It does not have "the whole nation of you." It may be that the consonants כלו הגם (instead of הגוי), which are written above the end of the line, may have been taken to end verse 8 to give the addition there. How that would be understood is difficult to see.

6   The Greek has πτερνίζετε.

Exegetical Notes

3:6

"Because."   The verse places the causal clause first; this is the reason that the descendants of Jacob are not destroyed.

"I do not change."   The form שָׁנִיתִי is the perfect tense — the first common singular; it is to be taken as a gnomic perfect, expressing a universal truth, that is, the immutability of God.

The apparent theological tension here is that if God does not change why does the text speak of his turning back, or other texts that say he repented over making mankind? The explanation lies in the scope of his immutability: he does not change his nature, the properties of which are to punish rebellious people but bless them if they repent. The language of God's *returning* is anthropomorphic to capture this pattern of divine dealing with people. The way God reveals his will sometimes gives the appearance of change. He may reveal only part of his plan, he may express it in human terms, or he may word it in such a way as to require faith. Scripture is clear enough to remind us that he carries out his plan — he knew it from the beginning.

"Jacob."   This name was probably chosen instead of "Israel" because the people have had a long history of disobedience and hesitancy to trust.

"destroyed."   The verb is כְלִיתֶם, the *qal* perfect tense, second person masculine plural from the *III he'* verb. It means "to be finished."

3:7

"you have turned away."   סַרְתֶּם is the *qal* perfect, second person masculine plural of סוּר, "to turn aside." The verb is figurative, comparing turning aside from a path with disobedience to the Law (hypocatastasis that became idiomatic along with "way"). The nuance would be present perfect, which means they have not turned back yet.

"From my decrees."   The word is מֵחֻקַּי; this word for laws and precepts presents them as binding.

"Return . . . and I will return."   The Lord uses the imperative, שׁוּבוּ, for an immediate response. He then follows this with the promise, וְאָשׁוּבָה, the *qal* cohortative, first person common singular: "and I shall return to you." The second clause is clearly based upon the first; this construction expresses purpose or result: "return that I may return to you." For them, returning was repentance and renewal; for the LORD, the returning would involve renewing his blessing.

"Wherein should we return."   This is the response of people who do not believe they need to return. The verb is נָשׁוּב, the *qal* imperfect, first person common plural. The question probably means "in what" or "from what" should we turn. The imperfect tense then would be a modal nuance of obligation.

3:8
_____

"Will a man rob God?"   The verb is הֲיִקְבַּע, the imperfect tense with the interrogative particle. The question is rhetorical (erotesis) because it is designed to say "No one would ever think of robbing God!" It would be sacrilege! It would be impossible because God would ultimately condemn! "Will a man even think of it?" The implication is that they rob God, but that has yet to be stated openly. So this is a very bold charge.

"you are robbing."   The plural participle is used as the predicate, and so stresses the durative, continual activity of robbing. This is an ongoing crime. And they are not convinced; they reply, "How do we rob you?" The verb is now the perfect tense with a suffix; the verb should be classified as a characteristic perfect because it picks up the participle's nuance and expresses the act as something they are currently doing.

"The tithe and the offering."   The words are singular nouns used collectively; they have the article attached to focus on the nature of the word. The sentence is elliptical: "(You are robbing me in) the tithes and offerings."

3:9
_____

"You are cursed with the curse."   The verb is expressed with the *niphal* participle נֵאָרִים serving as the predicate use. And the cognate word בַּמְּאֵרָה is in a prepositional phrase emphasizing the curse.

"me you are robbing."   The participle is used again as the predicate, but here the accusative "me" is placed first to stress the serious nature of the crime.

"the whole nation of you."   This is an interpretive rendering of הַגּוֹי כֻּלּוֹ that literally says, "The nation, all of it." There are variant readings for this Hebrew expression in other versions. The phrase is meant to expand on the pronoun "you," with "the nation," and that is clarified with "all of it."

3:10

"Bring in."   After the charges are made, the solution is simple: "bring in all the tithe." The verb הָבִיאוּ is the *hiphil* imperative, calling for immediate action. The nation is already under a curse for the violation, so the nation should resolve it quickly.

"that there may be."   The verb of the second clause is וִיהִי, the *qal* jussive, third person masculine singular, with the *waw* after the imperative form expressing purpose or result. This is the volitional sequence.

"and prove me."   The form is וּבְחָנוּנִי, the *qal* imperative, masculine plural, with the pronominal suffix. The verb means "test, try, prove." This is a call for the people to act in faith by giving the tithes so that the promise of God can be proven trustworthy.

"[and see] if I will not."   Some versions add the verbal idea "and see" to clarify the clause, which simply has "If I will not open." The Hebrew expression is framed like the oath formula to affirm that God was promising to send the rain if they believed and proved his word.

"floodgates."   The word is figurative, an implied comparison. It would not simply rain; it would pour as if floodgates holding back the water were finally opened.

"and pour out."   The verb is וַהֲרִיקֹתִי, the *hiphil* perfect, first person common singular, from the hollow verb רִיק (the *waw* consecutive on the perfect is only spelled with a *pathah* here by vowel harmony with the compound *shewa*, which came by propretonic reduction). The translation "pour out" is fine, but the verb means "empty out."

"blessing."   This noun is a figure of speech, a metonymy of cause, when the effect is intended — in this case, the harvest. The rain will provide a harvest too large to be stored in the ordinary ways.

3:11

"I will rebuke."   The verb is the perfect tense with a *waw* consecutive, and so receives the future tense translation. The form is וְגָעַרְתִּי, properly "and I will rebuke," but the meaning is to stop something by command, and so it is often translated "I will prevent."

"devouring pests."   This is another interpretive translation, because the word is the participle אֹכֵל, "eater," used collectively here. The line refers to something eating the crops, perhaps locusts. "Pests" may not be strong enough, but it at least helps communicate what the eater might be.

"they will not ruin."   The verb is יַשְׁחִת, the *hiphil* imperfect, third person masculine singular to match the singular "eater." The pests will not ruin the fruit of the field.

"cast."   The verb is תְשַׁכֵּל is the *piel* imperfect; the word means "to be bereaved" and here "to show abortion." The translation "will not cast their fruit" captures the idea of the vine losing the fruit prematurely.

3:12

"will call you blessed."   וְאִשְּׁרוּ is the *piel* perfect, third person common plural, with *waw* consecutive giving the future translation. The verb is "to bless, to call blessed." It refers to joy and satisfaction that comes from being right with God. Others will recognize the blessing of God on the land.

"delightful land."   The construction is "land of delight," the genitive being attributive.

Exegetical Outline

I. On the basis of his unchanging care for his people, the LORD calls for their repentance over their unfaithfulness in order that they might enjoy his great blessings (6–7).
   A. Israel has not been destroyed because of God's unchanging love for them (6).
   B. Israel must turn from its unfaithful ways if they are to enjoy God's great bounty (7).

II. Because of the failure of the nation to pay their tithes and their offerings, the LORD was cursing them for robbing him (8–9).
   A. The nation had been robbing God of the tithes and offerings (8).
   B. The LORD had been punishing them for the sin of in gratitude (9).
III. In order that they might see his bountiful blessing and protection of their crops that will make their land a delightful place, the LORD challenges the people to prove his promise true by being faithful stewards (10–12).
   A. The LORD challenges the people to prove his word true by bringing the whole tithe into the storehouse (10a).
   B. If they do this they will receive his bounty and protection in their crops (10b–11).
   C. And the nations will see that Israel is a delightful land (12).

Exegetical Summary

> *Because of his unfailing love for Israel, the LORD called for them to repent of their unfaithfulness in paying their tribute to him, and to prove his promise true that if they were faithful stewards they would enjoy his bounty and protection and their land would be known as a delightful place.*

Commentary in Expository Form

I.   *God's faithfulness protects his covenant people but his great blessings depend on their faithfulness (3:6–7).*

A. BECAUSE OF GOD'S UNCHANGING LOVE, HIS PEOPLE
ARE NOT DESTROYED (6).

This section of the message on the faithfulness of God begins with a firm doctrinal statement: God does not change. The wording is emphatic — "Because I, the LORD, change not" (לֹא שָׁנִיתִי). The statement forms a transition from the last section, where people thought that God was no longer judging sin, to this section, which shows that he has not changed. In spite of their failures God does not change; if he had changed, they would have been destroyed (כָּלָה, "to be finished, destroyed").

The second half of the verse is the result of the fact that God remains constant in his love (see chapter 1) and righteousness. The point is that God is faithful to the covenants that he makes, and he will not allow others to destroy them or the covenant people. Those who belong to him will not be judged; even if they prove to be unfaithful, he remains faithful because he cannot deny himself.

B. BUT IF HIS PEOPLE WANT HIS GREAT BLESSINGS THEY MUST SHOW THEMSELVES FAITHFUL (7).

God then reminds the people that they have been unfaithful, just as their ancestors were in the past, because they turned aside from God's statutes. But the LORD has always been there to call them to repentance so that they could enjoy his blessings and not just exist with difficulties and opposition. Here he calls for them to return, so that he might return to them. This verb "return" in Hebrew is often a call for repentance, to turn back from sins and return to obeying the LORD. Repentance is not merely feeling sorry for sins; it is a conscious decision to turn around, to change, to amend one's ways. The prophet has yet to clarify what it is they have done wrong. But on the basis of this call they would have concluded that God was requiring a great change.

If these people were to return to the LORD, then he would turn back to them. The idea of his turning to them is figurative (an implied comparison as well) of his pouring out blessings on them once again. Throughout the Bible, the explanation of divine blessings was expressed in terms of God's presence with his people, or visiting them, or returning to them. Here the idea is that God would turn from his course of action that he had begun — punishment for their sins — and begin blessing them again.

II. *God withholds his blessing as a punishment for ingratitude and disloyalty (3:8–9).*

A. BY BEING UNFAITHFUL IN STEWARDSHIP THE PEOPLE DEMONSTRATE THEIR INGRATITUDE (8).

Once again Malachi's audience was indignant: "How should we return?" They did not see that they had any need to repent. From what should they turn? And so the word of the LORD comes through Malachi with the indictment that they have been robbing God. The prophet first reasons, "Will a man rob God?" Then he flatly condemns them: "But you are robbing me!"

This charge certainly touched a nerve, because they responded sharply, saying, "Wherein have we robbed you?" And the LORD's answer is simple, having two nouns, but clear: "the tithe and the offering." The tithe was the regular portion of their income that went to the LORD; and their offering (תְּרוּמָה) was an additional gift that they were to give, often identified as the priest's due. The so-called tithe ("a tenth") added up to far more than a simple 10% annually, because there was a second tithe annually, and a third tithe in the third and fifth years; and the offering for the priest was either an additional 2% (possibly 10%), but there were also sacrificial offerings. In the Old Testament economy all the giving covered the sanctuary offerings for God, the taxes for the nation, and charitable gifts all rolled together. Their failure to bring these to God, or to bring worthless gifts and offerings, was a clear sign of their ingratitude and disloyalty. Their unfaithfulness to God was evidenced, therefore, in their lack of giving, which for Israel was serious, because giving was at the heart of the covenant in view of the fact that they owed their lives and their possessions to God. Giving properly was a sign that they acknowledged this, and that they were demonstrating their dependence on him for everything they needed.

B. WHEN THE PEOPLE ARE UNFAITHFUL, GOD WITHHOLDS
HIS BLESSINGS FROM THEM (9).

The people had not been paying their tithes, and so the whole land was under a curse, an actual dry spell where nothing was growing. The point is emphasized by the repetition of the word "curse," as a noun and as a verb. As we have already seen in this study, the word "curse" (אָרַר) means "to remove from the place of blessing." Here, since the entire nation has been robbing God, the whole land is cursed. We do not know how many disobedient people it takes to bring down a national curse, but this is clearly widespread throughout the land. It may be that in the difficulty of rebuilding the country they cut back on what they gave at the sanctuary, or gave imperfect offerings or nothing at all. But that excuse may be too easy, because they had been back in the land for about seventy-five years.

The prophet will remind them that if they thought that keeping back their money was the frugal thing to do for their livelihood, then they had misunderstood the covenant program. If they gave by faith what was due to God they would receive his bountiful provisions in ways that holding back could never produce. First and foremost, it would rain! And then, the devouring pests would not come.

These concerns apply to Israel; in later times as the people of God spread throughout the world, God dealt with them differently. These concerns were for the people living in a small geographical area with a desperate need for the seasonal rains. God was teaching them to depend on him for the rain and the crops, and when he provided for them to show their gratitude with their tithes and offerings (the tithes would be in proportion to the way God prospered them).

III. *God challenges his people to prove his promises by being faithful stewards (3:10–12).*

A. GOD CHALLENGES HIS PEOPLE TO ACT IN FAITH ON HIS PROMISES OF PROVISION AND PROTECTION (10).

The command of the LORD is simply a reminder of their covenant duties under the Law: "Bring all the tithe into the storehouse." The inclusion of the word "all" suggests that they may have been bringing something, but not nearly enough. And the purpose of their doing this was that there might be food in his house. The food in the temple would be a constant supply for the offerings, for the priests' share and their families' share, for the Levites, musicians, temple servants, and the poor. It was important for the economy as well as the religious activities that the people bring what was required.

Then, as if to motivate the people with a challenge, the LORD called for them to "test him and see" if he would provide for them if they gave. The word "test" (בָּחַן) would have the sense here of proving something, such as testing a new product or a plan. To test God would here be an act of faith; and that would be very different from the wilderness generation who tested God because they did not believe him. God was calling the people to act on his promises, to prove them true.

What they would discover if they did was that he would open the flood-gates of heaven and pour blessings upon them. We have a couple of figures of speech here. The floodgates are an implied comparison (a hypocatastasis) for the clouds that will open and pour down the rain; and the blessing is the result of the rain (so a metonymy of effect) that will come. The Law had warned the nation that if they were disobedient, God would withhold the rain; if they were obedient, he would send the rain. God was here calling the people to trust him to send the rain, but they would have to demonstrate their trust in him by giving him his proper due.

B. GOD DECLARES THAT IF HIS PEOPLE ARE FAITHFUL, HE WILL BE FAITHFUL TO THEM (11–12).

The last two verses elaborate on the promised blessings that were in store for them if they returned to him (which they were probably not enjoying at the moment). The LORD would first rebuke the devourer. The verb "rebuke" (גָּעַר) is a decree that would stop the activity from continuing. The devourer, simply the participle of the verb "to eat," probably refers to devouring pests, perhaps locusts. God would stop them from ruining the fruit of the land. The LORD also promised to prevent the vines in the fields from casting their fruit. He promised that what grew on the vines would grow to maturity and be harvested — there would be no loss of produce.

And as a result of God's blessing on the land, the nations would pronounce them blessed. The verb אָשַׁר means "to bless" or "to pronounce blessed" in the sense of recognizing and enjoying the gifts God bestowed because he was pleased with them. The frequent expression "blessed is [the one]" (as in Ps. 1:1) means that the faithful not only enjoy God's gifts but know that they are blessed because they are right with God. It is much greater than the idea of happy, which depends on the circumstances. The word in the text indicates that those blessed are right with God, no matter what the circumstances might be. Here we have the verb in the *piel* stem, meaning "pronounce blessed" (as in Psalm 126 when the nations declared that the LORD had done great things for them). The reason they will do this is because Israel will be a "land of delight," a place that is most desirable because of its rich produce and healthy crops. Thus, God was reminding the people of the covenant promises that were there from the beginning — blessing for obedience, but for disobedience a removal of the blessing. Nevertheless, because the LORD loved them constantly, he was always ready to pour out his blessings if they returned to him. And now, in the future when they do, the land will become as delightful as Eden (Isa. 51:3).

(Malachi 3:6–12)

Expository Idea and Application

Expository Idea

Malachi calls for the people to test God's faithfulness. This is a call to live by faith. They were to give to God first what was due him, trusting that he would take care of them and provide for them. The expository idea could be written this way to capture the message of the passage:

<blockquote>
The LORD promises to take care of his people
if they demonstrate faithfulness to him in their stewardship;
but he warns his people that he will withhold his blessing
if they are ungrateful.
</blockquote>

Application

I do not think we can apply the passage directly to our circumstance because it was a message to a nation living in the land of Israel to whom God made promises of sending the rain, producing crops, and giving prosperity in the land if the people faithfully tithed. The system was geared to their weather patterns and the need of the seasonal rains. In other countries like ours there may be droughts in regions from time to time, but it would be hard to prove that was because the region was not tithing. The application to the people of God today will have to be explained very carefully; the general principle may be retained, but the details of its working out may be different, perhaps more individual than collective. It is best to say that believers, not the secular country we live in, must demonstrate faith by being faithful in their stewardship and other expressions of loyalty, trusting that God will provide all their needs, spiritually as well as materially.

But if we refuse to show our loyalty and faithfulness to God in even such a simple thing as stewardship of our time, our talents, and our income in gratitude to him, then he may very well prevent his greatest blessings from being given to us. And we must be careful not to treat stewardship as an investment for sure returns, for the blessing of God on his people today could be spiritual, and it could be heavenly. It may be material—but it may not.

People were to give by faith out of gratitude, not as a way of manipulating God to give more back. But the Law of Israel promised blessing for obedience and a curse for disobedience (see Lev. 26). They could pray for rain, but they were to be faithful as well, if they wanted God to provide for their livelihood in the land. If they persisted in disobedience, there would be no divine provision or protection. It would not matter if they gave money; if they were divorcing their spouses, marrying pagans, not teaching the word right, ruining worship, or treating poor people with contempt, then tithing would not bring a blessing.

Stewardship in the Old and New Covenants

It is important for people to understand what Israel's tithes and offerings included. The Israelite under the Law had to bring first the priest's due (either 2% or 10%). Then he brought the basic tithe, 10%. But he was also required to pay a second tithe (another 10%) that was to go to Jerusalem and its needs — it could be spent in Jerusalem on the three annual pilgrimages, somewhat of a pilgrimage budget. But if they could not go to the holy city, they had to send the money. And then, every third and fifth year of the seven-year cycle there was a third tithe that went to the poor. So the basic tithing was probably more than 22% any given year, possibly 27%. Now this did not include the offerings, the animals that were to be brought to the three festivals. It did not include the extra money to be paid for sin and trespass offerings, which could be high, based on the sin. The tithing system also called for the people to have a sabbath year, one-seventh of their income over a seven-year period would be given up, as well as a forty-ninth of it over a forty-nine-year period if they kept the Jubilee. Then they were to leave the corners of their fields for the poor to glean; they were to give to charity; and they were to take care of the widow, orphan, poor and the stranger. On top of all that, they could at any time offer a freewill thank offering, which required more animals and gifts. So then, if someone today wanted to live under Israel's laws of tithes and offerings, the amount would exceed 40% a year. That amount was for giving to the LORD, but it was also for charities and taxes since Israel was a theocracy.

In the New Testament stewardship the economic system and the outlook are totally different; so we do not ask how much we should give, but rather how much can we keep and what we are to do with it, because everything we have and everything we are belong to God and are given to us in trust. As with Israel, we are to give proportionately as a token of our acknowledgment of how the Lord prospers. Our time, our possessions, our abilities — all part of the stewardship — are gifts from God. So we live in the light of the spirit of the Law, not the letter, which is in fact a much higher requirement than Israel's Law.

Key Words

"To Return"

The word שׁוּב is a very common word in the Bible, occurring more than a thousand times. It has the basic idea of "turn back, return." Derived nouns include תְּשׁוּבָה which means "return, answer," including the returning of the year or springtime; מְשׁוּבָה, "turning back" in the sense of apostasy; as well as the adjectives שׁוֹבֵב and שׁוֹבָב, both meaning "back-turning, apostate."

(1) The verb has both literal and figurative meanings. Literally, it is used for any simple act of turning back (Ruth 1:16), returning (Gen. 14:17), or returning to something (Exod. 4:20 and 21).

(2) In the figurative uses it can be used of human relations and conditions, such as returning to a physical condition (Job 33:25; 1 Kings 13:6), being refreshed (Ps. 23:3), returning to a divorced wife (Jer. 3:1), or restoring allegiance to a leader (Judg. 11:8).

(3) It has many uses for the spiritual relationship with God. The verb, as well as nouns and adjectives, can be used for turning away from God in apostasy (Judg. 2:19), and returning to God, meaning seek penitently (Hos. 6:1; Ps. 51:15). In this light the word can mean "to repent," that is, change the mind and direction (Jer. 3:7). The object of repentance is to return to the original covenant relationship with the LORD. It is not completely a restoration of the old, but more a starting point of a new or renewed relationship. Closely related is the emphasis on turning back from evil (1 Kings 8:35; Jonah 3:9), especially in the prophets where there is an urgent need to turn away from idolatry and corruption.

(4) The verb is also used of the LORD's returning to his people, meaning to show them favor and bless them once again (Gen. 18:10; Isa. 63:17). There are also a number of uses concerning inanimate subjects, such as a prayer turning back (Ps. 35:13), or the word returning (Isa. 45:23), or judgment (Ps. 94:15).[7]

---

7 See further W. L. Holladay, *The Root* ŠUBH *in the Old Testament* (1958); and "שׁוּב *šub*

"To Rebuke"

The verb "rebuke," גָּעַר, may be used with either humans or God as the subject, and the force of the word differs accordingly. G. Liedke suggests that the basic meaning is "to cry aloud, scream at" or "to raise a commotion" about something.[8]

(1) When we read that Jacob rebuked Joseph his son (Gen. 37:10), it would mean scold or criticize with the intent of stopping or preventing something from continuing or going too far. When Boaz warned his workers not to rebuke Ruth (Ruth 2:16), it means they were not to scold or reprimand Ruth if she got too close to the harvested grain.

(2) But when God is the subject it often is more than an intense scolding. For example, it is used in connection with the LORD's conflict with chaos (Pss. 104:7; 68:31, etc.). The effect of this divine rebuke is that the sea, the waters, the deep, recede or dry up.

In Zechariah 3:3 the LORD rebukes Satan, who was opposing his plan, and the rebuke effectively stops Satan's accusations. In Malachi 2:3 when God rebukes the seed (assuming that is the correct reading and not "shoulder"), it means either that he prevents the harvest or he removes the priests — the seed of Aaron.

In Psalm 76:6 the LORD rebuked the wicked, that is, they were destroyed in the war. But on the other hand, the divine reprimand of the nations (as in Ps. 9:6) or the proud (as in Ps. 119:21) is more of an announcement of what is going to happen than an immediate interruption of their lives.

"To Test"

The verb בָּחַן means "examine, try."

(1) One of its categories of meaning is simply "examine, try," such as the eyelids of the LORD examining the sons of man (Ps. 11:4). This is probably the emphasis in Psalm 139:23 as well: "examine me."

(2) The verb can also mean "test, prove" someone or something. God is said to test people, as one tries gold (Zech. 13:9). It is also found in passages

---

"to return," by J. A. Soggin, in *Theological Lexicon of the Old Testament,* ed. Jenni and Westermann, 3:1312–17.

8 S.v. גער *g'r* "to scold," in *Theological Lexicon of the Old Testament,* ed. Jenni and Westermann, 1:322; see also A. A. Macintosh, "A Consideration of Hebrew *g'r,*" *Vetus Testamentum* 19 (1969):471–79.

(Malachi 3:6–12)

where the analogy with gold or silver is not present but implied; in Malachi 3:10 and 15 God will test his people to make them fit for service. Isaiah 28:16 refers to a tested stone, one that was approved to be used in the foundation.

(3) The word can also be used for people testing or tempting God (Ps. 95:9, for the wilderness experience). They tested God even though they had seen his works. So in that case their testing God came from their unbelief or weak faith; when God tested people it was to discover faith in them.

Preparing for the Day of the Lord

Introduction

Translation and Textual Notes

¹³ "Your words have been harsh against me," says the Lord.[2]
  "But you say, 'What have we said against you?'
¹⁴ You have said, 'It is futile to serve God.
    What did we gain when we kept his requirements
    and went about like mourners before the Lord of armies?
¹⁵ But now we are calling the arrogant blessed.
    Certainly the evildoers prosper;
    moreover they test God and escape.'"

¹⁶ Then[3] those who feared the Lord talked with each other,
    and the Lord paid attention and heard.
  And a scroll of remembrance was written in his presence
    for those who fear the Lord
    and for those who esteem his name.

¹⁷ "They will be mine," says the Lord of armies,
    "in the day when I make up my treasured possession.
  And I will have compassion on them,

---

1 The Hebrew text does not have a chapter 4; the passage would be simply 3:13–24. The English references would be 3:13–18 and 4:1–6.

2 Some English Bibles follow one of the Greek manuscripts (*G^L*) in adding "armies" to fit the pattern of the passage. There is no reason to do this.

3 Greek has ταῦτα, "thus."

just as in compassion a man has compassion
on his son who serves him.
¹⁸ And you will again see the distinction
between the righteous and the ungodly,
between the one who serves God
and the one who does not serve him.

¹ Surely the day is coming, burning like a furnace.⁴
All the arrogant and every evildoer will be stubble,
and that day that is coming will set them on fire,"
says the LORD of armies,
"so that it will not leave⁵ for them root or branch.

² But for you who fear my name,
the sun of righteousness will rise with healing in his wings.
And you will go out and gambol like calves released from the stall.
³ Then you will trample down the wicked;
for they will be ashes under the soles of your feet
on the day I do these things," says the LORD of armies.

⁴ "Remember the Law of my servant Moses,
the decrees and laws I gave him at Horeb for all Israel.
⁵ See, I am about to send you the prophet Elijah
before that great and dreadful day of the LORD comes;
⁶ He will turn the hearts of the fathers to their children,
and the hearts of the children to their fathers,
or else I will come and strike the land with a curse."

Context and Composition

In the preceding message the prophet challenged the people to be faithful to the LORD in their personal stewardship and obedience. This represented the total commitment of the people to serve the LORD with all they had. The prophet held out the promise of God to them that their land would flourish

---

4 The Greek adds καὶ φλέξει αὐτούς, "and will burn them."
5 The Greek has ὑπολειφθῇ, which would reflect a form עֲזֹב. Many translations reflect the passive idea: "not a root or branch will be left to them."

if they were faithful, that all the nations would call them blessed, for the land would be a delightful land.

But the people Malachi addressed still had a wrong attitude; they still thought God was not administering things correctly and there was no pay-off for them. And so the prophet warned them about this and reminded them that the day of divine vengeance was coming. Their attitudes and actions revealed whether they had faith or not and that would be significant in light of what was coming.

Here we will have to deal with eschatology in brief form. The expositor will have to see how the prophecies given here fit into the total picture that Scripture gives, and this will require a good deal of study. Nevertheless, what is clear in the message is the devastation that awaits the unbeliever and the deliverance that awaits the believer.

Exegetical Notes

3:13

"have been harsh." The verb חָזְקוּ is the simple perfect tense, best taken as a present perfect. The word means "to be strong." The things they were saying were strong against God. They were not calm words, not words of faith and confidence. They were harsh criticisms.

"have we said." נִדְבַּרְנוּ is the *niphal* perfect, first person common plural, from דָּבַר. The *niphal* cannot be passive here, and so is probably reciprocal, meaning they have been conversing in their harsh criticisms.

3:14

"vain." The word is שָׁוְא, "vain" or "futile," to no good purpose. The form is the predicate adjective.

"to serve." The sentence actual reads "serving God is vain." The *qal* infinitive עֲבֹד functions as the subject of the sentence, and so is a substantival use: "serving God is vain."

"we kept." The verb שָׁמַרְנוּ is the simple *qal* perfect, first person common plural. It should be taken as a simple past tense, covering a period of time.

But it may also be either a present perfect or a characteristic perfect: "since we have kept" or "since we keep."

"and went."   The same classifications would apply to הָלַכְנוּ; what was used for the last verb should be used here as well.

"[in] mourning."   The noun "mourning" is used here as an adverbial accusative of manner. It is derived from the verb קָדַר, "to be dark." A related noun is the place name Kedar, as in the black or dark tents of Kedar.

3:15

"we are calling blessed."   מְאַשְּׁרִים is the *piel* participle, masculine plural. The word means "to bless," so in this stem would mean to pronounce or consider blessed. This word for "bless" means joy or happiness that comes from knowing one is right with God (Ps. 1:1).

"prosper."   נִבְנוּ is the *niphal* perfect, third person common plural, of בָּנָה; in this stem it means "to rebuild, restore."

"test."   בָּחַן means "to test, try." It can be in a good sense if it is motivated by faith. But if it is not, then it is rebellion against God. They were testing God by doing ungodly things, and they seemed to have escaped even the slightest rebuke ("escaped" is וַיִּמָּלֵטוּ). The nuance of the verb "test" may be taken as a characteristic perfect: "they test God." This harmonizes with the description of their using the participle as "doers of wickedness."

3:16

"talked."   Here too the verb is the *niphal* perfect, third person common plural, expressing the reciprocal nuance; "they talked with one another." The form has as its subject, "those who fear the LORD," and in apposition to that we have "each man with his fellow."

"Paid attention."   קָשַׁב is here in the *hiphil* preterite; it means "be inclined, pay attention," and so is an anthropomorphic expression. It emphasizes the intentional response of the LORD to his faithful.

"a scroll of remembrance."   The construction is סֵפֶר זִכָּרוֹן; the second word could be an attributive genitive, "a remembrance scroll," but more likely expresses the purpose, that is, "a scroll for remembrance." The word "remembrance" (and the verb "to remember") usually mean to act on what is being remembered, so not simply a record to keep in mind. These are the people God will deliver. But the whole expression is anthropomorphic, meaning the LORD does not need a scroll with names on it to remember whom to deliver. The writing in the scroll emphasizes the permanence of the LORD's intention.

"was written."   The form וַיִּכָּתֵב is the *niphal* preterite, third person masculine singular, with a *waw* consecutive. The subject is the "scroll of remembrance," which was written before him, literally, "to his face" or "in his presence."

"for those who esteem his name."   Parallel to the expression "for those who fear the LORD" we have this expression using the verb חָשַׁב in the *qal* active participle in the construct state. The verb "to esteem" is "to credit, to give him his proper due." This description explains further the faith of those who fear the LORD. These are the devout believers whom the LORD will deliver.

3:17

"when I make my treasured possession."   The believers will be the LORD's possession ("they shall be mine"), and this clause elaborates on when this will finally happen: אֲשֶׁר אֲנִי עֹשֶׂה סְגֻלָּה ("when I am making a treasure"). The deliverance from judgment is only one aspect of final salvation; the people will be turned into his prized possession.

"and I will have compassion."   The form is וְחָמַלְתִּי, the simple *qal* perfect with a *waw* consecutive. The verb means "to have compassion" with the idea of sparing the object of compassion. With the simile to follow, this word "compassion" is used three times in the verse. God has a relationship with believers — they are his sons who serve him faithfully. He will deliver them from the world of sin so that they might be with him.

3:18

"And you will again see."   Two verbs (functioning as a hendiadys) make this clause read וְשַׁבְתֶּם וּרְאִיתֶם, literally, "and you will return and you will see" (both being *qal* perfects with *waw* consecutives). The first becomes the adverb. The verb "see" here means "perceive, realize, understand."

"serves."   The form is the active participle, עֹבֵד. It is the calling of the believer to serve the Lord; and it is the highest description of the believer to be "the servant of the Lord." The "ungodly" or "wicked" (רָשָׁע), as popularly translated, do not serve him. The verb is the perfect tense, לֹא עֲבָדוֹ, probably best interpreted as a characteristic perfect.

4:1

"coming."   בָּא after the particle הִנֵּה expresses the imminent future. And **"surely,"** כִּי, underscores the certainty of it. The reference is to the day of the Lord when he comes to judge the world.

"burning."   The *qal* participle, masculine singular, from בָּעַר, also forms an imminent future in the announcement of the judgment, stressing what it will be like: "the day is about to come [and is about to] burn like an oven."

"stubble."   The word is figurative, an implied comparison, describing the arrogant and evil doers who will be destroyed as stubble. Stubble is not only of no value for the farmer, but is also easy to burn.

"set them on fire."   וְלִהַט is the *piel* perfect, third person masculine singular, with a *waw* consecutive to make the translation fall into sequence with the imminent future constructions preceding it. The verb is used elsewhere for fire "licking up" the things that it consumes. This idea of "set ablaze" then indicates complete burning. The subject of this verb is "the coming day"; it is a metonymy of subject, meaning the events that will occur on that coming day — the judgment of the wicked.

"so that."   The pronoun אֲשֶׁר is frequently a relative pronoun; but it has wider ranges of uses, serving in almost every type of clause. Here it introduces a result clause (or perhaps a purpose clause).

"root and branch."   The conflagration will be such that "it will not leave for them "root and branch." These two words are opposite ends of the tree, and so they form a merism, meaning the entire tree from the bottom root to the top branches. There is an implied comparison between the people and a tree. The destruction of the wicked will be complete.

4:2

"will rise."   The transition to the prospects of those who fear the name of the LORD begins with the verb, the *qal* perfect, third person feminine singular, with a *waw* consecutive to put it into the future translation. The verb וְזָרְחָה is often translated "and (the sun of righteousness) will rise." The verb means "to shine" or "glisten" like the blazing sun.

"The sun of righteousness."   The word "sun" is a figure of speech, comparing the actual sun to the coming Messiah; it is an implied comparison, signaling the dawning of a new day as well as all the benefits of his appearing. Here the primary benefit is righteousness. The word is a genitive after "sun," indicating not just his nature but what he will produce.

"with healing in his wings."   This is a nominal clause that begins with a *waw* conjunction: "and healing [will be] in his wings." The clause can be rendered as a circumstantial clause here: "with healing in his wings." The word "healing," מַרְפֵּא, can be used for physical as well as spiritual healing. And "wings" is part of the comparison of the Messiah to the sun; it understands the rising sun to be like a huge bird, its rays reaching across the skies as outstretched wings (so it is a zoomorphism). But the point is that wherever the sun's rays, wherever its light reaches, will enjoy the healing. This prophecy then is part of the larger revelation of a new creation.

"and you will go out."   וִיצָאתֶם is the *qal* perfect, second person masculine plural, with a *waw* consecutive to carry the future sequence. The root is יָצָא, and so with propretonic reduction there would have been a *shewa* under the first letter, but with the addition of the *waw* there was the rule of the *shewa* that changed the *yod* to be part of the prefix vowel. Here the going out is part of the imagery of being set free from bondage.

"and gambol."   The form is וּפִשְׁתֶּם, the *qal* perfect, second person masculine plural, with the *waw* consecutive, from the verb פּוּשׁ, "to spring about." Here the simile "like calves" clarifies that this verb refers to their gamboling when set free from the stalls. It is a picture of freedom and delight.

4:3

"Then you will trample."   וַעֲסוֹתֶם is another *waw* consecutive on a perfect, this time a geminate root meaning "trample." The word is likely figurative, a symbol of victory over the wicked.

"ashes."   The idea of trampling the wicked is expanded now to add that they will be ashes under their feet. If taken literally, with all the other imagery of the passage, the wicked will be consumed by fire, and wherever the remnant survived, they would walk on ashes. If figurative, it would be an implied comparison with the imagery of fire and ashes. In either case, the verse says that the people of God will have complete victory.

4:4

"Remember."   זִכְרוּ is the *qal* imperative from the verb "remember." This word does not merely mean memory; it includes the idea of acting on what is remembered. To remember the Law (תּוֹרַת) of Moses is to act on it, that is, live righteously and obediently to the Law. The instruction is intensified with the reference to Moses as "my servant," and the delineation of the Law as decrees (חֻקִּים) and decisions (וּמִשְׁפָּטִים), which are binding inscribed decisions.

4:5

"I am about to send."   Once again we have the participle in the construction that marks imminent future action: הִנֵּה אָנֹכִי שֹׁלֵחַ, "here I am sending." While this is imminent future, meaning it was always about to happen, it has now been over 2,000 years. But we only know that in hindsight. It is still imminent.

"Elijah the prophet."   The word הַנָּבִיא is in apposition to the accusative "Elijah."

"before the coming of the day of the Lord."   This half of the verse begins with the temporal clause: the preposition "before," followed by the *qal* infinitive construct בּוֹא, and then the subjective genitive, "the day of the Lord."

"great and dreadful."   These two words, the adjective הַגָּדוֹל and the *niphal* participle וְהַנּוֹרָא from יָרֵא, "to fear," modify the word "day." It helps clarify the fact that the day of the Lord is not the first coming, but a great and dreadful event at the end of the age.

4:6

"And he [Elijah] will turn."   וְהֵשִׁיב is the *hiphil* perfect, third person masculine singular, from שׁוּב plus the *waw* consecutive. The verb is often used for repentance, turning away from sin and turning or returning to God. Here the prophet will bring about such a spiritual change. To say he will turn the hearts of fathers and children involves the use of a metonymy of effect: there will be an actual change of heart, a new spiritual relation. But the cause of it is implied by the effect — they will repent and turn back to the historic faith.

"lest I come."   פֶּן־אָבוֹא uses the *qal* imperfect to express the consequences of refusing to obey the message through the prophet. The actual coming of the Lord to judge is certain and planned, but from the human perspective it could happen any time. This clause indicates that people should listen to God's warnings to be prepared, lest he comes (when they are not prepared) and strikes the earth.

"and strike."   The verb is וְהִכֵּיתִי, the *hiphil* (it is always *hiphil*) perfect, first person common singular, with a *waw* consecutive. It can mean "to kill," but it often means "to strike, smite, or attack." The word "earth" is a metonymy of subject, for to strike the earth with a curse means to strike it and everything in it, that is, the people in particular.

"curse."   This word חֵרֶם is new to the book of Malachi. The term is translated elsewhere as "ban," "devoted," as well as "curse." Whatever is put under this ban belongs to the Lord and people cannot have it; the Lord then can either take it into service or utterly destroy it. Here it describes the destruction of the world by God.

Exegetical Outline

I. The people were harsh in their criticism of God's justice, complaining that the wicked were blessed and they were not (3:13–15).
   A. The Lord said that their words were harsh against him (13).

       B. They had said it was futile to serve God or even appear devout (14).

       C. They had concluded that the wicked must be blessed because they prospered (14).

II. The devout believers talked about the LORD with faith and fear, prompting the LORD to promise them his compassion and protection when the day of judgment comes (3:16–18).

       A. The LORD paid attention to the way the devout believers talked with each other and guaranteed their preservation (16).

       B. The LORD declared that he would have compassion on them and make them his treasured possession (17).

       C. The LORD assured them that they would see the great division he would make between the righteous and the wicked in the judgment (18).

III. At the coming of the Messiah the wicked will be completely destroyed but the righteous will finally be free and victorious over them, a glorious prospect that calls for spiritual preparation for that coming day (4:1–6).

       A. The coming day of the LORD will bring complete destruction to the arrogant unbelievers in the world (1).

       B. The Messiah will bring healing to the world and freedom and victory to those who fear his name (2–3).

       C. The anticipation of the coming day calls for spiritual preparation (4–6).

          1. The people should live in harmony with Scripture (4).

          2. God will send Elijah to bring about spiritual renewal (5–6).

Exegetical Summary

Although many people misunderstand God's justice and think faithfulness to him futile, there is coming a day when the wicked will be destroyed but the faithful who fear the LORD and esteem his name will be set free from this world's bondage and share in the victory over it, a glorious prospect that calls for spiritual preparation.

Commentary in Expository Form

I. *Second guessing: People with selfish expectations will be frustrated with God (3:13–15).*

A. THEY OFTEN SAY INSOLENT THINGS (13).

The prophet immediately addressed the problem of those people who criticized the faith (and therefore the LORD) because things were not what they expected or thought they should be. The LORD said to them through Malachi, "Your words have been insolent against me" (חָזַק). The people that the prophet addressed here were skeptics; they had their doubts about the validity of the faith. But because many of them were not committed to the LORD, they had false and selfish expectations. They were expecting an immediate payoff, rewards, or benefits for becoming part of the congregation and living under the Law. They thought that God owed them something for their presence. They probably were not true believers; but if they were believers, their whole approach to the worship and service of God was mercenary — they wanted to know what was in it for them. The great saints of the ages who endured all kinds of suffering and deprivation would have been very hesitant to say such impudent things. But these people revealed impiety in their words, their attitudes, and their method of spreading their discontent.

Their insolent reply regarding the LORD was, "What have we been saying among ourselves against you?" The form of the verb indicates they were saying this to each other, complaining among themselves.

B. THEY EVEN CONCLUDE THAT IT IS FUTILE TO SERVE GOD (14–15).

These "make-believers" began to do what the LORD said to do in a way, that is, to test him and see if he was faithful. But because of their spiritual hardness, they concluded that he was not. Their insolent words formulated three claims. The first is the dramatic statement that it is vain to serve the LORD. The word "vain" (שָׁוְא) means "empty, vain, futile" or "to a false purpose" (found in the Ten Commandments for not taking the name of the LORD "in vain"). Their statement claims that all service of God is a futile endeavor on any level.

This is followed up with the claim that there is no profit (בֶּצַע) in keeping God's Law. The claim is expressed by means of a rhetorical question to indicate that there was no profit in it, no reward or benefit, no pay, no return on their investment. They are like some modern folk who give to God only because they expect to get double or triple their money back, a special reward.

In fact, they were truly surprised that there was no payoff since they had even gone about "[in] mourning" (קְדֹרַנִּית). They apparently went through the motions of appearing to have grief and sorrow for the sin of their nation, perhaps dressing in black sackcloth and looking dark and gloomy. But it was fake. They did it expecting some reward from God, almost as if they were professional mourners. But God always inspects the motives of mourners, or worshipers, to see if they are genuine, and if they are doing it for a reward or recognition.

But the most impudent statement they made concerns the justice of God. They claimed that the reality was just the opposite of what was said in verse 10, and they claimed that it was the arrogant whom they had to acknowledge were "blessed" by God. After all, these people who were doing wicked or godless things were actually flourishing; in fact, they were challenging God and escaping any judgment or rebuke. The implication of these comments is that God was either too weak to stop them, or was not interested in clamping down on the wicked or in making a distinction between the righteous and the wicked, or good and evil. God had promised to bless those who obeyed, but now he was blessing those who were wicked. So they concluded. These sharp words reflect a tragically unspiritual attitude, probably that of unbelievers (since the rest of the book seems to assume they are the ungodly).

II. *Second opinion: Those who love the LORD will be spared when the LORD comes to judge the wicked (3:16–18).*

A. THE LORD REMEMBERS THOSE WHO ARE FAITHFUL BELIEVERS (16).

There are others who see things differently. At the same time ("then") that people were criticizing the LORD, the righteous believers ("the fearers of the LORD") spoke to one another, but their conversation was very different. They loved and adored the LORD because of who he is and what he does, but they also treat him with reverential fear and obedience. When they spoke with their companions, their words were not insolent and self-seeking. Consequently, the text says the LORD paid attention (קָשַׁב, "pay attention to, regard, heed") and heard (שָׁמַע) what these folks were saying. The two verbs could be taken as a hendiadys, that is, he listened attentively to them.

Then we read that a book of remembrance was written concerning them.

This is certainly a figurative description, an implied comparison (hypoca-tastasis), for divine omniscience does not need to keep written records, and physical books would not be in the heavenly courts. But the imagery stresses the point that God does not forget his own. He knows everything instantly and completely; and he never forgets anything. But more is being stressed here by the word "remembrance" (זִכָּרֹון). It goes beyond a simple recollec-tion to mean "action based on the remembrance." If God remembers his people it means he will do something for them on the basis of the covenant he has with them. He will spare them in the day of judgment because he promised them eternal life with him.

The rest of the verse emphasizes that these people are those who "fear Yahweh" and "who think on his name." This verb "think" (חָשַׁב) means "to esteem, regard, plan, think." These folks give the proper due to God in all their thinking; they esteem him. But instead of saying they think on God, it says they think on his name. The name of the LORD, as we have seen, re-fers to his nature, his character, that is, the attributes of God (power, glory, wisdom, love, mercy, righteousness, goodness, eternality, omniscience, om-nipresence, infinity, and so on). And so "name" is a metonymy of subject. Therefore, these people are not simply good people, they are true believers whose thoughts are on God's nature. This was what built their pious devo-tion; it was like taking inventory on what God is like, or reckoning how those attributes work out in real life. The implication is that true believers value God as their prized possession.

B.   HE WILL SPARE HIS POSSESSION (17).

God announces that these people shall be his own possession (see Exod. 19:5) on the day that he makes up his treasure. Accordingly, when the day of judgment comes, God will remember his own people Israel, that is, spare them from the judgment. The security of those believers, as with all believers, is based on the fact that they belong to God as his prized treasure.

C.   HE WILL ENABLE PEOPLE TO DISCERN THE RIGHTEOUS AND THE WICKED (18).

When he does judge, then everyone will see the real difference between the righteous and the wicked. The skeptics claimed that there was no difference because they had false expectations of a simple payoff. But in the eternal plan the benefit of faith is much greater than a few rewards now. Everyone will discern between the one who is saved and the one who is not, and will fully realize the importance of fearing and serving the LORD.

III. *Second coming: The faithful should prepare for the day when the LORD will come to judge arrogant evildoers but deliver those who fear him (4:1–6).*

A. THE LORD WILL BRING HIS PEOPLE INTO A GLORIOUS NEW AGE WHEN HE COMES TO JUDGE THE ARROGANT EVILDOERS IN THE WORLD (4:1–3).

1. *The wicked will be burnt up (4:1).* The present announcement continues the theme of "the day of the LORD," a theme that prophets in each of the last few centuries of the monarchy stressed. The "day of the LORD" can refer to any divine intervention to judge and to bless; but the great day of the LORD refers to the last intervention, what begins with the second coming, when the Lord will come to judge the world by fire and establish a universal reign of righteousness. This day includes judgment on the wicked and blessing for the righteous; therefore, it is not only the second coming when the Lord will judge the earth, but the subsequent reign of Christ and the restoration of blessing to the earth as well.

The text again uses the construction of הִנֵּה with the participle (בָּא) to express the imminent future: "The day is about to come." It is certain, it is coming. And it will be a day that will burn like an oven. The day itself will not burn, but on that day the judgment will burn up the wicked (so we have a metonymy of subject for the events of the day). The comparison with an oven (a simile) indicates that the burning will be intense and consuming because confined to its intended use.

What will be burned up are the wicked: all the arrogant (זֵדִים) and every doer of wickedness (עֹשֵׂה רִשְׁעָה). The first word emphasizes their attitude as self-sufficient, in no need of God; and the second construction points out the fruit of their arrogance: they practice godlessness, or, they live an ungodly life. They want no part with God (arrogance), and they do not keep his laws (ungodly). They, then, will be judged in the great conflagration. The text says they will be "stubble" (קַשׁ), the metaphor not only signifying how easily they will be consumed, but also their worthlessness to God (see also "chaff" in Ps. 1).

To reinforce the idea the warning is repeated: "The coming day will set them ablaze." But to make sure that the meaning is not missed, a result clause is added: "so that it will not leave root or branch to them." The imagery used here falls into line with the metaphor "stubble." These are implied comparisons (hypocatastases), because it will not be roots or branches consumed, but the wicked in their totality. The expression "root and branch" is also a merism, meaning the entire tree from root to branch. There will be nothing left of the wicked when the day comes.

The imagery of burning in conjunction with judgment is used by Malachi and the other prophets, and later by John the Baptist when he declared that the wicked would be burned like chaff with unquenchable fire (as the Lord's baptism with fire would signify [Matt. 3:11–12]). Those judged are the proud and the wicked. The word "proud" must not be trivialized; it refers to people who think they do not need God, who live independently of God without faith or obedience. But their good works, whatever good works they have, will not be good enough to enable them to escape the judgment.

The prophets sometimes linked this judgment of fire with the final great war that will be raging at the time that the Lord descends to the Mount of Olives (see Zech. 14:3–4, 12–15). The plague that Zechariah describes may be a description of some kind of devastating holocaust that will bring human history to a close and be the means of removing the wicked from the earth. In that case the intense heat and the fire would be real, and so the expressions would be metonymies and not implied metaphors. But it will be focused as many of the plagues in Egypt were so that the righteous will not perish. Through it all the LORD will begin to renovate the earth.

We must not forget to relate this to general theology. The wicked may be destroyed at the coming of the LORD, perhaps in a dreadful war, or perhaps by his power. But they will not be annihilated; their spirits will go to *she'ol*, or hell, and their bodies to the grave, to wait for their resurrection to be judged and finally condemned.

2. Those who fear the LORD *will have a glorious deliverance (4:2–3).* The contrast is now made with the true believers: "to you who fear my name." These are not the arrogant, ungodly people. These are true believers who worship the LORD with reverence and obey his word in fear. This does not mean that they live in terror of judgment; they will not be in the last judgment. It is a healthy fear. Those with reverential fear draw near to the powerful and glorious God with adoration and amazement, but seek to obey him because he is also the awesome sovereign God of the universe. Once again the object of this reverential fear is the LORD's "name" (the character of God; see passages like Exod. 34:5–7 and Isa. 9:6). To fear the "name of the LORD" is the proper response of the faithful to God in all his glory, power, and majesty — all that he is and all that he does. So these are the devout believers who are faithful.

What do they have to look forward to? The coming of the Messiah and all the changes that will bring! To them the "sun of righteousness will rise with healing in his wings." The word "sun" (שֶׁמֶשׁ) is an implied comparison (hypocatastasis), comparing the appearance of the Messiah with the rising sun. But the following genitive "righteousness" (צְדָקָה) qualifies the nature and the effect of this rising sun. This could be an attributive genitive, a righteous sun, which is certainly true of the Lord. But in the context it is more likely an objective genitive, that is, this "sun" would produce righteousness throughout the world. The people had challenged God that there was no justice and that evil was rampant; the Messiah will change all that. He will "shine" (זָרַח), that is, as the sun rises in the sky so his brightness glistens and lights up the whole earth. Zacharias, the father of John the Baptist, accordingly referred to the Messiah as the "sunrise" (dayspring from on high) in his great song (Luke 1:76–79).

One further clause adds to this qualification: "with healing in his wings." The image of wings continues the comparison of Messiah with the rising sun, the rays of light shooting out from the sun appearing as wings across the sky (zoomorphism). This means that the whole world will come under the direct influence of this rising light. And that influence will bring "healing," that is, removing the problem of the presence of evil, its causes and its effects. The word "heal" (מַרְפֵּא) can be used for physical healing, mending of utensils and nets, or spiritual healing (cf. Exod. 15:26).

At the glorious appearing of the long-awaited Messiah, the great release from the bondage of the world, sin, and oppression will cause the righteous to celebrate enthusiastically. Here a different image is used, one that compares the people of God to calves that have been penned up too long in this evil world: "you shall go forth and gambol (skip) as calves from the stall." Calves that have been penned up closely for winter months will skip in their running (פּיּשׁ) when they are set free from the stalls. So the point of the simile is that the righteous when they are finally set free from all the effects of the curse will leap for joy in great celebration.

The righteous will also be victorious through faith; they will tread on the wicked, who will be ashes under the soles of their feet. Isaiah 63:1–6 portrays the Messiah with a similar but different image: he will trod them underfoot as in a winepress of his wrath. But here the prophet sees the righteous sharing in that great victory, perhaps because it was promised that the human race, the seed of the woman, would destroy the seed of the serpent in Genesis

3:15 (see also Rom. 16:20). However, since the human race has already been defeated, the Lord would have to destroy the evil one himself; but he would do it as a human. The righteous will not actually destroy the wicked because the Lord will do that. But it will appear that way when they accompany him in his victorious conquest (see Ps. 110). The verse here simply says that the wicked will be ashes under the feet of the righteous. Perhaps the battle is already over, and the symbolism of treading on the ashes indicates sharing in the conquest. In that case it would be a metonymy of the adjunct in which something connected with the victory is put for the victory itself. The righteous will triumph over the wicked, because they are on the side of the Lord.

B. THE LORD PREPARES HIS PEOPLE FOR THAT GREAT DAY TO COME (4:4–6).

1. Instruction: Obey the word of God (4). The first part of God's plan is for the righteous to prepare themselves spiritually by living out the word of God. Malachi calls on the righteous to "remember" (זְכַר) the Law of Moses. As noted above, the verb means more than mental reflection; it means to act upon what is remembered as may be seen by its usage, especially in prayers when people call on God to remember them. The call is for them to obey the Law of Moses, which was the foundation of all Scripture. People could not willfully disobey the Law and claim to be the righteous. We of course have much more Scripture. But Jesus said he did not come to annul or destroy the Law, but to fulfill it. So we interpret the Law through the fulfillment of Christ, and learn that the revelation in the Law is still profitable for instruction in righteousness, as the apostle says (2 Tim. 3:16).

The principle is that we who are looking for the second coming of Jesus the Messiah should be living soberly and righteously in obedience to Scripture. The apostle John says that whoever has this hope purifies himself (1 John 3:3). To live daily in the expectancy of the second coming, watching and waiting, means that we will be found faithful.

2. Provision: Elijah will unite the people in the covenant (4:5–6). Now the Lord announces that he is planning to prepare people in a special way: he is about to send "Elijah the prophet" before the coming of that great and terrible day. At the beginning of chapter 3 God said, "I am sending my messenger"; and now in similar words he says, "I am sending Elijah the prophet." Malachi does not say that these two are one and the same, although if we only had this book we might say they could be the same person because of parallel constructions. But there seems here to be a deliberate ambiguity.

We know from the New Testament that the messenger of Malachi 3:1 was

John the Baptist. But was John also Elijah? In the Gospels, John the Baptist came preaching repentance in the desert, preparing people for the coming of the Lord. Luke 1:17 says that he came in the spirit and power of Elijah. In the Old Testament, Elijah, we may recall, never died, but was taken up in a chariot of fire (2 Kings 2:11). But before he left he gave his mantel to Elisha, so that Elisha could have a double portion of the power of Elijah. Elijah was the first full prophet in the classical sense (although Abraham is called a prophet, and Samuel and David and Nathan and Gad were prophets). He stands at the head of a long list of prophets, so that all the prophets coming after him have something of the spirit and power of Elijah, but they were not Elijah the Tishbite. When John was asked who he was, he stated very clearly, "I am not Elijah" (John 1:21 and 23). In Matthew 11:13 Jesus said of John, "If you receive it" — this was Elijah who was to come. There is a deliberate contingency here as well. John may have come in the spirit and power of Elijah, but he was not Elijah, and he did not do what Malachi 4 said: turn the people right just before the great and terrible day of judgment. "If you receive it" may very well refer to receiving the message of the kingdom, that is, receiving Christ. But we know that Jesus came to his own, and his own received him not, but to as many as received him he gave the authority to be the sons of God (John 1:11 and 12). Jesus may have meant that had the people repented and received the Messiah, John would have fit the requirements. But of course they did not receive him, and Scripture was clear that they would not. But Jesus' offer of himself to his people was still a legitimate offer, even if he knew they would reject him — he had to offer himself to be rejected.

The context supports this idea for Jesus then goes on to explain why the nation did not believe. Then at the transfiguration (see Mark 9:2; Matt. 17:11), Jesus announced that Elijah does indeed come and restores all things. But then he added that Elijah already came. So here we have another example of what has become known as the "already/not yet" arrangement of prophecy. John came in the spirit of Elijah, and people killed him. But Elijah must yet come. Many commentators identify one of the two witnesses in Revelation 12 as Elijah — either the real Elijah (otherwise, why did he not die?), or one like John who will come in the spirit of Elijah. But there will be two of them. That chapter goes on to say that these witnesses have the power to shut up heaven so it will not rain, which is exactly what Elijah did at the beginning of his ministry.

But whoever he may be, when this "Elijah" comes at the end of the age, before the coming of that great and terrible day, he will bring about true repentance and change in the faith of the nation so that they will be ready for the coming of the Lord. The imagery of turning the hearts of fathers and children to each other is a spiritual change, the hearts referring to their wills. As they turn their hearts, it will be in obedience to the Law, and so they will be in fact turning their hearts to the Lord.

People everywhere must return to the historic faith, before the Messiah comes and smites the earth with the curse (חֵרֶם). This word for "curse" basically means "banned" (it is off limits to humans) or "devoted" (given to God for his use or to be destroyed). In holy war, things would be put under this "ban." That meant they belonged to the Lord, but no human could have them (see the sin of Achan in Joshua, and the sin of Saul in 1 Samuel — both took for themselves "cursed" things that should have been destroyed). So Malachi is thinking in terms of holy war, that when the Lord comes he will destroy the world, but will spare his faithful people.

Expository Idea and Application

Expository Idea

If people do not think God is ruling in fairness today, and they choose to reject him for that reason, they will have a sad future awakening. When the Lord comes again, he will come to judge, separating the righteous from the guilty, that is, the sinners who have not found forgiveness by his grace. Exactly how the coming in judgment will work out is not clear to us, but the language used is always of war and fire and devastation. That is how our human history will end.

But before he comes he will send guides to bring about harmony and righteousness in the families, a restoration to the historic faith. One of those guides is certainly Holy Scripture; it is full of instructions to watch and pray for his appearance. The faithful must work to bring people to repentance and to a proper spiritual level. But God is also preparing one last great guide, his messenger. Many will come in the spirit and power of Elijah over the ages; but after they are long gone, and just at the eve of the coming, Elijah (or one like Elijah) will appear and draw people back to God (this is the eve of the second coming). Those who do not respond will remain part of the cursed world.

The central expository idea could be worded this way:

(Malachi 3:13 – 4:6)

> Those who live in the hope of the coming of the Lord
> to judge the world and deliver the believers
> will prepare themselves spiritually for that day.

Application

First, we may say that criticizing and complaining to the LORD harshly is wrong. At best it shows a weak faith that cannot understand and does not like the way that God does things. But as people mature in the faith they learn that the LORD has an eternal plan — he knows what he is doing, and when and how it will be done. That does not mean that believers should never cry out, "How long, O Lord?" But that is a prayer, not a murmuring criticism. God has his reasons for not destroying the wicked and wickedness right now, and it is up to those who trust in him not simply to try to understand his ways, but to accept what he does as right and wise.

Second, believers must also do the work of the prophet in proclaiming the word of the LORD to prepare people for the coming day. It is the task of the church to warn people of the terrifying devastation to come on those who in arrogant unbelief reject the LORD and care nothing for his word. What lies ahead for the world and those who are of the world is a great judgment most dreadful; and though they might die in some end-time conflagration they must know that they are not gone forever, but will still stand in the judgment. Unfortunately, just as the world is in need today to hear the warning and the call to repentance, the church is strangely silent.

The corollary of this prophetic witness is for believers to encourage one another that the glorious day of deliverance is at hand, that those who trust and obey are destined to be part of his treasure when he appears as the Sun of Righteousness, bringing healing and deliverance from the bondage of this world.

And third, as part of this anticipation of the coming of the Lord, those living in hope are called to be waiting and watching, namely, preparing themselves for the coming of the Lord. They do this for two reasons. One is because that preparation will confirm that they are in the faith and that they belong to God. And the other is that the hope reminds them to purify themselves to be found faithful at his coming. They must "remember" the word of the LORD, that is, keep it in mind and act on it in obedience.

Key Words

"Vain"

The word שָׁוְא occurs 53 times in the Bible; it has as its basic meaning "deceit" or "wickedness" or "falsehood."

(1) In the Law it can refer to a false report (Exod. 23:1), a false witness (Deut. 5:20), or idol worship (Isa. 1:13). The commandment not to take the name of the LORD "in vain" (לַשָּׁוְא) would then mean speaking the name for a false or deceitful purpose.

(2) The verb seems to have the sense of "be evil, foul," although it occurs more in the cognate languages. There are a couple of rare uses where the verb (in the *hiphil*) means "to treat badly" (Pss. 55:16 and 89:23).

(3) The idea of vain may have come into English from the Latin rendering. Brown, Driver, and Briggs suggested that the basic meaning of the word was emptiness, rather than deceit, meaning then that false witness or idolatry was empty and therefore vain. Sawyer says that the meaning of deceit has been narrowed to the idea of nothingness or for naught, or in vain, through the Latin translation into English. In contrast to other words meaning vain or worthless, this word would retain the connotation of evil or deceit. The usage in Psalm 127 does not go this far; rather, it seems to mean that building without the LORD's participation is futile or worthless, closer to the idea of emptiness.[6]

"To Esteem"

The verb חָשַׁב has meaning in the semantic field of calculation, that is, compute, account, charge, reckon. It also has meaning in the field of thinking something out, that is, conceiving and inventing, and often carrying it out. We may survey the usage in several areas.

(1) First, there is the meaning "think." In Genesis 38:15 the word is used in the sense of taking someone to be a certain kind of person (e.g., he thought she was a prostitute). In Jonah 1:4 personification is used to say the creaky boat thought it was going to be broken.

(2) More common are uses with the sense of "plan." Proverbs 16:9 says the

---

6 See J. F. A. Sawyer, "שׁוא šāw' **deceit**," in *The Theological Lexicon of the Old Testament*, ed. Jenni and Westermann, 3:1310–12.

mind plans the way, but the Lord directs the steps. A common use of this meaning concerns people who devise evil things or make plans that turn into action (Hos. 7:15).

(3) A third meaning is "consider, value." It is used in Isaiah 40:15 and 17 with the sense of weighing or regarding the nations as all but worthless. First Kings 10:21 says that silver was not counted because it was not considered valuable in Solomon's day. And Malachi uses the word to describe people who esteem (by faith and obedience) the name of the Lord (3:16).

(4) Finally, the word is used in passages with the meaning "reckon, account." Genesis 15:6 uses the word this way: Abram believed in the Lord and the Lord "reckoned" to him righteousness. And in Psalm 32 true forgiveness means that the Lord does not reckon or impute iniquity.

"To Remember"

The verb זָכַר, "to remember," and its derivative is used frequently throughout the Old Testament. It always involves the memory in one way or another, but it has extended nuances in its usage.

(1) It can mean simply a mental recollection, the basic idea of "to remember."

(2) But it often has the added emphasis of acting on the basis of what is remembered. For example, in the prayers of people we might find expressions such as, "O Lord, remember me." We find this emphasis in passages such as Genesis 8:1 where we read, "And God remembered Noah." This means that in the height of the flood God began to act on behalf of Noah and the ark, and everything after this reversed what was described before 8:1. Of special interest is the statement that God will remember our sins no more. Being omniscient, God cannot forget. Rather, it means that he will never act on them if they are forgiven.

(3) Likewise the noun אַזְכָּרָה, "memorial," has the same import. Portions of some of the Levitical sacrifices were offered as a "memorial," intended to remind God of the worshiper's devotion, and to remind the worshiper of God's grace and the stipulations of the covenant. It made the ritual a covenant renewal service (as the admonition in the New Testament, "do this in remembrance of me"). The memorial reminded the Lord of covenant promises to be fulfilled (so it formed a prayer), and the redeemer of obligations yet to be met (so it formed a vow as well). It went far beyond a mere remembering.

(4) The noun זִכָּרוֹן, "remembrance," has the same force. A scroll of re-membrance would list (figuratively speaking) the faithful believers who were to be kept from the judgment to come.

(5) The noun זֵכֶר, "memorial, remembrance," came to signify what was being remembered. We find this, for example, as a substitute for the divine name: in Exodus 3:15 the word זִכְרִי, "my memorial," is parallel to "my name." The words refer to the nature of the LORD that is to be preserved by creed and praise.

(6) In the *hiphil* it can also mean "to praise," that is, "to cause (people) to remember" the LORD (see Isa. 43:26; Ps. 71:16) through what was said. But the verb can also be an internal causative with the sense of "keeping something in mind, meditating, or pondering" (Ps. 20:7). This word clarifies how praise has the important function of preserving in the memory the acts of the LORD and the expected acts of devotion and service of the worshiper.[7]

---

7 See Brevard S. Childs, *Memory and Tradition* (Naperville, IL: Alec R. Allenson, 1962), pp. 1–8.

Conclusion:
The Biblical and Theological Emphases of Malachi

The Seven Messages

These seven messages by the prophet Malachi are filled with doctrinal and practical themes, and although they were delivered to an Israelite congregation several centuries before Christ, they are as meaningful and applicable today as they were then in the following ways:

1. *God's Faithful Covenant Love (1:1–5)*

The love of God is the basis for his covenant with his people — Israel then, and the church today. And that love will sustain the faithful through all persecution and trouble. With the new covenant in Christ Jesus we have a better understanding of the love of God.

2. *Worship That Dishonors God (1:6–17)*

The principles that inform this message are timeless — believers must fear and honor the Lord in the way that they worship. The outer form of worship with sacrifices and altars has been fulfilled in Christ's sacrifice, and this makes the standard for worship even higher. Treating the sacrifice as worthless and the ritual as drudgery betrays a corrupt minister and profane service.

3. *Teaching God's Word Faithfully (2:1–9)*

Those who are entrusted to teach the word have a sacred duty — they must believe it, live it, teach it faithfully, and apply it to turn people to righteousness. This has not changed, neither have the failures and violations of teachers from the days of the apostles now. What has changed is that we have more Scripture to proclaim, and therefore the material in the prophetic literature has to be seen through the revelation of the new covenant.

4.   *Profaning the Holy Covenant of Marriage (2:10–16)*

Here too the message is still valid. In fact, it is more urgent given the modern corruption of the idea of marriage as it was instituted by God. The reminder of Malachi of the relationship between the man and the woman in marriage fits very well with pastoral counseling for marriage. And violation of marriage still is a sin, still causes great pain to people, and still ruins worship. All of this calls for diligence not to act treacherously and break the marriage vows.

5.   *God's Justice and Faithfulness (2:17–3:5)*

People still want God to come and judge the wickedness in the world. But the cry for the God of justice can reflect a spirit of self-righteousness as much as a cry of pain. He is coming and no one can stand. But by his grace he has preserved his people from the destruction to come. In this passage we move from a purely Old Testament setting to the prophecy of the coming of Christ. We therefore have the advantage of looking back to see John the Baptist and Jesus Christ as the prophecy becomes clearer. That should not simply clear up some questions; it should inspire to greater faith as we realize the truth of God's word.

6.   *God's Faithfulness to the Faithful (3:6–12)*

Here we focus on stewardship. It is one passage in Malachi that is used most frequently in the churches today. The principle is clear: devout worshipers are called to honor God with their stewardship. The details of Israelite sacrifices, offerings, and tithing may not all be carried forward literally to the New Testament, but the principles behind them are. Giving to God is an act of gratitude and faith — gratitude for all that he has provided and faith that he will continue to meet our needs. But the details of God's blessings for the faithful might change, especially if we are thinking of other countries where rain is in abundance already. God provides physical and material blessings in different ways, and he gives spiritual blessings for the faithful, now in this life and in the rewards in the life to come. So again, the principles remain, but the details are expanded in the new covenant.

7. *Preparing for the Coming of the LORD (3:13–4:6)*

The message of this passage is the same for us as it was for Israel. The difference is that we know much more about the first coming and the second coming. But we know of the great judgments on earth to come and the final judgment on the wicked. The church, like the earlier messengers of God, must encourage one another in the faith and warn people of the judgment to come. These principles do not change, even though we have a better knowledge of salvation and judgment because of the new covenant.

The Theological Ideas

The following survey of the doctrinal themes will use the categories of God, his creation (basically people), and the relationship between God and his creation.

I. *The Doctrine of God*

The book presents the LORD God as sovereign, powerful, holy, righteous, merciful, loving, and faithful. These characteristics come out naturally and powerfully in the flow of the messages through the prophet. Because the book is so brief, we must read it against the background of the Law and the Prophets. And because the book anticipates future fulfillment, we must link many of its themes to the New Testament to clarify the theology. We will begin with the doctrine of God.

THE NAMES OF GOD

In general the holy name Yahweh, translated "LORD," is used throughout the book (17 times by itself). It was the personal name of God in the Old Testament from the very beginning. But because its significance was explained to Moses in conjunction with the fulfillment of the promises (Exod. 3:14), it also identifies him as the covenant God. The repetition of the declaration "I am Yahweh your God" in the Law (see, for example, Exod. 20:1 and Lev. 19) shows how significant this association was. The holy name was a constant reminder of the covenant and its stipulations. And since there is a strong emphasis in the book on the covenant, it is natural that the name was used throughout.

God himself explained the significance of the name to Moses in Exodus 3:14 by using a word play based on the name: "I am that I am." The name "Yahweh" would properly be the third person of the verb, "he is," and not the first person "I am" (that would be *'ehyeh*). In the explanation God reveals himself to be sovereignly independent of all creation and always present to act. When the faithful refer to him by name, they are confessing their faith in all that he is. It is a distinct identity, for the name opposes all that is merely naturalistic, impersonal, and corrupt.

The holy name is used about a dozen more times in conjunction with the word "armies" (or "hosts"). The title "Yahweh of armies" (rendered "LORD of hosts" often) denotes God as powerful. He is like a warrior who has armies at his disposal — armies in heaven and on earth. The title was used by the prophets to emphasize that what the LORD declares he is fully able to do. And in Malachi, as well as other prophets, the title appears when God is in opposition to what Israel or the nations were doing. In such cases people would be reminded that God will defend and fulfill the covenants with all the power in heaven and on earth. The title in a prophetic sermon would alert the people that something has gone terribly wrong and that God was about to set it right.

The meaning of the holy name is associated with Christ Jesus in the New Testament. The deity of Christ is certainly a key doctrine in the New Testament, but several times that doctrine takes the form of Christ's self-revelation as "I am" in a distinct way (e.g., John 8:58). Such a reference harmonizes with his claim to be equal to the Father (John 10:30). And the power that God commanded in the Old Testament as "LORD of hosts" is the property of the Son as well. At his ascension he declared that all power was given to him in heaven and on earth (Matt. 28:18–20). By his mighty works he demonstrated he was indeed "the Mighty God" (one of the names for the Messiah in Isa. 9:6). Those who put their faith in Christ must therefore believe that Jesus is Lord (Rom. 10:9–10), not just Lord in the sense of master, but Yahweh God revealed in the Old Testament.

In Malachi the "messenger of the covenant" that the people desired (the

Messiah) we know to be Jesus Christ (Mal. 3:1), primarily because the mes-senger who was to prepare the way was a prophecy of John the Baptist (see also Isa. 40:3–5). Accordingly, the covenant that he was to bring was the new covenant (Heb. 12:24). But most importantly the oracle announces that this messenger will come to his temple. This is a clear indication of his deity because the temple was always known as the house of the LORD. So in Malachi 3 we have Yahweh sending two messengers — one fully human to prepare the way, the other human and divine to come to his temple and inaugurate the new covenant.

The other prophecy of the Messiah also reveals him as supernatural in power and authority. He is referred to as the "sun of righteousness who rises with healing in his wings" (4:3). He comes to restore creation to its intended condition, to set his people free from the bondage of the world, and to judge the wicked once and for all. This is no ordinary messenger.

The Spirit is also mentioned in the book, but it occurs in a difficult pas-sage that has been given a variety of translations. The traditional interpre-tation is that when God created one (woman for the man), he "had the residue of the Spirit." He was not limited in the possible ways he could have created. If this translation stands, then the reference is to the Holy Spirit in the creation account.

In the book of Malachi the LORD is also referred to as Father. This is not a common designation for God in the Old Testament; nonetheless, its signif-icance is clear. It is a human description that points to him as the sovereign Creator, a covenant God, and a person related to believers. All of these em-phases come together in the prophet's message on divorce as a violation of the holy covenant and a repudiation of God as Father and Lord. Israel had been designated as God's son by covenant (Exod. 4:22) and as his servant by calling (Isa. 41:8). In the new covenant believers have been given the right to be called the children of God (John 1:12). We therefore have been taught to address him as "our Father."

Two other designations of the LORD reveal his relationship to his people. He is referred to as "the God of Israel" and "King." Both of these would remind the people of their loyalty to the covenant by obedience to their sovereign.

But a couple of times "God" is used in a way that suggests some of the people were not members of the covenant. In the words of the belligerent people listening to the prophet, the way God was dealing with the nation (with them in particular) was seen as unjust: "Where is the God of justice?" And in the last section of the book their complaint is that it was futile to serve God. They may have been so-called believers who made a profession of faith but had not submitted to doing the will of God. But it may be stronger, because in the end they are contrasted with those who fear the name of the LORD and find security through the coming judgment. Were they also hesitant to use the personal covenant name?

THE WORKS OF GOD

Creation

The doctrine of creation does not receive a lot of attention in Malachi, but its brief references show it to be foundational to the message. In 2:10 the prophet reasons with the people that one God created them. The point could be in reference to creation (Gen. 1–2), but it more likely refers to the creation of the people of Israel into one nation at Sinai. The foundation of the nation is therefore supernatural: God created them as a people through redemption from Egypt and the granting of a covenant. It was a creation as in the beginning.

The other reference to creation probably does recall Genesis. The statement that God made one could refer to the nation (or the spiritual seed), but in the context probably refers to one woman (or one union), since the man and the woman became one (2:15). The way God created in Genesis formed the pattern for the creation of the nation. If God had wanted to create more than one wife, or make a variation to the designation of one flesh for the union of the man and the woman, he could have done so. But marriage according to Malachi is one man and one woman united for life in the faith to produce a godly seed.

This emphasis is not lost in the New Testament. Jesus himself affirmed that God joined the man and the woman together and what he has joined no one should separate (Matt. 19:1–6). And Paul clearly relies on God's creation of the man and the woman in his instructions for marriage.

Election

Israel actually became the chosen people of God long before Sinai. Malachi reminds the people that God elected them when he chose Jacob over Esau (Gen. 25:23). He loved Jacob but he hated Esau. Since this was prior to their births, the emphasis is on the election of Jacob and rejection of Esau. The point is not that the Israelites were righteous and the Edomites sinful, but on the election of one line over another for the covenant plan. Salvation was always a separate, individual matter of faith. However, Paul uses this election of Jacob to teach the general truth of divine election (Rom. 9:13). So the church, like Israel, owes its existence to creation and election (Eph. 1:14). There is no other path to becoming the people of God.

Redemption

Redemption begins with the love of God and his compassion for his people. For Israel this love was central to their existence as the people of God (see Deut. 7:7–8; Hos. 11:1; Isa. 48:11; and especially Jer. 31:13). The love of God exhibited in forming the nation did not guarantee all Israelites were saved, but no Israelite could be saved without responding by faith to the love of God. One central point of Malachi is that God is always ready to show compassion and grace to those who seek it (1:9). To that end he calls those who have wandered from him to return to him so that he might return to them (1:6–7). He does not change, otherwise they would have been consumed.

There is no difference in this point in the New Testament, only the developed meaning of the love and grace of God. Salvation is only possible because God loved us and sent his Son to die for the sins of the world (John 3:16). But his death is only effectual for those who believe in him. His love is everlasting because atonement was once for all (John 13:1). And that love preserves us through life and secures our eternal redemption (Rom. 8:37–39).

God chose the line of Jacob to carry on the covenant plan to bring blessing to the nations (Gen. 12:1–3). To that end he ordained Levites to be messengers of the covenant, to teach Israel the Law, and to lead them in their spiritual service (Deut. 33:8–11). They were to minister life and peace to others, which they themselves received (Num. 25:12–13; Ps. 106:30). They did this by demonstrating their own reverential fear of the Lord, faithfully teaching of his word, walking with God in obedience, and turning many to righteousness (2:1–9).

It was always God's plan that the chosen people be a blessing to the nations. In the case of Israel's refusal to serve the Lord in faithfulness, God announced that he would turn to the nations. The oracle proclaimed that the nations would demonstrate faith by living out the fear of the Lord and acknowledging the greatness of his name. This prophecy would be fully realized in the New Testament, for Jesus himself said that the kingdom was being taken from faithless Israel and being given to a people who bear fruit (Matt. 21:42–45). But the beginnings of this prophetic word are in the Old Testament (see Isa. 11:1–16; 66:20; Zeph. 2:11; Zech. 9:10). And so nations are included in the praise and service of the LORD (see Ps. 113:3; Isa. 42:6; 45:6; 49:6). But it would take the new covenant to break down the partition between Jews and Gentiles and unite believers in one faith (Eph. 2:14).

Covenants

The means of confirming the certainty of a promise or an agreement was by a covenant in which people swore by the living God. But when God made covenants with people since there was no higher power he swore by himself — he staked his life on it, as it were. The covenant guaranteed the fulfillment of the promises.

In Malachi we have first a reference to "the covenant of our fathers," the patriarchs, which would mean Abraham, Isaac, and Jacob (2:10; cf. Gen. 12:1–3; chaps. 15, 18, etc.). The promises that God swore to Abraham form the foundation of all subsequent biblical covenants, as well as the stipulations for participants to observe. The covenant of the fathers established a great nation, Israel, through whom all the families of the earth would be blessed. Violation of marriage would profane the covenant and they would no longer be a holy nation.

Another covenant mentioned is the covenant with Levi, probably a reference to the selection and ordination of the priests to serve in the sanctuary and administer the ritual of the covenant (see Lev. 8–10; 21–22; and Num. 25:12–13). The standard for the priests was that God be sanctified in the eyes of the people (Lev. 10:10).

A third covenant in the book is marriage. It is a covenant made between a man and his wife with God as the witness (2:14). And because the LORD hates divorce (2:16) and loves the sanctity of marriage in the faith (2:11), his witness against the treachery of those who violate the marriage covenant, and therefore the covenant program God has for his people, will bring about a curse in place of blessing. The marriage covenant was to reflect the main covenant of the fathers — to break it was treachery, to keep it was faithfulness. God had instituted holy marriage for the covenant people between one man and one woman in order to produce a godly seed (2:15; Gen. 2:24; Prov. 2:17; 5:15–21). The future of the covenant people was in jeopardy if people married devotees of paganism, which was the result of divorce in Malachi's day (see Ezra 9:2–6 and 10:18–19; Neh. 10:30 and 13:23–27).

Conclusion

The New Testament confirms this plan of God for marriage. Jesus reminded the people that God had ordained the institution of marriage from the beginning. God put the man and the woman together, and no one dare destroy marriage (Matt. 19:4–6). He added that Moses permitted divorce for serious violation of the sanctity of marriage, but that allowance was necessitated by the people's hardness of heart. Divorce is one thing, but marrying a devotee of pagan religion is another. Paul warned about being unequally yoked with false beliefs, and that surely applied to marriage (2 Cor. 6:15–16). Furthermore, he stressed the need for godly influence in the home so that the children might be sanctified (1 Cor. 7:14). The marriage covenant was important enough to be symbolic of the covenant of redemption (cf. 2 Cor. 11:2–3).

The people were not faithful to the covenants. They violated the stipulations through their corrupt and profane worship, which was permitted by the priests (cf. 1 Sam. 2:12–26 for one example). The priests violated the priestly role by their false teaching and corrupt living; they did not emulate the early priests in personal faith, faithful teaching, obedient living, and bringing many to righteousness (see Ezek. 34:1–16; Lev. 10:10–11). The people and the priests violated the code of marriage, which was the stability of the nation, as well as the laws of tithing that expressed their gratitude and allegiance. In sum, they were not living according to the laws of God, and they were not really looking for the coming of the Lord.

Covenant is also central to the message of the New Testament: Jesus is the mediator of the new covenant because all of the promises of God are fulfilled in and through him (Heb. 12:24 and 2 Cor. 1:20; for the new covenant, see Jer. 31; Isa. 54; and Ezek. 36). The new covenant forms believers into a new kingdom of priests (compare Exod. 19:5–6 and 1 Peter 2:4–5). This was a work of God by creation, a new creation (2 Cor. 5:17) and election (Eph. 1:4). And it calls for faith to keep its stipulations and to look for its coming fulfillment (cf. Eph. 1:12; 2:22; 4:17–23).

The covenant promises and stipulations were announced from the beginning. Besides Moses, the lawgiver and covenant maker (Mal. 4:5), and the priests who were messengers of the covenant (2:7), he promised to send a messenger to prepare for the coming of the Lord (3:1). That preparation would be through a call to repentance — to return to the Lord — and the reiteration of the promise of ultimate salvation.

God will send another messenger, Elijah, before the great day of the Lord at the end of the age (4:3; cf. also Rev. 11:1–12). He will turn hearts back to the covenant faith, warning people to escape the judgment that is to follow.

Judgments

The warnings of judgment for sin in the book are very clear, but their application is general. It will be helpful to divide them into two categories. First, we have God's dealing with people who profess to be believers. They are there in the sanctuary participating in the ritual, and they think of themselves as righteous because they are troubled that God does not judge the wicked.

The warnings of an immediate, temporal judgment first concerns the priests: God was beginning to curse their blessings because they did not honor him (2:1–9). Their priestly family would come to an end. Temporal judgment was also proclaimed for those who violated marriage by marrying pagans (2:12). And finally, temporal judgment in the form of pests (locusts?) and failed crops are in view for the nation because of its failure to bring the tithes and offerings (3:11–12).

The New Testament carries forward these warnings but with slight changes in the application. The church is not a nation living in a land as Israel was, so the warning is that a failure to give to God will result in a smaller blessing, a loss of blessing as it were (cf. 2 Cor. 8 and 9:6–15). And if in giving to God the people try to deceive everyone, we have the warning through the experience of Ananias and Sapphira who tried to deceive in the amount they were giving (Acts. 5:1–5; cf. Mal. 2:14). Then failed or ruined ministries receive a punishment remarkably similar to Malachi's announcement: God would remove the lampstand (Rev. 2–3), meaning those churches would continue to exist but have no influence for God. Finally, we have the apostle's instructions for those who corrupt marriage in various ways (cf. 1 Cor. 5 and 6).

Believers will not be destroyed in the great judgment of the day of the Lord. But the Lord will purge them as a refiner so that they would again offer pure and righteous service (Mal. 3:3–4). This prophecy is illustrated dramatically in the night vision of Zechariah in which the high priest is cleansed and re-installed (Zech. 3). He represents the priestly nation and its renewal to service. The purification in that passage is linked ultimately to the death of the Messiah, the Branch. Ultimately this will happen with the coming of the Lord, but along the way there would be partial fulfillments (cf. 1 Cor. 3:11–15; note also the priests who came to faith in Acts 6:7).

In the second place we read about the wicked, people who do not fear the name of the Lord (Mal. 3:5). The Lord is coming to be a swift witness against them, destroying all those who have no faith but live out major violations of God's righteousness. The violations selected in the announcement refer to the customary practices of unbelievers, not occasional violations. All of the sins mentioned are the exact opposite of what the righteous were to be doing. And even though some of these people might have been giving the appearance of faith, the coming of the LORD in judgment would enable everyone to distinguish the righteous from the wicked (3:18). The wicked will be consumed by fire in the day of the LORD, and the true believers will be spared to celebrate their salvation.

II. *The Creation of God*

Apart from references throughout the book to God's control of his creation, namely, the blessing of crops with the sending of rain or the removal of devouring pests, the focus on the creation of God is on people. Some of the discussion of humans has necessarily been included above, but here we can consider Malachi's descriptions categorically.

BELIEVERS

The references in Malachi essentially describe people who have genuine faith. In general, true believers are those who "fear the LORD" (3:16; 4:2). This is reverential fear — adoration and thanksgiving to the great God and a serious commitment to obey him. In Malachi 3:16 we learn how these people encourage one another as they talk together. And their faith is rewarded by the LORD's promise to deliver them from judgment, for they belong to him and are part of his treasure (see Eph. 1:14, 18).

There is clear evidence for genuine faith. Believers are the righteous who honor the name of the LORD in their worship and obedience. And in the priesthood, the faithfulness of the earlier priests exemplifies what the priests and the priestly nation were to be doing: they feared the LORD, taught the Scriptures, lived out the faith, and turned many to righteousness. That is what it means to be a kingdom of priests in the New Testament as well as in the Old.

In Malachi we also have prophecies that Gentiles will come to faith — they will fear the LORD and acknowledge the greatness of the name of the LORD, that is, the LORD himself (see Exod. 34:5–7; and for the power and the authority of the name, 23:20–21; Matt. 7:22; and Acts 4:7). This prophecy began to be fulfilled in their time as references to the faith of the nations confirm (cf. Pss. 35:27; 113:3), but will receive its greatest fulfillment through the new covenant. Jesus announced that the kingdom was to be taken from the Jews and given to a people who would produce fruit (Matt. 21:42–45).

God provides promises to the believers so that they have assurance of their faith. He makes a "book of remembrance" to ensure their deliverance in the day of judgment (3:16). They will not be destroyed with the wicked (see also Rom. 8:1, 19–24). God will remember them, for they belong to him.

UNFAITHFUL BELIEVERS

In any congregation there are many who profess to believe and be part of the community, but it is never certain. Malachi addresses a particularly belligerent crowd who challenge everything he says. They are arrogant and self-righteous, weak in faith, and ignorant of the ways of God. This led to disobedience at every turn. The description of all their violations does not need to be rehearsed again; here we may look at some of the telling descriptions.

They complained that believing in God did not pay off — they did not gain any benefits from it. And they complained that wicked people thrived and were not destroyed: "Where is the God of justice" was an accusation that God was unjust (2:17). They were convinced that they were right, and so they should be rewarded for it and not rebuked. They did worship, but they corrupted it with their worthless gifts and profane activities (see the standard in Exod. 12:5; 29:1; Lev. 1:3, 19; 22:18–25 for a few examples — they could not have missed the point). They continued to worship but nullified it by divorcing their wives and marrying pagan devotees (Deut. 24:1; Prov. 5–7; along this line, see 1 Peter 3:7). They complained that God was not profiting them (3:14), but they were robbing God by not paying their tithes and offerings. Theirs was a faith of convenience. In the final analysis, they were hypocrites (cf. Matt. 23). The LORD warned them that they had to change immediately — to return to the LORD. But how were they to do that? First and foremost, they were to cry out for mercy to avail themselves of his compassion (1:9). They were then to amend their living, in marriages, tithing, offerings to God, and living in hope.

The prophecy announced that when the Lord comes to his temple, he will then sit as a refiner and washer, thoroughly purging Israel and restoring them to a faithful ministry in which they will again worship with righteousness. This purging is not the same as the absolute destruction of the wicked.

UNBELIEVERS

Among those who were violating God's laws were people who never came to faith and so were not members of the covenant. In God's assessment, they stand as wicked, condemned sinners. We first see such antagonism to God and his people in the Edomites who opposed Israel and wanted it ruined (Mal. 1:2–5). But God chose Israel, and would continue to protect them from Edom and other enemies.

The prophecy also announces that the LORD would draw near in judgment against the doers of wickedness who did not fear his name (3:5). They eventually will be utterly destroyed by fire that would turn them to dust, leaving no trace of them. That will be the great day of the LORD.

III. *The Relation of the Creator to the Creation*

Here we are concerned with the outworking of the covenant promises. The LORD, for his part, promises not only blessings in this life (Mal. 3:10–12), but ultimate deliverance from the bondage of this world (4:3). All of that will come by his grace declared through the promises of his word. And because he does not change (3:6), the promises will be fulfilled. Even if his people are unfaithful, he remains faithful to his word, for he cannot deny himself.

The people, on their part, had to respond to his word by faith, and then demonstrate that faith through obedience. The fulfillment of the promises of God is sure and unconditional, but participation in them required faithfulness — a life of faith lived out in righteousness. And so God sent messengers to help the people walk with the LORD. The first were the priests, messengers of the LORD, who were to teach the truth and turn many from wickedness. But over time they had become complacent and corrupt, showing respect of persons in their application of the Law. And since they failed so often, he sent the prophets to call people to repentance. Malachi is the messenger God sent to this particular crowd; his name means "my messenger." He reproved, rebuked, warned, and instructed the people, but we have little information about the lasting effect of his ministry. His reforms may have had little more success than those of Ezra or Nehemiah.

Malachi's vision turned to the future, partially because the self-righteous demanded, "Where is the God of justice?" The prophet's answer was clear: "If you want him, look, he is coming! But no one can stand when he appears, because he will come to judge the world." They clearly did not know what they were asking. But Malachi prophesied that a messenger was going to be sent first — John the Baptist — who would prepare the way before the LORD. It was a messenger who would call people to repentance, make them aware of their sin, and prepare them for the one who could bring forgiveness. That one — Jesus Christ–was going to be a messenger as well, and his message will be the new covenant, offering life and peace to those who believe. Then, under the new covenant God made some to be apostles, some prophets, some evangelists and teachers, to spread the gospel and to inspire faithful worship and service in the believers.

The oracle slowly changes to the judgment that will come at the end of the age. There too God will send a messenger, called Elijah by the prophecy. He will bring about spiritual renewal prior to the terrible day of the LORD, when judgment will be poured out on the unbelievers (see Isa. 63:1–6; Joel 2:11; and Amos 5:18).

What the covenant promised to people who believed was eternal salvation. When the LORD comes to judge the wicked, the true believers, those who fear his name and follow after righteousness, will be delivered from the judgment and set free from the bondage of the world (4:2–3). They will look in triumph over the destruction of wickedness in all the earth.

In the meantime they are kept in his "book of remembrance," known to him as his treasured possession (see Eph. 1:14; 2 Thess. 2:14; Titus 2:14; 1 Peter 2:9). They now enjoy the life they have been given because they have also been given peace with God through redemption. So they seek to live righteously, awaiting the coming of the Lord. It is the hope that inspires them to purify themselves (cf. 1 John 3:3). And so the messengers of the covenant were designated to teach the Law. The faithful would honor God in their worship by bringing the best sacrifice they had and to treat the ritual with humility and sincerity. They were to follow the teachings of the Law even if the teachers were showing respect of persons in its application (cf. Matt. 23:2–3). They were to take heed not to deal treacherously in their marriages, but to fulfill the intent of God and remain faithful to their word and produce a godly seed. And they were to honor God with their stewardship, trusting that he would provide. The themes of these messages were not only relevant for Malachi's audience, but they are still the constant touchstones of faithfulness.

IV. *Eschatology*

It should be clear by now that Malachi referred to several general themes of eschatology. Here we need simply to arrange them in order based on comparisons with other passages, notably New Testament passages. Without the full revelation of the New Testament it would be difficult to sort out the material in Malachi.

First, Malachi tells us that the LORD is coming to judge the world and destroy the wicked completely by fire. But before that terrible day of the LORD he is sending messengers to warn people. The prophecy at the beginning of chapter 3 announces a messenger who will prepare the way before the LORD. A second messenger will be the Lord whom the people desire, who will come to his temple, who will bring a new covenant, and who will purge his people. Then at the end of chapter 4 we have the promise that the LORD will send Elijah before the great day of the LORD and he will unite the nation in the faith. For the Old Testament believer who was thinking only of one coming, the forerunner (3:1) and Elijah could be the same person. The text does not say they are, but the parallel ideas leave it as a possibility.

By comparing these oracles with other Old Testament prophecies and by using the complete revelation of the New Testament as our framework, we are now able to clarify this material. There would be two comings of the LORD. In the first coming, the LORD sent the messenger of the covenant who would come to his temple. He would be introduced by a forerunner, the messenger who would prepare the way. The New Testament is absolutely clear that the forerunner was John the Baptist. And the messenger of the covenant was Jesus the Messiah. Because Jesus would go to his temple, we can only conclude he is divine because the temple was the house of the LORD. So in the first coming we have God (the Father) sending God (the Son) into the world to establish the new covenant. And John would have a ministry of repentance to prepare people for the coming of the Lord.

But the great and terrible day of the LORD was not fulfilled or even begun in the first advent of Christ. It is a prophetic designation that refers to the coming of the Messiah to judge the world and bring in an age of blessing. The prophet Elijah (whether Elijah himself or one in the power of Elijah is debated) will come before that great and terrible day. This cannot be John, because the great day of wrath did not come and John did not bring about spiritual renewal in Israel.

When the Lord appears he will make up his treasure of people who belong to his covenant and that includes the faithful of Israel and the Gentile world. He will purge his priestly people like a refiner, so that they might worship in purity and righteousness. This primarily refers to the conversion of Israel at the end of the age (Rom. 11). This was partially fulfilled at the return from the exile, and gradually fulfilled down through history as people came to faith. All believers today have been grafted into the covenant and are also a kingdom of priests; but to function as such requires purification to be a holy people.

The Lord will also come to destroy once and for all the wicked and wickedness in a most dramatic and convincing way. This has not happened yet. In fact, in the parable of the wheat and the weeds (Matt. 13: 24–30), the Lord of the harvest told his servants not to root out the weeds lest they damage the wheat. So in the developing program of God the righteous must live in and among the wicked until the second coming. But when the LORD comes he will divide between the wheat and the weeds so that the weeds will be burned up with an unquenchable fire, but the wheat (the righteous) will flourish in his kingdom.